IMMIGRATION AND ASYLUM LAW AND POLICY IN EUROPE

Volume 3

Editors

Elspeth Guild
Kingsley Napley Solicitors, London,
Centre for Migration Law, Katholieke Universiteit, Nijmegen

Jan Niessen
Migration Policy Group, Brussels

The series is a venue for books on European immigration and asylum law and policies where academics, policy makers, law practitioners and others look to find detailed analysis of this dynamic field. Works in the series will start from a European perspective. The increased co-operation within the European Union and the Council of Europe on matters related to immigration and asylum requires the publication of theoretical and empirical research. The series will contribute to well-informed policy debates by analysing and interpreting the evolving European legislation and its effects on national law and policies. The series brings together the various stakeholders in these policy debates: the legal profession, researchers, employers, trade unions, human rights and other civil society organisations.

The titles publised in this series are listed at the end of this volume.

NEGOTIATING EUROPE'S IMMIGRATION FRONTIERS

Negotiating Europe's Immigration Frontiers

by

BARBARA MELIS

KLUWER LAW INTERNATIONAL
THE HAGUE / LONDON / NEW YORK

A C.I.P. Catalogue record for this book is available from the Library of Congress.

ISBN 90-411-1614-1

Published by Kluwer Law International,
P.O. Box 85889, 2508 CN The Hague, The Netherlands.

Sold and distributed in North, Central and South America
by Kluwer Law International,
101 Philip Drive, Norwell, MA 02061, U.S.A.
kluwerlaw@wkap.com

In all other countries, sold and distributed
by Kluwer Law International, Distribution Centre,
P.O. Box 322, 3300 AH Dordrecht, The Netherlands.

Printed on acid-free paper

Lay-out and camera-ready copy:
Anne-Marie Krens – Tekstbeeld – Oegstgeest – The Netherlands

Printed in the Netherlands.

TABLE OF CONTENTS

LIST OF ABBREVIATIONS

CCME	Churches Commission for Migrants in Europe
CEEC	Central and Eastern European Countries
CFSP	Common Foreign and Security Policy
EC	European Community
ECHR	European Convention on Human Rights and Freedoms
ECSC	European Coal and Steel Community
ECR	European Court Reports
ECJ	European Court of Justice
EDU	European Drugs Unit
EEA	European Economic Area
EFTA	European Free Trade Association
EIS	European Information System
EP	European Parliament
EU	European Union
EUROPOL	European Police Office
ILPA	Immigration Law Practitioners' Association
IMADRIS	International Movement against all Forms of Discrimination and Racism
IOM	International Migration Organisation
JHA	Justice and Home Affairs
OJ	Official Journal
SEA	Single European Act
SIS	Schengen Information System
TCN	Third Country National
TEU	Treaty on European Union

TABLE OF CASES
(chronological order)

Case 29/69 *Erich Stauder v City of Ulm, Socialamt* [1969] ECR 419, 19
Case 41/73 *J. Nold, Kohlen-und Baustoffgroßhandlung v Commission of the European Communities* [1974] ECR 491, 19
Case 181/73 *R. & V. Haegeman v Belgian State* [1974] ECR 449, 32
Case 21/74 *Jeanne Airola v Commission of the European Communities* [1975] ECR 221, 43
Joined Cases 62 and 63/81 *Seco SA and Desquenne & Giral SA v Etablissement d'Assurance contre la Vieillesse et l'Invalidité*, [1982] ECR 223, 81
Case 53/81 *Levin v Staatssecretaris van Justitie* [1982] ECR 1035, 114
Joined Cases 35 and 36/82 *Elestina Esselina Christina Morson v State the Netherlands and Head of the Plaastelijke Politie within the meaning of the Vreemdelingenwet; Sewradije Jhanjan v State of the Netherlands* [1982] ECR 3723, 74
Joined Cases 286/82 and 26/83 *Luisi and Carbone v Ministero del Tesoro* [1984] ECR 377, 71
Joined Cases 60 and 61/84 *Cinéthèque Sa and Others v Fédération nationale des cinémas français*, [1985] ECR 2605, 19
Case 267/83 *Aissatou Diatta v Land Berlin* [1985] ECR 567, 78ff, 90
Case 59/85 *State of the Netherlands v Ann Florence Reed* [1986] ECR 1283, 77
Case 139/85 *Kempf v Staatssecretaris van Justitie* [1986] ECR 1741, 114
Case 66/85 *Lawrie-Blum v Land Baden-Württeberg* [1986] ER 2121, 114
Case 131/85. *Emir Gül v Regierungspräsident Düsseldorf* [1986] ECR 1573, 81
Case 316/85 *Centre public d'aide sociale de Courcelles v Marie-Christine Lebon* [1987] ECR 284, 78
Case 12/86 *Meryem Demirel v Stadt Schwäbisch Gmünd* [1987] ECR 3719, 32, 33, 96, 207

Joined Cases 281, 283, 285 and 287/85 *Germany et al. v Commission* [1987] ECR 3203, 88

Case 186/87 *Ian William Cowan v Trésor Public* [1989] ECR 195, 71

Case 321/87 *Commission v. Belgium* [1989] 997, 198

Case 344/87 *Bettray v Staatssecretaris van Justitie* [1989] ECR 1621, 114

Case 30/88 *Hellenic Republic v Commission of the European Communities* [1989] ECR 3711, 32

Case C-233/88 *Grimaldi v Fonds des Maladies Professionelles* [1989] ECR 4407, 126

Case C-113/89 *Rush Portuguesa Lda v Office National d'Immigration* [1990] ECR I-1417, 82 ff

Case C-192/89 *Sevince v Staatsecretaris van Justitie*[1990] ECR 3497, 33, 111 ff

Case C-369/90 *Micheletti and others v Delegaciòn del Gobierno en Cantabria* [1990] ECR I-4239, 43, 98

Case C-292/89 *The Queen v Immigration Appeal Tribunal, ex part Gustaff Desiderious Antonissen* [1991] ECR I-745, 114

Case C-260/89 *Elliniki Radiophonia Tiléorassi AE and Panellinia Omospondia Syllogon Prossopikou v Dimotiki Etairia Pliroforissis and Sotirio Kouvelas and Nicolaos Avdellas and others* [1991] ECR I-2925, 19

Case C-18/90 *Office nationale de l'emploi (Onem) v Bahia Kziber* [1991] ECR I-199, 96

Case C-379/90 *The Queen v Immigration Appeal et Surinder Singh, ex parte Secretary of State for Home Department* (1992) ECR I-4265, 78, 90

Case C-237/91 *Kazim Kus v Landeshauptsadt Wiesbaden* [1992] ECR I-6781, 112

Case C-171/91 *Tsiotras v Landeshauptstadt Stuttgart* [1993] ECR I-2925, 115

Case C-43/93 *Van der Elst v Office des Migrations Internationaux* [1994] ECR I-3803, 82

Case C-58/93 *Zoubir Yousfi v Belgian State* ECR [1994] I-1353, 96

Case C-103/94 *Zoulika Krid v Caisse Nationale d'Assurance vieillesse des Travailleurs salariés* ECR [1995] I-719, 96

Case C-434/93 *Ahmet Bozkurt v Staatssecretaris van Justitie* [1995] ECR I-1475, 114 ff

Case C-126/95 *Hallouzi- Chocho v Bestuur van de Sociale Verzekeringsbank* ECR [1996] I-4807, 97

Case C-277/94 *Z. Taflan-Met and Others v Bestuur van Social Verzekeringsbank and O. Akol v Bestuur van de Nieuwe Algemene Bedrijfsvereniging* [1996] ECR I-4085, 94

Case C-171/95 *Recep Tetik. v Land Berlin* [1997] ECR I-0329, 114

INTRODUCTION

Western Europe is presently a region of intense immigration; great numbers of people coming from difficult political, social and economic situations, choose Europe as their safe haven. For many it is, to some extent, a choice and they can decide to go back to their original countries whenever they want, while others are forced to emigrate in order to escape persecution in their home countries.

The movement of third country national TCN is not a new phenomenon for Western Europe as Western countries have always experienced continuous migration and given refuge to asylum seekers.

Nevertheless, only since the late 1980s have such migratory movements become a major concern due to changes of internal and international factors, and are now regarded to be of primary and common interest for the Member States of the European Union (EU).[1]

The research analyses the development of the legal framework of the European common immigration policy. An EU integrated policy covering all aspects related to TCNs does not exist but very important steps, consolidated in the Amsterdam Treaty, have been taken in the last decade (1989-1999). The strategy to adopt at EU level in the area of immigration is still not very clear and coherent due to the complexity of the area itself and because of the different approaches of the EU institutions on the answer to give to immigration issues.

The research covers the study of the migratory flows and the evolution of their regulation under EU and EC law in a historical perspective with projections looking at the inevitable enlargement of the EU towards Central and Eastern Europe. Specific reference to international agreements and to national immigration rules is made when necessary.

1 Presently over a third of the current meetings which the Council Secretariat services and over 40 per cent of the paper which circulated are concerned with justice and home affairs. House of Lords Debates, 1747, 6.11.1998.

The analysis also examines the main factors that have contributed to the adoption of such a European immigration policy in fifty years of Community history, namely economic, security and racial factors. In particular, it evaluates the impact of the new restrictive policy towards third country nationals, focusing on racial and ethnic minority groups. Among these groups special attention is reserved to the position of women. The research demonstrates how the new rules on immigration although not directly sexist or racist can, however, have an enormous impact on racial and ethnic minorities and women.

Several reasons justify the decision to concentrate on TCNs belonging to ethnic minority groups and female migrants. First of all, it is important to remember that the large majority of TCNs already settled or arriving in the EU (70% of the migrant population of which around 50% are women) are from poor developing countries. They possess a different "ethnicity" compared to what is assumed to be European, although an increasing number of the extra-Community population arrives from the white, rich and developed world. This latter group, composed of managers, diplomats, specialists of multinational companies is barely regarded as a problem contrary to the non privileged TCN labour migrants. Moreover, notwithstanding the wide concern and protection guaranteed under the most important human rights conventions, to which the majority of the European Union States have acceded, *sex* and *race* are among the most relevant factors of discrimination, whether direct or indirect.[2]

Finally, the decision to evaluate the position of women, which must be considered as a sub-category, is justified by the fact that women often suffer racial discrimination as do their male counterparts due to the emerging restrictive European rules *however* taking into account that "both societies of origin and societies of immigration are to a different extent and different ways marked by sexist ideologies"[3] they also suffer a more specific, gender-related discrimination, which is worth investigating, whenever it is possible.

For practical reasons the study is divided into four parts. The first part deals with issues and problems of a general character, which are required in order to introduce and to place in the historical context the matters analysed in depth in the following sections. By means of the study of the immigration figures, it is possible to distinguish three main periods in the migratory movements and of their regulation in Europe, which have been influenced by economic, security and race

2 As Greenberg recalls "mere inspection of the basic international human rights documents demonstrates that racial, sexual, and religious discrimination are, certainly in terms of attention paid on the face of the agreements, the overarching human right concern of the international community". Greenberg J., "Race, Sex, and Religious Discrimination in International Law", in Meron T. (ed), *Human Rights in International Law, Legal and Policy Issues*, Oxford Clarendon Press, 1989, 309.

3 Morokvasic M., "Fortress Europe and Migrant Women", *Feminist Review*, 1991, Vol. 39, 71.

factors. The research shows how in the last phase of immigration, from 1989 onwards, race factors have become very important in the elaboration of the common immigration policy. It follows the analysis of the compatibility of the EU immigration policy with the best European democratic and liberal traditions. The second part analyses the relevant provisions of the EC/EU regulation related to TCNs legally settled within the Union. The analysis shows the divergence in the regulation of the position of EC migrants and TCNs in the evolution of immigration rules and the increasing gap between the two categories. The research likewise shows the contradictions in the development of immigration rules as regards the EU commitment to the fight against phenomena concerning sex and race discrimination because as has been demonstrated, the rules adopted, whether directly or indirectly, are often racist and sexist. Discrimination of the extra-Community population compared to EC citizens can take place in other important areas, because, only incidentally, EC provisions on free movement of persons and in the social field, are applicable to TCNs. Until recently, the lack of any planning at EU level has made the regulation in this area of immigration very chaotic but it is always possible to identify certain patterns, which are also confirmed by the several agreements signed by the Community and third countries. The Amsterdam Treaty (1998) does not represent a U-turn in this area but a further confirmation of the tendency of exclusion of the extra-Community population, although some important concessions have been made. Unexpected evolution can nonetheless occur by the extension of Community competence to these areas, from pressure coming from the European Commission but, especially, from the European Parliament. In this respect it should be noted that Member States have committed themselves in the European Council held in Tampere (15-16 October 1999) to adopt a more liberal and generous policy in the area of immigration.

The third part analyses immigration policies and rules related to TCNs admission from outside the Union. This area of immigration has been subject to a growing and more organised EC/EU involvement in the last decade. It results clearly that, except for very few concessions, largely due to the influence of the European Commission or the European Parliament, a very restricted approach has been privileged. Despite general statements and commitments about the respect for democratic and liberal values, EU policy is aimed at creating a fortress Europe, particularly unreachable for certain migrants. It has in fact been demonstrated that the new rules are concerned with the *quantity* as well as the *quality* of new arrivals, in order not to get the *wrong* migrants. TCNs arriving from Black countries are the most unwanted. Such an exclusionary tendency is present in the elaboration of all rules concerning admission, including family reunion immigration.

The last part concerns EU policing and expulsion measures. The creation of a fortress Europe has required the Member States, which have dedicated important energies and funds, to set up and enforce a system of controls in order to avoid TCNs from eluding stricter immigration rules. Again, it has been demonstrated that, although often disguised, the new rules are more likely to affect racial and ethnic minority groups and women.

PART 1

IMMIGRATION IN EUROPE: AN INTRODUCTION

I

IMMIGRATION IN EUROPE

The movement of Third Country Nationals is presently a matter of primary interest to the Member States of the European Union.

Many international and national reasons justify this concern among which some are of particular relevance.

I.1 IMMIGRATION TOWARDS THE EUROPEAN UNION: FIGURES

When dealing with immigration the first problem a specialist must face is the lack of the necessary up-dated information on the movement of people. Yet statistical information is often instrumentalised in political propaganda to justify the adoption of specific immigration measures. The collection of data related to immigration at European Union level in order to evaluate the number of TCNs present within its boundaries or willing to enter into the EU is a particularly hard task because the systems to collect this information differ widely among Member States due to many variables. Finally, there is not a common and usable definition of an "international migrant"; although progress is now being made to achieve this goal. Therefore, data often give only an approximate picture of the real situation, which is in fact more complex. Accordingly, the Council has given great importance to this area.

> "An overall priority should be to improve the exchange of statistics and information on asylum and immigration: this exchange should include statistics on asylum and immigration, information on the status of third country nationals and national legislation."[4]

---

4 Council Document, Action Plan on Establishing an Area of Freedom, Security and Justice, 12028/1/98.

According to EUROSTAT sources,[5] all Member States are facing the same problems related to immigration.

All EU countries have become immigration countries. Also southern European countries such as Italy, Spain, Portugal and Greece, which have traditionally been countries of net emigration are slowly becoming countries of net immigration.[6] In 1998, the migrant population in the EEA space was 5.1% of which 3.5% were non-EEA nationals.[7]

The analysis of the figures shows that there has been a steady increase of the migrant population until the end of the 1890s but the rhythm has accelerated since then.

Overall, the increased number of aliens knocking at the European Union's doors, in the past decade (1989/99), has often been the direct and immediate consequence of the dissolution of the Soviet empire that upset the EU after the fall of the Berlin wall. The war in Kosovo can also be seen as a legacy of the end of the cold war between the two blocks.

However, many governments and people in the EU feel that aliens are a present and permanent threat. They fear massive migratory movements of people no longer prisoners of Communist regimes and wanting a share in the rich EU. Added to these are the movements from southern developing countries. It must be expected that growing numbers of people from all over the world, but mainly from developing countries, will try to enter the EU in the future, despite the official ban on primary migrants, because of a "combination of modern travel possibilities and the readiness of unscrupulous traffickers in human beings to exploit their desperation".[8]

The majority of these aliens, as has become clear since the 1970s, normally arrive in the Member States planning to live *there* for just a few years and then, hoping in changes in the economic and political situation, whether personal or

5 In the past decade EUROSTAT has published various surveys: EUROSTAT Non-Nationals make up less than 5% of the Population of the European Union on 1.1.1993, 1996/2; EUROSTAT, Decline in Migration stopped in 1995. Principal demographic trends in the EU in 1995, 1996/6. More recently, EUROSTAT, European Social Statistics, Luxembourg, 2000.

6 For further information on the new migration flows in the Mediterranean Europe see De Filippo E. & Pugliese E., "Le Nuove Migrazioni Internazionali e i Modelli Migratori nei Paesi del Sud Europa", *Mediterraneo*, luglio-settembre 1996, 49-71. Baldwin-Edwards M., "The Emerging European Immigration Regime: Some Reflections on Implications for Southern Europe", *Journal of Common Market Studies*, 1997, Vol. 35, No 4, 497-519. King R. "Southern Europe and the International Division of Labour: From Emigration to Immigration", in King R. (ed), *The New Geography of European Migrations,* Belhaven Press, 1993.

7 EUROSTAT, European Social Statistics, see supra note 10.

8 European Commission, Communication from the Commission to the Council and the European Parliament on Immigration and Asylum Policies, COM (94) 23 final.

of the country they come from, to go back to the country of origin. But once settled, although contrary to their original plans, they choose Europe as their definitive home, so their stay can no longer be considered temporary.[9] From the figures, it is evident that, even though Western European countries do not like to consider themselves as immigration countries, they now are, nonetheless, the destination of thousands of immigrants every year.

In the perspective of the enlargement of the European Union to Central and Eastern Europe the threat of migratory movements from ex-Communist countries has been partially neutralised. It should be remembered that for many years the European Community did not have any contact with the countries of Central and Eastern Europe, satellites of the Soviet Union. It was only in 1988 that the Community put the basis for a fruitful cooperation. By means of these accords – the most recent preparing for the accession of these countries to the Union – migration clauses are included in order to regulate flows from these countries. Furthermore, the concession of aid for the democratic and economic restructuring of this part of Europe has worked as a braking factor. Western Europe, however, still fears that the introduction of freedom of movement of labour for Central and Eastern European nationals might lead to strong unwanted migratory pressures. The Community as a whole is experiencing a very high unemployment rate, around 9%,[10] and the arrival of a cheap labour force in the Union, it is believed, would cause more unemployment. The strategy followed by the Community is therefore to accord such rights in different stages.[11] But some candidate states are pushing in order to eliminate the transitional period and to apply the freedom of movement of workers from the day of accession.[12]

---

9 Collinson S., *Beyond the Borders: West European Migration Policy towards the 21st Century*, Royal Institute of International Affairs, 1995. See also Coleman D.A., "Europe under Pressure: Some Facts on Immigration", in Uçarer E.M. & Puchala D. J., (eds), *Immigration into Western Societies: Problems and Policies*, Pinter, 1997, 121-147.

10 According to EUROSTAT source, in March 1999, the unemployment rate in the Union amounted to 9.6%, http://www.europa.eu.int/en/comm/eurostat/compres/en/4699/6304699a.htm.

11 Krenzler G.H., *The EU and Central-East Europe: The Implications of Enlargement in Stages*, The Robert Schuman Centre, Policy Paper 97/2, European University Institute, 23.

12 "The head of the Polish team negotiating the country's accession to the EU, Jan Kulakowski, has said that Poland will insist during the negotiations on the grant freedom of movement for Polish workers in the EU from the day of the accession. The Polish government's objective is to negotiate application of the principle of free movement without any transitional period". Agence Europe No 7170, 28.02.1998. Also the Czech Republic has demanded the integral application of the principles and rules of the Internal Market since the day of the accession and, therefore, of the four freedoms. Agence Europe No 7192, 01.04.1998.

Migratory movements from Africa and Asia are the most likely and most feared in the long-term. The explosive combination of very poor resources, badly exploited, with a very high birth rate of these areas of the world, represent an extremely relevant push factor towards the rich European Union. The strongest pressure is to be expected from the countries of the Mediterranean basin, both for geographical and economic reasons. There is in fact a gap between the EC and these neighbours which stands at around ten to one. Such a situation is able to provoke a flow of economic (and political) migrants, especially from North Africa, seeking a better life in the European Community.[13]

Aware of this, the European Community has reinforced its Mediterranean policy since the mid 1990s.[14]

I.2 Evolution of the migratory flows and their regulation

International migratory movements are notably caused by social and economic reasons, by pull/push, demand/supply factors. Historically, Western European governments, from the 1950s to the 1960s, encouraged migratory movements in order to rebuild post-war Europe. As discussed in the next sections, migratory movements from outside the European Community were strictly governed by Member States' legislation.

EC law was only competent to regulate movements of specific categories of EC nationals. Only *incidentally* the regulation of the legal status of TCNs was covered by EC law. Regulating the flows of both EC nationals and TCNs responded mainly to economic logic.

In a second phase, from 1973/4 onwards, due to the international recession, mainly caused by the oil crisis, Member States tried to regulate migratory flows more actively but they found it impossible to eliminate the growing foreign population. Most governments in Western Europe immediately froze the attribution or renewal of labour permits and since residence was usually contingent upon work, they expected a substantial drop in the foreign population. But, notwithstanding the recession, many migrants decided to stay and to bring their families. Such incapab-

13 According to EUROSTAT sources TCNs from the Mediterranean area represents 1.3% of the total population of the Union. Those already settled are estimated to be five millions. Also, major migration pressures come from this area. EUROSTAT, Migration entre le Bassin Méditerranéen, 3/98.

14 See King R., "The Mediterranean: Europe's Rio Grande", in Anderson M. & Bort E. (eds), *The Frontiers of Europe*, Pinter, 1998, 109-131.

ility to reduce immigration pressures and to carry out repatriation programmes seriously alarmed all Northern Western countries.

Member States therefore reacted to this *unexpected* and *unwanted* reality in a defensive way. They started elaborating very restrictive measures directed at stopping new entrants either individually or commonly through the several intergovernmental fora created for this aim. The new restrictive policies provoked a rise in illegal immigration which, in turn, determined the adoption of much stricter rules. Governments responded by imposing more restrictive admission policies in order to avoid abuse of legal channels of migration. Furthermore, repatriation programmes started but incentives to return for migrants already settled within the host country had little effect and their forced removal, frequently, proved impossible for political and humanitarian reasons, as is clear from the growth in the number of aliens.

In this context, the obligation contained in the Single European Act (SEA) in 1987 to remove all internal frontiers among the Member States by 1992[15] acted as a "speed-up" factor as it raised security problems connected to the free movement of persons. The achievement of the freedom of movement of persons originally thought to benefit EC citizens was capable of having important consequences also for third country nationals. According to the SEA, Member States were to remove all controls at the internal borders on persons whether EC nationals or TCNs. *If* Member States maintain their national powers to control international movements of TCNs, the real significance of the freedom of movement of persons would be frustrated as internal movement of EC citizens would have to be controlled to avoid being abused by TCNs.[16] The fear of uncontrolled movements of TCNs as a result of the suppression of internal borders slowly modified the attitude of the Member States in this field.

Migration slowly started to be seen not only as an economic problem but also as a *security matter* which, given the international character of the problem, required a more coordinated answer. Since the 1970s, therefore, all matters concerning TCNs were recognised as issues to be tackled on a co-operative basis. In different intergovernmental fora outside the EC framework, among which special reference must be made to the Trevi Group (1975),[17] the AD HOC Group on Im-

15 European Commission, White Paper, Completing the Internal Market, COM (85) 310 final.

16 See on this point Evans A., "Third Country Nationals and the Treaty on European Union", *European Journal of International Law*, 1994, Vol. 5, 199-219; Garbagnati M.L., "Immigrazione, Diritto di Asilo e Libertà di Circolazione delle Persone nella Prospettiva dell' Unione Europea", *Diritto Comunitario e degli Scambi Internazionali*, 1995, Vol. 34, 7-45.

17 Mainly concerned with the fight against terrorism and international crime, the TREVI Group was set up in 1975. Its scope was occasionally extended to include immigration and asylum matters when connected with its aims.

migration (1986),[18] the Schengen Agreements (1985)[19] and the Co-ordinators' Group on the Free Movement of Persons (1988),[20] Member States slowly recognised immigration as a prominent issue both in their internal and external politics and therefore they decided to face it *commonly* in a more institutionalised framework.[21]

I.3 THE NEW IMMIGRATION AND ITS REGULATION IN THE EU

According to Koser and Lutz "the origins of the new migration are normally traced to 1989, the date that witnessed the conclusion of the Cold War and the collapse of Communist regimes resulting in the end of Europe's political division and in the opening of borders between East and West".[22] Due to the turmoil that followed the fall of the Iron Curtain, in particular in the area of the Balkans, migration has assumed a growing importance on the EU political agenda.

Until the late eighties, Member States' governments considered the control on the movements of the extra-Community population to and within their territory a clear expression of their sovereignty. They were therefore very reluctant to allow Community competence to regulate the field of immigration.

Finally, at the end of the 1980s, the Member States decided to give up a few areas of competence under the EC framework. Unfortunately, major disagreements

18 The AD HOC Group on Immigration, set up in 1986, principally dealt with the control of EC external borders and co-ordination of the national immigration and asylum policies.

19 The Schengen Agreements represent the first attempt to realise the objective of creating, among some Member States, an area without internal frontiers. There are two Schengen Agreements. The first one on the gradual abolition of Controls at the Common Frontiers was signed in June 1985 and the second one, the Schengen Implementing Agreement, was signed in 1990. These two Agreements responded to the frustration of some Member States about the impossibility of making any progress towards the removal of the internal frontiers within the European Union because of the controversy on the meaning of Article 7a of the EC Treaty. The Schengen Agreements were formulated completely outside the EU framework, as international law instruments. But the connection with the EU structure was made evident since their elaboration. They were to achieve a Community aim, i.e. the realisation of the internal market, and, for that reason, their provisions were hold to be compatible with EC legislation (Article 134 of the Schengen Implementing Agreement).

20 The Co-ordinators' Group on the Free Movement of Persons was established by the Rhodes European Council (1988) with the objective of co-ordinating the confusing range of groups dealing with all aspects of the free movement of persons and justice and home affairs in general.

21 Walker N., "The New Frontiers of European Policing", in Anderson M. & Bort E. (eds), see note 14, 165-186.

22 Koser K. & Lutz H., "The New Migration in Europe: Context, Constructions and Realities", in Koser K. & Lutz H.(eds), *The New Migration in Europe, Social Constructions and Social Realities,* MacMillan Press LTD, 1998, 2-4.

between Member States led to the adoption of the Maastricht Treaty compromise which created the European Union (1992), where provisions on migration were scattered in different parts of the Treaty in detriment of a single coherent framework.

It should be noted that by means of the Maastricht Treaty along with an increasing number of areas of action included in the European Community, the Member States decided to set up a framework for intergovernmental cooperation in the field of security and foreign policy (CFSP), on the one hand, and in the area of justice and home affairs (JHA), on the other. However, they did not reach an agreement to extend Community competence to those areas. Instead, the Member States created a Pillar structure where the three Communities make the first Pillar, the CFSP the second, and finally the JHA constituted the third Pillar. With the exception of very few areas related to visas, matters related to TCNs were to be regarded as matters of common interest but they *were not* subject to EC competence. They were to be regulated under the third Pillar (old Title VI TEU). Although under the EU cloak, EC law system was denied any competence. That meant that the EC Institutions, even though Article C TEU[23] referred to a single institutional framework, were attributed different functions in relation to the Pillar in which they operated and, more precisely, the Council, expression of Member States' will, had the greatest powers. The European Commission shared its right of initiative with the Member States, a right that is exclusive under the first Pillar, the European Parliament (EP) had only a consultative role while the European Court of Justice (ECJ) was in principle excluded.[24]

23 Old Article C TEU stated "the Union shall be served by a single institutional framework which shall ensure the consistency and the continuity of the activities carried out in order to attain its objectives while respecting and building upon the 'acquis communautaire'. The Union shall in particular ensure the consistency of its external activities as a whole in the context of its external relations, security, economic and development policies. The Council and the Commission shall be responsible for ensuring such consistency and shall cooperate to this end. They shall ensure the implementation of these policies, each in accordance with its respective powers." (New Article 3 TEU).

24 Old Article L TEU provided that "the provisions of the Treaty establishing the European Community, the Treaty establishing the European Coal and Steel Community and the Treaty establishing the European Atomic Energy Community concerning the powers of the Court of Justice of the European Communities and the exercise of those powers shall apply only to the following provisions of this Treaty: a) provisions amending the Treaty establishing the European Economic Community with a view to establishing the European Community, the Treaty establishing the European Coal and Steel Community and the Treaty establishing the European Atomic Energy Community; b) the third subparagraph of Article K.3(2)(c); c) Articles L to S." (New Article 46).

In only a few years, several documents were adopted dealing with important areas in this field, such as admission policies for students, workers, self-employed persons, family members, refugees and asylum seekers, measures of expulsion.

The regulation adopted in the area of immigration proved to be ineffective not only because of the instruments chosen to deal with it, often lacking any legally binding force, but also because it was ad hoc: a more coherent and systematic approach was needed.

The inefficacy of the system introduced by the Maastricht Treaty in dealing with immigration related issues was soon evident. Strong criticisms as regards the functioning of the TEU were advanced not only by some Institutions such as the European Commission[25] and the EP[26] but also by several Member States that insisted on the necessity to transfer those issues under Community competence.

In fact, during the revision of the Maastricht Treaty which led to the signature of the Amsterdam Treaty, one of the main areas on top of the agenda was the reorganisation of the European Union Pillar structure. All but a few Member States, namely the UK and Denmark, agreed that all issues related to immigration were to be shifted into the core of the EC Treaty provisions and dealt with in a single framework.

Only time will show the efficacy of the revised TEU, which entered into force 1st May 1999,[27] in tackling these issues. Nevertheless, there are serious doubts as to whether the restrictive trend recorded in Europe under the Maastricht co-operation will be radically reversed in adopting immigration rules, although under EC competence.

The brief history summarised above, shows how the elaboration and adoption of a common immigration policy has proved to be a very difficult task and this objective is still far from being achieved. The regulation of the legal status of TCNs is therefore complicated and often incoherent. Few measures under the EC Treaty regulate incidentally the position of specific categories of TCNs, i.e. family members of EC migrant or posted workers. Also, by means of the numerous international agreements signed by the Community, TCNs may gain specific rights

25 During the intergovernmental Conference (IGC) that led to the adoption of the Amsterdam Treaty, Commissioner Gradin, responsible for the immigration, home affairs and justice area, and Commissioner Monti, responsible for internal market issues, agreed on the necessity of putting immigration and asylum matters under Community competence. Migration News Sheets, 151/95.

26 Great discussion accompanied the IGC in the EP and pressures were made to ensure the communitarisation of the matters related to TCNs, from the third Pillar into the EC framework. See EP, Resolution on the functioning of the Treaty on European Union with a view to the 1996 Intergovernmental Conference – Implementation and development of the Union, OJ 1996 C 151/56.

27 OJ 1999 C 120/24.

depending on their nationality. Finally, important measures have been adopted under the third Pillar. Such measures, apart from just a few aimed at the integration of non EC-migrants into the Union, are based on a very restrictive and repressive approach.

The result of this very defensive stance is creating the so-called fortress Europe[28] whereby the gap between EC migrants and TCN migrants settled within its boundaries is constantly increasing and for those seeking entry it is barely possible to gain access to the Union.

The Maastricht Treaty formalised the birth of European Citizenship to which important rights are linked, in particular, more extensive rights in the area of free movement and political rights (see section II.6). EC nationals are no longer just labour under EC law but they are considered in their social and political capacity. Citizenship, as discussed in the next sections, has been increasingly recognised as an autonomous right regardless of the economic position of the *EC citizen* in the market. The Amsterdam Treaty has confirmed this tendency. It seems that Member States want to create a European Union where citizens have a predominant role. This explains the concerns to protect human rights and fundamental freedoms more seriously. But this construction clashes with the shaping of the present immigration policy as third country nationals are still seen as just labour or recently a security threat to European societies as demonstrated by the very restrictive and repressive measures addressed to them.

Such a restrictive approach is often justified by economic reasons – in time of recession, Europe does not need unskilled labour – and security reasons – the removal of the internal frontiers can facilitate illegal immigration and in general illegal activities. It seems however that there is a process of "racialisation" in the elaboration of the new European immigration rules. The new reality is forcing Member States to reconsider the impact of ethnic and cultural diversity on social and political cohesion. Accordingly, in the shaping of the new immigration policy, factors such as race and, in more general terms, ethnic antecedents are given more and more consideration.

I.4 RACIALISATION OF THE NEW IMMIGRATION POLICY?

The new restrictive policy strongly affects all migrants or would-be migrants but it seems that there is a *hidden target* in these rules. Those TCNs distant from the "European" standard seem to be the target of the restrictive measures. In the

---

28 See Peers S., "Building Fortress Europe: The Development of EU Migration Law, *Common Market Law Review*, 1998, Vol. 35, 1235-1272.

European context, "European" appears to be white, rich and Christian. Those to whom this definition does not apply, in particular poor immigrants belonging to ethnic minority groups who are perceived as Blacks in contrast to the White Europeans are especially considered as undesirable. Not all Blacks are considered as such. The colour is not important *per se* but only in the way it is perceived. Martiniello makes some important remarks about the social construction of skin colour in the Italian context:

> "It is remarkable that Moroccans are considered as Blacks although they do not objectively differ phenotipically from many Italians. On the contrary, the Black American artists working for example for the state television channels are mainly regarded as Americans, not as Blacks".[29]

Such a phenomenon is not restricted to Italy but can be easily extended to all the Community's Member States. Blacks in France are the Algerians or Moroccans, in Germany they are Turks, while in the UK, people from the New Commonwealth are the target of racist attitudes.

The more distant they are from the "European" the more they are considered undesirable. This process is well known in any multi-cultural reality. According to Hagendoorn:

> "In a multi-ethnic context, each group will have stereotypes about several outgroups accentuating negative differences from the ingroup. Outgroups will be placed further away from or further below the ingroup, the larger and more important these differences are".[30]

This process of racialisation in the elaboration of the immigration policy is widespread throughout Western Europe.

To understand this reaction it must be noted that the majority of Western European countries have fought in the past to assume the unitary character that they presently proclaim and they therefore strongly resist this mutation, i.e. from fairly homogeneous nation-state into something which is still called a nation-state but which has acquired a multi-ethnic and multi-cultural dimension. Often the extra-Community population has a different ethnicity based on a distinct culture,

29 Martiniello M., "Italy: The Late Discovery of Immigration", in Miles R. & Tränhardt D. (eds), *Europe, a New Immigration Continent, Policies and Politics in Comparative Perspective*, LIT, 1992, 198.

30 Hagendoorn L., "Ethnic Categorisation and Outgroup Exclusion: Cultural Values and Social Stereotypes in the Construction of Ethnic Hierarchies", *Ethnic and Racial Studies*, 1993, Vol. 16, 36.

race, religion, language and national identity, which is considered to be incompatible with European societies. Where migrants were just a few and were also Europeans, integration was relatively easy and it was generally successfully accomplished by the second generation. But TCNs, by means of several years of family reunion, have created their own world, parallel to that of the host societies which makes their *assimilation* in the host countries more difficult. This seriously challenges the ethnically unitary concept of Western European societies, based on "presumed" common identity, culture, race, religion, etc. These concerns and, in particular, the degree of "assimilability", strictly linked to race and wealth factors, are shaping the emerging immigration policy. The temptation to keep immigrants out or as a second class citizens, as has been shown, is great.

In this last phase, economic, security and race factors work together in the elaboration of the immigration rules. Often it appears very difficult to find the dividing line among these factors and to decide which one plays the predominant role as many migrants come from very poor areas of the world, they possess a different ethnicity, are low-skilled or unskilled which situates them at the bottom of the social ladder in the host state, they find major integration problems in the host society and are often involved in crime. But when adopting such a restrictive immigration policy at EU level, it is believed that factors such as race and ethnic antecedents are becoming an increasingly important element in the elaboration of immigration measures.

The European Institutions do not often share the same position as regards the treatment to be accorded to TCNs. The EP and the European Commission have stressed the urgency to take steps towards the concession of political and social rights in specific situations similar to those conferred upon EC citizens but they have always faced Member States' reluctance to take such a step. The measures adopted by the Member States within the Council are largely aimed at stopping the flows or at increasing controls on immigrants. The most "generous" measures, whether adopted or only proposed, for the integration of immigrants have instead come from the Commission or the EP, as analysed in the next sections.

Overall, the tendency of exclusion seems to be prevailing as regards all policies aimed at regulating first entries, also including policies of family reunion and asylum, while few concessions have been accorded to those TCNs already settled within the EU.

I.5 COMPATIBILITY OF THE NEW RULES WITH EUROPEAN VALUES

This exclusionary tendency, whether justified by economic or security reasons, is however creating increasing uneasiness in Europe and the emerging immigration policy is questioned more and more in the light of the best "European" traditions such as democracy, tolerance, and the respect for human rights and fundamental freedoms.

In this respect, it should be noted that Europe is seen by its people and also governors as a realm of democratic and liberal values opposed to racist and totalitarian regimes all over the world. Member States have always emphasised the importance of such values against any kind of discrimination, exclusion and intolerance. In fact, it seems that there is a willingness to build a European Union based on democratic values and human rights. By definition the protection of such rights must be universal: this is to say all individuals should be covered equally. Keeping with these proclaimed values would, therefore, force Member States' governments to approach the area related to TCNs more liberally. But this is not the case. The trend is to limit the improvement and progress in the area of Community law only to EC citizens but TCNs are not included in this project. Community declarations in favour of real solidarity and against discrimination are under siege due to the increasing number of TCNs arriving in and settling into the EU.

However, a democratic and rich society, such as the European Union, cannot exclude important portions of its legal residents from the mainstream of society. It should be remembered that TCN migrants arrive mainly from developing countries. Often they possess few qualifications and they may not master the language of the host State, which puts them in a very vulnerable position at the bottom of host societies. But they also possess a different ethnicity, distinct from "Europeans". This latter aspect is capable of having a cumulative effect and it makes them more vulnerable in the host society. In fact, even when they possess comparable skills to those of nationals, they face greater difficulties to improve their economic and social status. They too often face a sort of disguised racism and xenophobia. Their "visible" difference becomes indeed an important factor hampering their concrete integration into the European Union.

Again, the new restrictive rules are justified for economic and security reasons but also, at EU level, there is great concern as to what to do with the large communities of migrants who, because of their characteristics, are "difficult" to assimilate in the host societies. There is in fact a racist and xenophobic approach, whether hidden or open, in the elaboration of the new rules in order to impede or at least make the settlement of certain migrants more difficult. In this latter phase of immigration, flows, real or feared, and their associated consequences, have become entangled with the extraordinary complications of building a new European identity.[31]

This is leading to great tension between two opposite tendencies: *inclusion*, on the one hand, justified by traditional democratic and liberal values aimed at integrating TCNs in the host societies, and *exclusion*, which would maintain TCNs as a class apart.

Apart from humanitarian considerations about the justice of a policy based on discrimination and exclusion, motivated often by racist justification, Member States must comply with international commitments to respect fundamental human rights. The new policy is being criticised more and more for its incompatibility with the principle of equality. Non-discrimination on the basis of race or ethnic origin, whether direct or indirect, is strictly forbidden by the major international instruments of human rights protection.

Although outside the scope of the present work, this area of Community law deserves some clarification.

I.6 HUMAN RIGHTS ISSUES

At the beginning of the process of integration, matters related to the respect and protection of fundamental freedoms and human rights, were considered as falling outside the scope of EC law. As the Commission pointed out:

> "Observance and protection of human rights and fundamental freedoms in the Community are matters which fall primarily within the jurisdiction of the Member States: the individual is protected by, on the one hand, national constitutional provisions and, on the other, the supervision which, as far as their powers allow, the bodies of the European Convention of Human Rights exercise over domestic legal systems".[32]

However, it was soon made clear that the deepening of the integration process required that these special rights were observed and safeguarded in Europe. The ECJ, although initially reluctant to protect them *overtly* has since the late 1960s affirmed its determination to protect, according to the *Stauder* case, "the fundamental human rights enshrined in the general principles of Community law."[33] Since then, in keeping with its previous judgments, the ECJ has always recognised

31 See on this point Papademetriou P.G., *Coming Together or Pulling Apart? The European Union's Struggle with Immigration and Asylum*, Carnegie Endowment for International Peace, 1996.

32 European Commission, The European Community and Human Rights, Official Publications of the European Communities, Luxembourg, 1993, 12.

33 Case 29/69 *Stauder* [1969] ECR 419.

its competence in protecting individual rights.[34] This competence is not general but is limited to the protection of human rights and fundamental freedoms from violation of the Member States when adopting or implementing EC legislation. The ECJ recognised in fact the principles contained in the European Convention of Human Rights (ECHR) as principles common to the Member States but it also declared itself powerless to examine the compatibility with the European Convention of national legislation which concerns an area that falls within the jurisdiction of the national legislator.[35] As Lenaerts highlights:

> "The 'European model' of protection of fundamental rights rests on a division of responsibilities between two supranational legal orders, i.e. the legal order of the European Community and the legal order established by the European Convention for the Protection of Human Rights and Fundamental Freedoms within the Council of Europe...The Court of Justice developed a coherent case law relating to the protection of fundamental rights only to possible infringements by the Community itself or by the Member States acting in the field of application of Community Law, while it denied any impact of the Community concept of fundamental rights upon the Member States' freedom of action outside this field".[36]

However, more recently, in the *ERT* case,[37] the Court also held "on the other hand, where such rules do fall within the scope of Community law, and reference is made to the Court for a preliminary ruling, it must provide all the criteria of interpretation needed by the national court to determine whether those rules are compatible with the fundamental rights the observance of which the Court ensures and which derive in particular from the ECHR". In the case of *Kremzow* the Court reaffirmed the position held in the case of *ERT* and it ruled that "it has no jurisdiction with regard to national legislation lying outside the scope of Community law" but "measures are not acceptable in the Community (if) incompatible with observance of the human rights thus recognised and guaranteed."[38]

Considering that immigration matters are to be regulated under Community competence according to the Amsterdam Treaty, freedom of action of Member States is decisively curtailed and the ECJ will be fully competent in this area of law.

---

34 Case 41/73 *Nold 2* [1974] ECR 491. On the evolution of the ECJ's stance as regards the protection of human rights see Ward I., *The Margins of European Law*, MacMillan Press LTD, 1996, 141-147.

35 Joined Cases 60 and 61/84 *Cinéthèque*, [1985] ECR 2605.

36 Lenaerts K., "Fundamental Rights to be Included in a Community Catalogue", *European Law Review*, 1991, Vol. 16, 371-372.

37 Case C-260/89 *ERT* [1991] ECR I-2925.

38 Case C-299/95 *Kremzow* [1997] ECR I-2629.

The Maastricht Treaty expressly recognised the importance of protecting fundamental human rights at European level with the greatest respect of the ECHR. "The Convention must remain the essential reference point for the protection of human rights and fundamental freedoms in Europe as a whole in terms of both guaranteed rights and judicial control of respect for these rights...the European Union and the Council of Europe share the same goals of the principles of liberty, democracy and respect for human rights and fundamental freedoms and the rule of law".[39] Accordingly, old Article F (2) TEU stated that "the Union shall respect fundamental rights, as guaranteed by the European Convention of Human Rights...and as they result from the constitutional traditions common to the Member States, as general principles of Community Law". However, old Article L TEU denied the ECJ any competence to interpret and enforce that provision. Therefore, the insertion in the common provisions of the TEU made that commitment nothing but a political declaration. A further step was taken during the revision of the TEU. The Amsterdam Treaty revised Article F TEU, new Article 6 TEU, and it inserted a new Article 7 TEU. The amended Article 6 TEU puts more emphasis on human rights as it declares that:

> "The Union is founded on the principles of liberty, democracy, respect for human rights and fundamental freedoms, and the rule of law, principles which are in common to the Member States".

Also, the insertion of Article 7 TEU must be mentioned, which provides for a system of sanctions in the case of a breach of fundamental rights.
Article 7 TEU states that:

> "1.The Council meeting in the composition of the Heads of State or Government and acting by unanimity on a proposal by one third of the Member States or by the Commission and after obtaining the assent of the European Parliament, may determine the existence of a serious breach by a Member State of principles mentioned in Article 6, after inviting the government of the Member State in question to submit its observations.
> 2. Where such a determination has been made, the Council, acting by a qualified majority, may decide to suspend certain of the rights deriving from the application of this Treaty to the Member State in question, including the voting rights of the representative of the Government of that Member States in the Council. In doing so, the Council shall take into account the possible consequences of such a suspension on the rights and obligations of natural and legal persons.
> The obligations of the Member State in question under this Treaty shall in any case continue to be binding on that State.

39 Council Press Release, 7745/99.

3. The Council, acting by a qualified majority, may decide subsequently to vary or revoke measures taken under paragraph 2 in response to changes in the situation which led to their being imposed.
4. For the purpose of this Article, the Council shall act without taking into account the vote of the representative of the government of the Member State in question. Abstentions by members present in person or represented shall not prevent the adoption of decision referred to in paragraph 1. A qualified majority shall be defined as the same proportion of the weighted votes of the members of the Council concerned as laid down in Article 205 (2) of the Treaty establishing the European Community.
This paragraph shall also apply in the event of voting rights being suspended pursuant paragraph 2.
5. For the purposes of this Article, the European Parliament shall act by a two-thirds majority of the votes cast, representing the majority of its members".

The proposal, therefore, must be presented by the Commission or one-third of the Member States, and to be adopted it requires the unanimous vote in the Council and a two-thirds majority of the votes cast, representing the majority of its members in the EP.

Some authors have already criticised the requirement of unanimity necessary to declare the breach of fundamental human rights pointing out that "it is unlikely that any Member State should be so isolated as to fail to have any friendly state which would be willing to block a censure motion".[40] However, the *gravity* of the consequences in particular from a political standpoint for the Member State concerned by the sanction, justifies this very complex procedure.

This very long Article is the internal response to the commitment to take matters related to fundamental rights seriously. In fact, in the external dimension, the increasingly strong emphasis placed on the protection of human rights and the democratic process has resulted in the context of European political cooperation in the Community's more and more numerous agreements with non-member countries. Gradually, but especially since 1990, the reference to the principles of the UN Charters contained in the preambles to such agreements have been reinforced by the inclusion of clauses on human rights in the actual body of the agreements. For instance, Article 5 of the Lomé Convention makes the democratic values and the respect of human rights a key element of the Convention itself. Such a provision has enabled the Community to take action in the event of serious and persistent breach of human rights on different occasions.[41]

---

40 ILPA, "European Update: July 1997. The Draft Treaty of Amsterdam", 1997, 3.

41 Financial and technical cooperation was frozen with Sudan (1990), former Zaire (1992), Nigeria (1995), OJ 1998 C 386/49. After democratic elections in Nigeria on May 1999, the Community repealed its sanctions against Nigeria, OJ 1999 L 133/5.

In the most recent negotiations to association or cooperation agreements the respect for human rights has been considered as a preliminary condition for the signature itself. Article 49 TEU (ex Article O TEU) on new accession, inserts a new clause for the candidates for accession which reflects this commitment. Not only they must belong to the European continent but they must also respect the principles set out in Article 6 (1) TEU, namely principles of liberty, democracy, respect for human rights and fundamental freedoms, and the rule of law, *in order* to apply to become members of the European Union.

Also, the Amsterdam Treaty introduced a new title, which is discussed in detail in the next sections, establishing an area of freedom, security and justice. It is agreed that freedom must be completed by the full range of fundamental human rights, including protection from any form of discrimination (Article 13 EC).

Member States must therefore honour these commitments and adopt a more positive action in the elaboration of a common immigration policy.

I.7 THE RE-BIRTH OF EUROCENTRIC ATTITUDES

The targeting of specific categories of migrants accompanied by the insufficient adoption of measures to ensure their inclusion and integration is only increasing racist and xenophobic attitudes everywhere in Europe. In fact, migratory movements towards the Union are closely linked to the growing levels of intolerance, racism and xenophobia, and "their more extreme forms of expression, unhappily known in many Member States in recent years, overt hatred and physical violence against ethnic minorities, leading in numerous cases to senseless murders".[42] The number of extreme right-wing political parties that expressly manifest their racist programmes has worryingly increased.[43] According to Eurobarometer,[44] in the last ten years there has been an intensification of ethnocentric attitudes and a rise of fears that "the boat is full and there are too many aliens in Europe".

Scenarios of ethnic and cultural infiltration have led to both hostility towards foreigners and to ethnocentric attitudes.

Member States' approach in this area whereby a few positive measures are taken and, on the contrary, policies result in the creation of a "white fortress Europe" can only fuel racism and xenophobia towards non-EC citizens.

42 EP, Report drawn up on behalf of the Committee of Inquiry into Racism and Xenophobia on the findings of the Committee of Inquiry, Luxembourg, 1991.

43 See on this point *Race and Class*, "The Far Right in Europe: A Guide", 32(2), 1991, 127-146.

44 Eurobarometer, 1/1988 and 1/1993.

The European Commission has recently presented an Action Plan against Racism in which important measures were suggested to tackle this phenomenon. The Commission states that:

> "Racism is diametrically opposed to everything that Europe stands for in terms of human dignity, mutual respect and understanding and Citizenship in the broadest sense. European societies are multicultural and multi-ethnic and their diversity, as reflected by the range of different cultures and traditions, is a positive and enriching factor. The fight against racism goes hand in hand with the promotion of a society for all, which actively encourages integration and full participation."[45]

It follows that the prime responsibility for combating racism lies with the Member States but taking into account the transnational dimension of the problem, action is needed and justified at European level. The Commission recalls indeed that "the right to equal treatment and freedom from discrimination is one of the core principles and common values underlying the process of European integration".[46]

It should be interesting to see how many Member States would recognise themselves in such a definition of multicultural and multiethnic society and to what extent they agree to give up substantial powers in this area.

As often happens at EC/EU level, developments in new areas of law are contradictory, *while* many measures disregard the actual effect on racial and ethnic minorities and therefore result in being discriminatory for them, *at the same time*, important measures have been taken in the past years to fight against racism and xenophobia. Great emphasis has been placed on the need to tackle the problem of discrimination and racism in the Union.

Since the 1980s, Member States have recognised the danger hidden in the rise of racism and xenophobia and, therefore, the importance of combating such phenomena Union-wide. In 1986, the European Parliament, the Council, the Representatives of the Member States meeting within the Council and the Commission adopted a Joint Declaration against racism and xenophobia whereby they vigorously condemned all forms of intolerance, hostility and use of force against persons or groups of persons on the ground of racial, religious, cultural, social or nationality differences.[47] Later, in 1990, another Resolution on the fight against racism and xenophobia of the Council and the Representatives of the Governments of the Member States, meeting within the Council, was adopted.[48] The consideration given to these issues at Union level is demonstrated by the mention of them

45 European Commission, An Action Plan against Racism, COM (98) 183 final.
46 Ibidem.
47 OJ 1986 C 176/62.
48 OJ 1990 C 157/1.

in other Resolutions since then, in particular, the Resolution of the Council and the Representatives of the Governments of the Member States, meeting within the Council on the fight against racism and xenophobia in the fields of employment and social affairs[49] and the Council Resolution of the Council and of the Representatives of Member States' Governments meeting within the Council on the response of educational systems to the problems of racism and xenophobia.[50] Furthermore, the Council adopted a Joint Action concerning action to combat racism and xenophobia under Title VI.[51] In June 1996, the Council adopted a Regulation for the creation of the observatory against racism with office in Vienna.[52] EU's commitment to combat these phenomena led the Member States to declare 1997 the European Year against Racism which opened a great discussion on these themes.[53] Further developments are envisaged in the Amsterdam Treaty which includes a general non-discrimination clause offering the legal basis to adopt legislation in this area (*infra* section II.4). However, to combat racism and discrimination it is necessary to provide the Community with legal instruments but, most importantly, to make the public aware of the problems related to these phenomena. Recently, the European Commission brought the attention to this point when it adopted the Action Plan against Racism[54] in which several measures are proposed and discussed. The Action Plan, although representing a platform for discussion, must nonetheless be criticised because it is likely to be incapable of reaching its ambitious objectives as "the Action Plan against Racism can scarcely be described as an action plan. There are no specific plans with objective, timetable and financing".[55] Member States are left largely with the responsibility of implementing the plan.

Overall, the elaboration of a common immigration policy in Europe is still at the embryonic stage and action is needed. First of all, positive or pro-active action is required in order to eliminate these internal contradictions but also to ensure legal certainty. From a legal standpoint the regulation of third country migrants or would-be migrants is very chaotic. Under specific circumstances, TCNs' legal status is regulated under EC provisions, sometimes under international

49 OJ 1995 C 296/13.

50 OJ 1995 C 312/1.

51 OJ 1996 L 185/5.

52 Commissione Europea, Relazione Generale sull' Attività dell' Unione Europea, 1997, Ufficio delle Pubblicazioni Ufficiali della CE, Lussenburgo, 1998, 27.

53 Resolution of the Council and the Representatives of the Governments of the Member States, meeting within the Council concerning the European Year against Racism, OJ 1996 C 237/1.

54 EP, Report on the Communication from the Commission on Action Plan against Racism", A4-0478/98.

55 Ibidem, 7.

agreements signed by the Community, and, finally, by specific measures adopted under the third Pillar. TCNs are accorded different treatment compared to EC migrants but greater distinction must be made between the different categories of TCNs.

For practical reasons the analysis of the immigration rules in Europe is carried out in three different sections. The first is dedicated to the study of the legal status of the extra-Community population already settled within the Union (*immigrant policy*);[56] the second is concerned with the analysis of the immigration policy *strictu sensu,* this is to say those measures dealing with the regulation of the flows from outside the European Union (*immigration policy*); and, finally, the third section is aimed at studying all those restrictive and repressive measures of control, policing, expulsion, that are considered necessary in order to ensure the correct functioning of the system so created.

56 The distinction between *immigrant* policies and *immigrati*on policies is borrowed from Puchala who refers to the first ones as "having to do with the treatment of residing aliens once admitted" and the latter "having to do with admission into receiving countries". Puchala D.J., "Immigration into Western Societies: Implications and Policy Choices", in Uçarer E.M. & Puchala D.J. (eds), *supra* note 9, 341.

PART 2

IMMIGRANT POLICIES IN THE EUROPEAN UNION

II

THE LEGAL STATUS OF THIRD COUNTRY NATIONALS IN THE EU

It is clear that the life of migrants in the host societies is determined by the rights, duties and opportunities granted to them by the host State. Neglected for decades under EC/EU law, TCNs have been, since the late 1980s, the object of an increasing number of restrictive provisions. Such interest has been justified by several reasons, economic as well as security. Member States have concentrated more on the elaboration of restrictive and repressive measures to keep TCNs out of the Union (*immigration policies*) than to define the status of those already settled within its boundaries (*immigrant policies*). Back in the 1970s, concerns on the integration of TCNs were discussed in different Social Action Plans but no specific action was taken because, from a political standpoint, times were not ready to take that direction at EU level.

The need for integration has appeared less urgent. In particular, progress in the external dimension of the immigration policy – restrictive measures to regulate the flows from outside the Community- has been considered a prerequisite for any integration policy. As Peers points out "on the whole Member States' negotiators have weakened the integration features of proposals before them and strengthened the restrictive ones, to the point where the overall effect of Union policy has been to hamper integration, not support it".[57]

II.1 EU INSTITUTIONS' POSITION IN THE ELABORATION OF IMMIGRATION RULES

Presently TCNs are accorded only very few limited rights. In this latter phase of immigration or in the new migration era, the need to regulate the area of immigration is perceived as more and more urgent by the European actors. But the approach of the European Institutions in this area differs widely.

---

57 Peers S., *supra* note 28.

The discussion within the EP stressed the urgency to elaborate immigration rules with a more liberal approach. In the proposal for the charter of TCNs' Rights it argued that in order to define clearly their status and bridge the growing gap between EC nationals and TCNs: "Migrants must be given a clear status that will enable them to live their own lives as participants in the society in which they live, they must not be considered merely as 'workers' or as an exploitable and transitory labour force".[58] In addition, TCNs legally resident in the EU should be granted equivalent rights to those rights possessed by EC citizens. The residence permit, therefore, "would enable them to move about, settle down and work throughout the Union".[59] These rights should be accompanied "with basic social, economic, cultural, legal and political rights and so put an end to discrimination of all kinds against migrants".[60] The EP has reiterated this position and has deplored the exclusively repressive nature of many of the recommendations, declarations and resolutions, which have been adopted or are currently being drawn up, at EU level. It has demanded without further delays that immigrants from outside the Community enjoy economic and social rights and gain the same civil, cultural and political rights as EC citizens. The equality of treatment principle, in the EP's opinion, shall apply without restriction to all people lawfully present on the territory of the European Union.[61]

The very liberal position of the EP is not supported by the other Institutions. The European Commission is in fact more cautious when dealing with TCNs rights. However, it is slowly moving towards the EP's positions. In the past, the Commission, aware that times were not ready for radical changes, did not incorporate measures comparable to those presented by the EP in its legislative proposals. The Commission's proposals were mainly directed at reaching the complete removal of the internal frontiers and they only indirectly benefited TCNs. But in late Declarations the Commission has overtly embraced the TCNs cause. "The integration of migrants is an imperative dictated by the democratic and humanitarian tradition of the Member States."[62] It has also remembered the need to reach equal treatment for migrant workers and to combat all discrimination:[63] "A further essential aspect is the economic and social integration of lawfully established non-Union nationals together with the principle of non-discrimination set in the Amsterdam

58 EP, Report on the Status of nationals of non-member countries in the European Union, A3-0332/93.

59 Ibidem.

60 Ibidem.

61 EP, Annual Report on Respect for Human Rights in the European Union (1996), A4-0034/98.

62 Proposal for a Decision of the Council establishing a Convention on Rules for the Admission of Third Country Nationals to the Member States, COM (97) 387 final.

63 European Commission, An Action Plan against Racism, *supra* note 45.

Treaty".[64] The Commission has recently accompanied these general declarations with more specific proposals, analysed in the next sections.

Finally, the Council of Ministers and the Member States have been very reluctant to adopt measures aimed at improving TCNs' legal status, concentrating more on proposals aimed at restricting and stopping the flows of newcomers. However, the Tampere Council seems to mark a change, at least in the language used in dealing with TCNs. It is stated that "The European Union must ensure fair treatment of third country nationals who reside legally on the territory of its Member States. A more vigorous integration policy should aim at granting them rights and obligations comparable to those of EU citizens. It should also enhance non-discrimination in economic, social and cultural life and develop measures against racism and xenophobia".

The often contrasting positions of the European Institutions have made progress in this area slow and inconsistent. This a very sensitive area in which the tension discussed above between the two tendencies of *inclusion* v *exclusion* is greater. It is more and more difficult to reconcile the Member States' tendency to exclude large numbers of legally residents, in particular those who are in the European Union on a permanent basis, from enjoying EU and EC rights *with* democratic values. Particularly, because the presence of those TCNs who are settled on a permanent basis within the EU has notably increased so that it is now possible to talk of a Sixteenth Member State. Many have gained important rights but whether voluntarily or not, they have not acquired citizenship from the host State. As the number of this category of TCNs has considerably increased, some authors have decided to distinguish them from the rest of the extra-Community population and to define them *denizens*, this is to say "persons who are foreign citizens with a legal and permanent status."[65]

II.2 THE REGULATION OF THE LEGAL STATUS OF TCNS WITHIN THE EU

Under EU and EC law, as they now stand, there is a great difference in the treatment between EC citizens and TCNs. EC migrants have been able to gain important rights and protection under EC social and free movement chapters. TCN migrants, on the contrary, are, except for a few categories, not covered by those provisions.

---

64 European Commission, Communication from the Commission, Towards an Area of Freedom, Security and Justice, COM (98) 459 final.

65 Hammar, T., *Democracy and the Nation State, Aliens, Denizens and Citizens in a World of International Migration*, Avebury, 1990, 12-18. .

More importantly, as discussed above, EC nationals are increasingly seen as social and political actors, not just as economic migrants, under EC/EU provisions. Such a change has taken place largely in the past decade but the approach as far as TCNs are concerned has remained unchanged. They are seen as guest workers and not as an integral part of the host society. Many Member States strongly refuse to accept this change and, consequently, to reserve energies for the integration of a larger extra-Community population, culturally and somatically different, who is present in their territory. They rather concentrate on provisions to keep them out. Taking into account that, until recently, the competence to deal with matters related to immigration was principally circumscribed to the third Pillar under which Member States had greater powers, very few measures have been adopted to regulate the legal status of those TCNs lawfully settled within the EU's territory.

Until the adoption of the Treaty of Amsterdam, with few irrelevant exceptions, no competence to regulate these matters was foreseen under EC law, regardless of the presence of more than ten million TCNs legally resident within the European Union. No specific reference was made in the original EC Treaty to any competence whatsoever as the regulation of the legal status of TCNs, the only exception is the old Article 59 EC. The regulation of the movement of migrants within the EU was limited to nationals of Member States, not migrants any more but, since the Maastricht Treaty, *citizens* exercising their freedom of movement's rights. Nevertheless, the EC Treaty, since its origin, has allowed for the granting of some rights to the extra-Community population living within the Community's boundaries, under a few specific sections, i.e. *freedom of movement of persons* and *social provisions*.

Also, great differences exist among the extra-Community population itself. There are only a few rules which are generally applicable to TCNs. Often their status is defined by means of international agreements concluded by the Community under Articles 228 EC (new Article 300 EC) and 238 EC (new Article 310 EC) with third countries. It should be remembered that such agreements are part of international law but the ECJ has made it clear on several occasions that such agreements are *acts* of the Institutions of the Community and, therefore, their provisions form an integral part of Community law.[66] More importantly, the ECJ has ruled that "provisions contained in these agreements are capable of having direct effect when having regard of its wording and the purpose and nature of the agreement itself such provisions contain a clear and precise obligation which is not subject, in its implementation or effects, to the adoption of any subsequent

66 Case 12/86 *Demirel* [1987] ECR 3719, para 7; Case 181/73, *Haegeman* [1974] ECR 449, para 4 and 5; Case 30/88, *Greece v Council* [1989] ECR 3711, para 12.

measure".[67] Individuals are, therefore, entitled to rely directly upon the provisions of the agreement in litigation in any of the Member States.

The majority of these accords is aimed at establishing economic cooperation; incidentally they may affect the national work force. TCNs are accorded a more or less favourable treatment in relation to the nationality they possess.

Finally, few measures have been adopted or are under discussion under the Title IV EC aimed at regulating the status of TCNs lawfully settled in the Union. In Tampere, the European Council stated its determination to develop the area of freedom, security and justice, established by the Amsterdam Treaty, and to bridge the existing gap between EU national and TCNs as far as possible. "The legal status of third country nationals should be approximated to that of Member States' nationals".

But, the principle of equality of treatment among the migrants in the Member States is far from being achieved.

From a legal standpoint, the regulation of the legal status of TCNs settled in the Union is therefore very chaotic.

More importantly, as discussed above, the construction of the European Union which often results in the discrimination of TCNs is hardly compatible with the protection of human rights and fundamental freedoms as guaranteed under both EC law and international law.

Among the extra-Community population, in particular female migrants seem to suffer the most, as they must face the double burden of being discriminated against due to their belonging to ethnic minority groups and because of their sex.

II.3 Gender discrimination in the Union

According to Fredman and Szyszczak[68] "for women there are two central causative features of sex discrimination: issues relating to child-care and domestic responsibilities, and issues relating to violence". TCN female migrants do not escape this scheme.

As regards the first point, it is important to remember that the traditional model of the family which sees men as the breadwinners and heads of family and women as responsible for the domestic sphere is often a reality: men are the economically active sex while women are confined to domestic responsibilities, outside the

---

67 *Demirel*, ibidem, para 14, and Case C-192/89 *Sevince* [1990] ECR 3497, para 13.

68 See Fredman S. and Szyszczak E., "The Interaction of Race and Gender", in Hepple B.A. & Szyszczak E. (eds), *Discrimination: the Limits of Law*, Mansell Publishing Limited, 1992, 218-219.

market, ancillary to male market actors.[69] This is even more true when dealing with ethnic minority groups, especially belonging to Muslem countries, where the conception of family can be particularly sexist: wives follow the destiny of their fathers or husbands and they are responsible for the domestic work which includes the upbringing of children as well.

Accordingly, although not all TCN female migrants arrive as spouses, many are wives who decide to follow their migrant husband for the well-being of the family and they therefore have a dependent status on men.

As regards *gender-related violence*, statistics in Europe show appalling records of violence against women, regardless their cultural, social and economic differences.[70] This comes in various forms, "pornography, sexual harassment at work and rape"[71] but, special mention must also be made of *domestic violence*. Violence, in general, is not gender specific but domestic violence is mainly suffered by women. According to the Women's European Lobby:

> "Violence against women is a crime. Yet, institutions and individuals still treat it as a private affair...Violence is a serious violation of women's human rights and an undeniable obstacle to women's full participation in society. Ignoring the issue of violence against women results in relegating a public crime to the private sphere. Violence kills; it shatters lives and families and contributes to social disintegration. Acts or threats of violence instil fear, impede upon women's mobility, limiting their access to resources and activities. Much energy, time and resources are invested in tolerating violence – giving a sense that it is an 'inevitable' part of society and something women alone should deal with".[72]

This long passage shows in very clear terms how violence represents a gross violation of human rights of women. It should be noted that often violence against women leads to the murder of the victim. For instance, in Northern Ireland, 40%

---

69 A wide literature on the position of women in the EU exists. To name but a few publications see: Churches Commission for Migrants in Europe, "Immigrants Women and Integration towards Equal Opportunities", *CCME Briefing Paper*, 1995, No 21. Mullen T., "Nationality and Immigration", in Mc Lean S. & Burrows N. (eds), *The Legal Relevance of Gender, Some Aspects of Sex-Based Discrimination*, MacMillan Press LTD, 1988, 147-169. Campbell T., "Sex Discrimination: Mistaking the Relevance of Gender", ibidem, 16-39. Hervey T., "A Gendered Perspective on the Right to Family Life", in Neuwahl N.A. & Rosas A. (eds), *The European Union and Human Rights*, 1995, 221-234. Wrench J. & Solomos J. (eds), *Racism & Migration in Western Europe*, Berg Publishers LTD, 1993. Moebius I & Szyszczak E., "Of Raising Pigs & Children", *Yearbook of European Law*, 1999, forthcoming.

70 Fédération Internationale des Ligues des Droits de l' Homme La Lettre (FIDH), *Violence Coniugale, une Réalité trop Banale*, 1999, Vol. 15.

71 See Fredman S. & Szyszczak E., *supra* note 68.

72 Http://www.womenlobby.org/en/action/projets/index.html.

of the murders are committed by men against their partners; in Finland 22% of the women interviewed declared to have been victim of violence by their partners, while in Austria one in five women has suffered violence inflicted by the partner at least once in her life.[73] As will be discussed in later sections, the denial of certain rights does not *obviously* increase the cases of violence against women but it is capable of weakening their reaction against all types of violence and abuse.

An old form of violence suffered mainly by women which has gained importance recently is the *trade in persons* into the European Union for slavery purposes. The trade of human beings, which largely concerns women and children, is becoming a very lucrative business for criminal networks that take advantage of the poverty and unsuspiciousness of their victims to force them into prostitution or slavery in a broader sense.

Notwithstanding its gender neutrality, EC/EU law as it now stands, does not take in due account the position of migrant women and that they are more easily subject to old and new forms of violence which makes them very vulnerable.

At this point, some preliminary remarks about the EC provisions related to protection against sex and race discrimination are necessary. There is a tendency at EC/EU level to establish analogies between race and gender discrimination and there is an effort to combat these two different forms of discrimination by using the same techniques and the same approach. "The experience derived from Community legislation and case law on equal treatment between women and men should serve as a model for future legislation against race discrimination."[74]

---

73 FIDH, *supra* note 70.

74 EP, Report on the Communication from the Commission on Action Plan against Racism, A4-0478/98. Also, see Commissioner Flynn's Speech, at a conference held in Vienna, 4 December 1998, which contained a package of proposals to fight discrimination. Mr Flynn affirmed in that occasion "this package would be reinforced by an approach which mainstreams anti-discrimination into all other EU policies". *Our thinking here draws heavily on our experience of gender legislation and action on the issue of equality* (emphasis added). http://europa.eu.int/rapid/cgi/rapci.ksh...gettxt=gt&doc=SPEECH/98/282/0/RAPID&lg=EN.

II.4 EC PROTECTION AGAINST RACE AND SEX DISCRIMINATION

Until the Treaty of Amsterdam, no general provisions were provided for under the treaties to prohibit race and sex discrimination. The non-discrimination clause contained in the original version of the EC Treaty, old Article 6 EC,[75] was very limited in scope and it concerned the obligation to not discriminate against EC nationals on grounds of their nationality. Specific mention of EC nationals was absent in the Article but this was interpreted as not covering TCNs. The lack of any revision during the IGC accompanied by the inclusion in the EC Treaty of a more general *non-discrimination* provision seems to confirm that the personal scope has not changed. Some could however argue that such a restriction is to be abolished under the Amsterdam Treaty as TCNs are now under the scope of the new Treaty and their exclusion can no longer be justified. But this appears not to be the case.

Protection against *sex discrimination* was guaranteed even before the signature of the Treaty of Amsterdam. The EC Treaty contained, in old Article 119 EC, a specific reference to sex discrimination in pay[76] but protection was also ensured by the ECJ activism in the area.[77]

Old Article 119 EC Treaty stated, in fact, that "each Member State shall during the first stage ensure and subsequently maintain the application of the principle that men and women should receive equal pay for equal work". This principle, i.e. principle of equal treatment, was extended to discrimination in employment and vocational training by Council Directive 76/207 that provides that "the principle of equal treatment shall mean that there shall be no discrimination whatsoever on grounds of sex either directly or indirectly by reference in particular to marital or family status".[78] TCN female migrants, as women, were able to benefit from

75 Old Article 6 EC (new Article 12 EC) states that "within the scope of application of this Treaty, and without prejudice to any special provisions contained therein, any discrimination on grounds of nationality shall be prohibited". Although this discrimination clause could have been included more generally in Article 13 EC, ex Article 6a EC, it seems that Member States decided not to eliminate it because of its direct effect.

76 For an analysis of EC legislation in this area see Rossilli M., "The European Community's Policy on the Equality of Women", *The European Journal of Women's Studies,* 1997, Vol. 4, 63-82.

77 On the contribution of the ECJ to sex equality see Fenwick H. & Hervey T.K., "Sex Equality in the Single Market: New Directions of the European Court of Justice", *Common Market Law Review*, 1995, 32, 443-470.

78 Article 2.1 of Council Directive on the implementation of the principle of equal treatment for men and women as regards access to employment, vocational training and promotion, and working conditions, OJ 1976 L 39/40.

the Community's policy to promote equal opportunities as between women and men.[79]

As far *as racism and xenophobia* are concerned, the fight against these phenomena has seen the active participation of the academic world[80] and several declarations and conclusions were adopted by the European Institutions, always in the form of soft law.[81] The need to provide clearer legal basis to combat any form of discrimination led to the insertion of a very general clause in the Amsterdam Treaty. Article 13 EC (ex Article 6a EC) states:

> "Without prejudice to the other provisions of this Treaty and within the limits of the powers conferred by it upon the Community, the Council, acting unanimously on a proposal from the Commission and after consulting the European Parliament, may take appropriate action to combat discrimination based on sex, racial or ethnic origin, religion or belief, disability, age or sexual orientation."

Such a clause must be welcomed because it is able to fill the lacuna providing the legal basis to adopt legislation in this area. Unfortunately, the compromised nature of this Article is evident by its wording: the clause "does not go so far as to prohibit discrimination, but simply makes provisions for appropriate action, which will moreover require a unanimous vote in the Council",[82] it is unlikely it will have any direct effect and without deadlines forcing the Council to act only

---

79 See on this point European Commission, The social situation and employment of migrant women, COM (88) 734 final.

80 A wide literature exists in this area, many scholars have, indeed, recognised the danger of the rise of racism and xenophobia in Western Europe and the importance to find an answer at European level. See Essed P., *Diversity Gender, Color, and Culture*, Braun Brumfield, 1996; Fridlizius S. & Peterson A., *Stranger or Guest? Racism and Nationalism in Contemporary Europe*, Almqvist & Wiksell International, 1996. An entire dossier has been dedicated to racism and xenophobia by the *Centre d' Information et d' Etudes sur les Migrations Internationales*, 1997, Vol. 9, No 49, 39-128.

81 All the European Institutions have participated to the debate but the EP has overtly expressed in several occasions great concern for these movements through many Reports and Resolutions. EP, Resolution on the resurgence of racism and xenophobia in Europe and the danger of right-wing extremist violence OJ 1993 C 150/127; EP, Resolution on the rise of racism in Europe and the criminal attacks against Turkish citizens in Germany OJ 1993 C 194/1; EP, Resolution on racism and xenophobia OJ 1993 C 342/7; EP, Resolution on the situation of Gypsies in the European Community OJ C 128/1; EP, Resolution on racism, xenophobia OJ 1994 C 323/154; EP, Resolution on the Racist Murders in Austria; OJ 1995 C 56/9; EP, Resolution on racism, xenophobia and anti-semitism OJ 1995 C 126/75. The EP in different occasions expressed its worries that these matters were dealt through intergovernmental methods and it called to adopt binding legal instruments to combat these phenomena under the First Pillar, namely a "anti-discrimination directive" see EP Resolution on the Communication from the Commission on racism, xenophobia and anti-semitism OJ 1996 C 152/57.

82 EP, Report on the Treaty of Amsterdam, A4-0347/97/ANNEX.

time will show the appropriateness of this formula to combat a delicate issue such as discrimination. Moreover, the implementation of this Article must be within the limits of the competence conferred by the EC Treaty as some authors have pointed out "one interpretation of which may be that anti-discrimination measures should only be adopted in areas of existing Community competence such as employment or social policy. It does not appear to create a free-standing principle or to be capable of direct effect, being framed as a classical legal base."[83] At the time of writing, the Council had not adopted any specific measure. The Commission, however, even before the Amsterdam Treaty entered into force, started elaborating a package of proposal to implement Article 13 EC. Also, according to the Action Plan,[84] it was agreed that, even though no deadline was established in the Amsterdam Treaty for the adoption of measures in this area, within five years of Treaty coming into force action against racism and xenophobia should be taken. Old Article 6 EC (Article 12 EC) has remained unchanged so that the fight against racial discrimination is limited and it does not include discrimination on the grounds of nationality, which exists in several important areas such as housing, education or employment.

The Amsterdam Treaty introduced wider protection for women against *sex discrimination*. Old Article 119 EC was revised so that it adds to the principle contained in the original version of Article 119 EC of equal pay for equal work the express mention that equal pay also applies to work of equal value.

Article 2 EC states "the Community shall have as its task...to promote...equality between men and women...". Also, Article 3 EC, which includes the objectives of the Community, has been amended in order to provide that "in all the activities referred to in this Article, the Community shall aim to eliminate inequalities, and to promote equality between men and women". The promotion of equality between men and women is recognised as one of the objectives of the Community. Article 3 EC, in particular, seems to include the principle of mainstreaming so as to eliminate any discrimination between men and women in all Community activities beyond the employment field.[85] And finally, Article 13 EC (ex Article 6a EC), which as seen above, provides a general non-discrimination clause.

---

83 Langrish S., "The Treaty of Amsterdam: Selected Highlights", *European Law Review*, 1998, Vol. 23, 15.

84 Action Plan of the Commission and the Council on how best to implement the provisions of the Treaty of Amsterdam on an Area of freedom, security and justice OJ 1998 C 19/1.

85 The principle of mainstreaming was previously defined in the 4th Action Programmeme for Equal Opportunities see European Commission, Equal Opportunities for Women and Men in the European Union, Annual Report 1996, COM (95) 381 final.

Article 13 EC (ex Article 6a EC), as has already been said above, does not have direct effect, it requires a unanimous vote in the Council, and it needs implementing measures without nonetheless agreed deadlines.

In respect of discrimination on the grounds of *race or ethnic origin*, apart from the protection afforded by the general clause contained in Article 13 EC (ex Article 6a EC), Member States committed themselves under the new Title VI to develop a common action among them to provide citizens with a high level of safety within an area of freedom, security and justice by preventing and combating racism and xenophobia (new Article 29 TEU).

New Article 29 TEU recognises those issues as matters that require a common action, but the reasons for the insertion in the amended Title VI undoubtedly proves that Member States want to maintain the control over these areas, free from any Community control. In fact, many problems concerning racism and xenophobia may surge in the field of immigration, but the new Title VI TEU deals with police and judicial co-operation in criminal matters, only. There is no mention in the sections referring to immigration and asylum, which have been communitarised. It is widely known that the second and the third Pillars, although amended, are the least effective and still represent a form of intergovernmental cooperation. Moreover, Article 29 TEU continues by stating that "that objective shall be achieved by preventing and combating crime, organised or otherwise, in particular terrorism, trafficking in persons, and offences against children, illicit drug trafficking and illicit arms trafficking, corruption and fraud". As it was argued "exactly how any of this helps combat racism is unclear. In any event, in the whole new third Pillar no further mention is made of racism or xenophobia".[86]

Finally, new Article 29 TEU limits its objective of preventing and combating racism "to provide citizens with a high level of safety, security and justice", how this specification must be interpreted is not clear but in keeping with the interpretation of the Treaties "citizens" are only those who are nationals of the Member States excluding TCN migrants. It seems though that the great majority of those in need of protection (70% of TCNs within the European Union belong to minority groups) are excluded.

Nowadays, the instruments provided for under EC and EU law do not seem to be adequate to protect TCNs against discrimination, whether overt or more hidden.

The measures adopted so far, whether directly aimed at regulating the status of TCNs or only incidentally affecting them, legally authorise a different treatment

86 ILPA, *supra* note 40.

of the extra-Community population compared to EC citizens, and they are able to produce undesirable discriminatory effects increasing the vulnerability and marginalisation of TCNs.

In the elaboration of a common immigration policy not only is the commitment of protection against discrimination not taken in due account but the same provisions are often the cause of their discrimination.

Eurocentric considerations are present in the elaboration of immigration measures. It seems that Member States are conscious of the necessity, due to political and security reasons as well as economic benefits, of the opening towards third countries but, at the same time, they are also concerned about the need to protect European culture and heritage. Such measures, therefore, sometimes mirror the "white fortress approach" severely affecting racial and ethnic minority groups.

II.5 PROGRESS TOWARDS A MORE "HUMAN" EUROPEAN UNION

Member States, through several revisions to the original Treaties, particularly by means of the Maastricht Treaty (1993) and the Amsterdam Treaty (1999), have decided to formalise the tendency of creating a Union not *purely* economic and consequently included more areas under the EC/EU competence. This process has as its focal point the *citizen*, as a human being and not just as an economic factor in the production process. As old Article A TEU stated:

> "This Treaty marks a new stage in the process of creating an ever closer Union among the peoples of Europe, in which decisions are taken as closely as possible to the citizen".

This Article, which has become Article 1 TEU, has been reinforced under the Amsterdam Treaty which refers to the need for more transparency in the decision making process as it states "...decisions are taken as *openly* as possible and as closely as possible to the citizen" (emphasis added).

Accordingly, although some authors may disagree,[87] citizens are increasingly conferred more important rights. This view was confirmed during the Cardiff European Council (1998) where it was declared that "a sustained effort is needed

---

87 In the light of the development made in the IGC, Weiler argues "there is much rhetoric on a commitment to employment, there are a few significant proposals on free movement, elimination of gender discrimination and other rights...But overall, the net gainers are, again, the governments". Weiler J.H.H., "The European Union Belongs to Its Citizens: Three Immodest Proposals", *European Law Review*, 1997, Vol. 22, 151-152.

by the Member States and all the institutions to bring the Union closer to people by making it more open, more understandable and more relevant to daily life".[88]

> "The people of Europe are now no longer considered simply as a factor of economic production and, as the Community has diversified its role and activities, Community law conferred upon these people some features of Citizenship of a nation state."[89]

The EC Treaty, as modified by the Maastricht Treaty, was very clear in this respect. Old Article 8 EC stated:

> "Every person holding the nationality of a Member State shall be a citizen of the Union: Citizens of the Union shall enjoy the rights conferred by this Treaty and shall be subject to the duties imposed thereby".[90]

The following Articles 8a, 8b, 8c, 8d EC (new Articles 18, 19, 20, 21 EC) enumerated the new rights conferred upon EC citizens by the TEU. Under the Amsterdam Treaty, this was not an area subject to radical changes.

Moreover, there is a tendency to consider EC citizens' rights in a new light. In the case *Martínez Sala*,[91] the material scope of Article 8a was questioned and the Commission suggested that, since the entry into force of the Maastricht Treaty, every EC citizen must be recognised a right of residence in any Member State. If the Commission's construction of Article 8a is its correct interpretation it is undoubtedly a major advancement towards a more human Europe. This seems, indeed, to imply an *autonomous* right for EC citizens to enter and reside in other Member States *regardless* of their position in the labour market. Unfortunately, the Court did not clarify this point as it did not consider "necessary to examine whether the person concerned can rely on Article 8a of the Treaty in order to obtain recognition of a new right to reside in the territory of the Member State concerned, since it is common ground that she has already been authorised to reside there".[92] Even if the Court had accepted the Commission's reasoning in the *Martínez Sala* case and ruled that all EC citizens had a general right to reside anywhere in the Union, such a right when not accompanied by all the benefits available for the national population would have not improved the situation

88 Cardiff European Council Conclusions, June 1998.
89 Pollard D. & Ross M. cited in Shaw J. "The Interpretation of European Union Citizenship", *The Modern Law Review,* 1998, Vol. 61, No 3, 303.
90 Article 8.1 and 2 EC Treaty.
91 Case C-85/96 *Martínez Sala* [1998] ECR I-2691.
92 Ibidem, para 60.

significantly.[93] But the Commission's interpretation of the Article 8 EC is nonetheless important from a political standpoint as presumably it responds to the will to expand EC citizens' rights.

But as things now stand, the Court still privileges an economic interpretation of EC rules and, therefore, EC *economic* migrants are the most privileged. The Court's economic approach in this area is reflected *particularly* when dealing with the rights of the extra-Community population.

The creation of European Citizenship by the Maastricht Treaty has been the centre of a very controversial debate in Europe. As made clear from the wording of old Article 8 EC it only covers nationals of the Member States. Therefore, as the majority of the extra-Community population keeps the nationality of the country of origin, either because they want to maintain the ties with their mother country[94] or because in many Member States naturalisation is a long and difficult process, they are excluded from its scope.

II.6 RELEVANCE OF NATIONALITY CONCEPT FOR COMMUNITY PURPOSES

The nationality of the person concerned has become extremely important under Community law as it entitles the holder to exercise a wide range of old and new rights. But although the criterion of nationality has special relevance at Community level, its acquisition and loss belongs exclusively to the competence of each Member State. This was made evident by the annexation to the Maastricht Treaty of the "Declaration on Nationality of a Member State" where Member States, concerned to keep nationality matters outside the scope of Community law, declared that questions regarding nationality would be solved solely by reference to national laws.[95]

---

93 On this point see Moebius I. & Szyszczak E., *supra* note 69.

94 According to Soysal "restrictive procedures for Citizenship are only a partial explanation for their foreignness. Survey have repeatedly shown that there has not been an urgent demand among immigrants themselves to take on the Citizenship of their country of residence, either, when there is a demand, it is usually accompanied by demands for dual Citizenship". Soysal Y.N., "Changing Citizenship in Europe", in Cesarani D. & Fulbrook M. (eds), *Citizenship, Nationality and Migration in Europe,* Routledge, 1996, 20.

95 "The Conference declares that, wherever in the Treaty establishing the European Community reference is made to nationals of the Member States, the question whether an individual possesses the nationality of a Member State shall be settled solely by reference to the national law of the Member concerned. Member States may declare, for information, who are to be considered their nationals for Community purposes by way of a declaration lodged with the Presidency and may amend any declaration when necessary". Declaration on Nationality of a Member State annexed

The absence of Community interference on nationality matters has allowed some Member States to make declarations adopting a definition of nationality for the purposes of Community law different from that which applies in their domestic law.[96] But *if*, as regards the acquisition of nationality, Member States have wide powers, *its loss* must respect European law. In the *Airola*[97] case, the ECJ for the first time clearly broke the principle that the dispositions related to nationality made by a Member State were always and under any circumstance to be recognised and applied. The ECJ further developed this reasoning in the *Micheletti*[98] case ruling that the power of Member States to make dispositions of their nationality is a competence which must be exercised with due regard to Community law.[99] It, indeed, held that "whenever a Member State, having due regard for Community law, has granted its nationality to a person, another Member State may not, by imposing an additional condition for its recognition, restrict the effects of the grant of that nationality with a view to the exercise of a fundamental freedom provided for in the Treaty, particularly since the consequence of allowing such a possibility would be that the class of persons to whom the Community rules on freedom of establishment were applied might vary from one Member State to another".[100] Despite these very cautious attempts of the ECJ to limit Member States' discretion, nationality remains a very important expression of their sovereign powers.

The construction of the concept of nationality implies the creation of boundaries and, therefore, it defines those who belong to the Member State and share a

to the TEU.

96 Two Member States have made such declarations: the Federal Republic of Germany and the United Kingdom. The earliest of these declarations is the unilateral declaration made by Germany upon signing the EEC Treaty and the Euratom Treaty in 1957, by which it was declared that "All Germans as defined in the Basic Law for the Federal Republic of Germany shall be considered as nationals of the Federal Republic of Germany". Declarations to identical effect were made upon signing the Treaty of Accession 1979 and the Treaty of Accession 1985. The UK made a unilateral declaration on nationality upon signing the Treaty of Accession in 1972. It replaced that Declaration in 1983 with another unilateral declaration upon the entry into force of the British Nationality Act 1981. For further information on this point see Hall S., *Nationality, Migration Rights and Citizenship of the Union*, Martinus Nijoff Publisher, 1995.

97 Case 21/74 *Airola* [1974] ECR 221.

98 Case C-369/90 *Micheletti* [1992] ECR I- 4239.

99 For a further comment of this judgment see Hall S., "Loss of Union Citizenship in Breach of Fundamental Rights", *European Law Review*, 1996, Vol. 21, No. 2, 129-143.

100 For further information see O' Leary S., "Nationality Law and Community Citizens: A Tale of two Uneasy Bedfellows", *Yearbook of European Law*, 1992, No 12, 354-384, Greenwood C., "Nationality and the Limits of the Free Movement of Persons in Community Law", *Yearbook of European Law*, 1987, No 7, 185-210. Simmonds C.R., "The British Nationality Act 1981 and the Definition of the Term 'National' for Community Purposes", *Common Market Law Review,* 1984, No 21, 675-686.

common set of values, i.e. insiders, and those who do not, i.e. outsiders. This construction is reflected at European level in the elaboration of the European Citizenship,[101] which is based on the nationality of the Member States, but the dividing line between insiders and outsiders in the European dimension is more extreme. In fact, while at national level Member States slowly began to recognise the position of TCNs, at least, those who are legally settled on a permanent basis, within their territory, granting them a few rights, the requirement to hold the nationality of a Member State immediately deprives TCNs of an important set of Community rights.

II.7 EUROPEAN CITIZENSHIP: EXCLUSION OF THE EXTRA-COMMUNITY POPULATION

The very controversial decision to limit European Citizenship only to nationals of Member States can only be justified by presuming the existence of an European identity based on a cultural, ethnic and racial homogeneity not shared by the extra-Community population. EC citizens share an important set of values, such as common democratic beliefs, common culture, religion, race, etc.[102]

This presumed homogeneity is to be stimulated and protected. But many authors have criticised these presumptions. Pieterse[103] argues that the definition of the European culture based on common values "from Plato to Nato" is "in addition to being chauvinist, elitist, pernicious and alienating, wrong". He argues that:

> "It is wrong as regards the origins of European culture; it is wrong in so representing European culture that European regional cultures and subcultures are overlooked; it is wrong in representing elite culture as culture tout court and in denying popular culture;

101 There is a great confusion of the two terms nationality and Citizenship. According to O' Leary, nationality is a positive legal prescription of membership of that state and it refers to the fact that the individual is subject to the public authority and legal order of that state, while Citizenship is defined as the legal and political status of belonging to and participating in the shaping of the polity of that state. However, she acknowledges, such definitions are not applicable to all Member States as, for instance in Italy, nationality and Citizenship are synonymous but in the UK Citizenship rights and duties are more closely linked to the immigration status of the holder than to nationality aspects. For further information on this point see O' Leary S., *European Union Citizenship. The Options for Reform*, IPPR, 1996, 11-13.

102 The view of the existing common culture is reflected in the Title IX as introduced by the Maastricht Treaty, that states "The Community shall contribute to the flowering of the cultures of the Member States, while respecting their national and regional diversity and at the same time bringing the common cultural heritage to the fore" (Article 151 EC, ex Article 128 EC).

103 Pieterse J.N., "Fictions of Europe", *Race and Class*, 1991, Vol. 32(3), 3-10.

> it is wrong in defining European culture in terms of the past ('inherited civilisation') and in totally ignoring Europe's contemporary multicultural realties".[104]

Nevertheless it is true that Western Europe shared a common history and culture.

More importantly, Member States have built themselves on the same basis. They are *all* democracies based on the respect of fundamental human rights, they are market economies, and they rely on welfare systems.

Europeans, in the strict sense of the term, do not exist and it is doubtful that they will in the near future: Europeans still maintain their national dimension, they are Britons, Italians, Spaniards, etc. However in a wider international dimension they will probably tend to recognise themselves as Europeans.

The creation of European Citizenship *per se* therefore must be welcomed as it could introduce a greater sense of belonging and create a real solidarity among Union citizens. In this sense is questionable the argument of Kristeva[105] "that the search for identity is always a hate reaction, a determination to isolate, exclude and oppress Others" is questionable.

Such a very positive element however has been instrumentalised to discriminate against those who are excluded from this construction. What therefore should be feared is who the construction of the European identity can serve as a tool to exclude those that are not considered Europeans under the stricter sense of European Citizenship. It is this "instrumentalisation" that must be revised.

It is worth noting that, as other authors have remarked, strengthening the concept of Europeness, in the attempt to define the characteristics of Europeans, has implied the accentuation of non Europeans, the Others.[106] Europeaness is associated with *whiteness, wealth* and *legality*. Such presumption of white supremacy in the European context is shaping not only the Citizenship concept but more importantly immigration policies. Accordingly, there is no place for the great majority of poor TCNs, who belong to ethnic minority groups, originally from developing countries, indistinctly perceived, as noted above, as Blacks. The extra-

104 Ibidem, 3-4.

105 Kristeva cited in Ward I, "Law and the Other Europeans", *Journal of Common Market Studies*, 1997, Vol. 35, 79-96.

106 Weiler J.H.H., "Thou Shalt Not a Oppress Stranger: On the Judicial Protection of the Human Rights of Non-EC nationals – A critique", *European Journal of International Law*, 1992/2, 53-64 and Ward I., *supra* note 105, 117.

Community population perceived as "Blacks " or "Others" is often socially and economically marginalised. Such marginalisation is more remarkable taking into account that many foreigners in Europe have spent an important part of their life in the host country or have been born there and lived there all their lives. Many of them have close and intense relation with the host country. Their exclusion is highly discriminatory, in particular, if in this process of exclusion matters such as *race* or *ethnicity* play an important role.

As Geddes points out:

> "Millions of people...live and work in the new Europe, but are denied the status of being 'European', normally because of their ethnic antecedents and the colour of their skin".[107]

It seems that, in recent decades, in Europe, race and ethnic origin have been strongly used when shaping immigration policies. There is a presumption that immigration and race are closely linked. *Third Country National* is a neutral term but it is generally used to define certain migrants, generally Blacks. As Rasmussen observes "nowadays, the term 'foreigner' has become fairly meaningless as well as discriminatory when used".[108] On this point Huysman is to be criticised when he argues:

> "In the dialectic of inclusion and exclusion the natives overcome the differences among migrants by putting them all into one single category: the Migrant... Differences between them, for example, sex, wealth, culture, religion etc., are hidden inside the box which is labelled 'migrant' or 'refugee' or 'asylum seeker'."[109]

But in line with Miles and Tränhardt "the vast category of non-EU nationals and citizens is effectively divided into two groups: those originating from other centres of the world economy (i.e. nation states who belong to the OECD), who retain the rights of privileged access to the EU, and those originating from the peripheries of the world economy, who face an ever more coordinated structure of exclusion".[110] This division is motivated by economic, security as well as cultural factors. Indeed, as Ward argues "certain antecedents and certain colours, in particu-

107 Geddes cited in Ward I, *supra* note 105, 48.

108 Rasmussen H.K, *No Entry. Immigration Policy in Europe*, Copenhagen Business School Press, 1997, 30.

109 Huysman J., "Migrant as a Security Problem", in Miles R. & Tränhardt D. (eds), *Migration and European Integration in Europe*, Pinter 1995, 61.

110 Miles R. & Thrähardt D., *supra* note 109, 3.

lar, are deemed to be inappropriate".[111] As Carens points out in a slightly different context:

> "Citizenship in the modern world is a lot like a feudal status in the medieval world. It is assigned at birth; for the most part it is not subject to change by the individual's will and efforts; and it has a major impact upon that person's life chances. To be born a citizen of an affluent country like Canada is like being born into the nobility (even although many belong to the lesser nobility). To be born a citizen of a poor country like Bangladesh is (for most) like being born into the peasantry in the Middle Ages. In this context, limiting entry to countries like Canada is a way of protecting a birthright privilege".[112]

The lack of European Citizenship deprives TCNs of EC judicial protection, allowing Member States to discriminate against them in important areas such as employment, housing or education, in breach of the equality principle, recognised as a fundamental human right.[113] Their "denizen" status, until the Amsterdam Treaty's provisions are implemented, leaves them unprotected against race discrimination at European level. Such a culture of exclusion, reflected in the instrumentalisation of the creation of European Citizenship, has, indeed, fed racist and xenophobic attitudes. The introduction of Article 13 EC, as discussed in details in section II.4, offers a valid legal basis to combat against race discrimination.

The Amsterdam Treaty could improve the position of the TCNs legally settled within the European Union not only because of the insertion of Article 13 EC but also because the matters related to immigration are presently under Community competence. However, as will be discussed in the next sections, there is no clear commitment or willingness of the Member States to extend EC rights to TCNs in the same form as they presently apply to EC citizens. In the European Council in Tampere, a timid progress in that direction has been made. Is was in fact decided that EC nationals and TCNs should be treated equally as far as that is possible. In particular, in respect to TCNs with a long-term residence status. "A person, who has resided legally in a Member State for a period of time to be

111 Ward I, *supra* note 105.

112 Carens J.H., "Migration and Morality: A Liberal Egalitarian Perspective", in Barry B. & Goodin R.E. (eds), *Free Movement, Ethical Issues in the Transnational Migration of People and of Money*, Harvester, 1992, 26-27.

113 Notwithstanding the absence in Community law of an enumerated or codified bill of rights, thanks to a wide interpretation by the ECJ of the Treaties, fundamental rights are protected by referring to some sources of inspiration. According to O' Leary "a rough list of fundamental rights to which the Community adheres would include...equality...", in O' Leary S., *The Evolving Concept of Community Citizenship. From the Free Movement of Persons to Union Citizenship*, Kluwer International Law, 1996, 293.

determined and who holds a long-term residence permit, should be granted in that Member State a set of uniform rights which are as near as possible to those enjoyed by EU citizens; the right to reside, receive education, and work as an employee or self-employed person, as well as the principle of non-discrimination vis-à-vis the citizens of the State of residence." Unfortunately, as often happens in the area of immigration generous commitments and declarations are not translated into legislation.

Few measures were adopted or proposed to lessen their exclusion, not only by means of the Amsterdam Treaty but even before, under the third Pillar of the European Union. The way chosen by Member States however has not been, as was suggested during the IGC,which led to the adoption of the Treaty of Amsterdam, a redetermination of the concept of European Citizenship.[114] On the contrary, the construction of the concept of European Citizenship was used to keep TCNs as second class citizens. New Article 17 EC (ex Article 8 EC) stated that "Citizenship of the Union shall complement and not replace national Citizenship". Obviously, it is necessary to be a national of one Member State in order to enjoy Citizenship of the Union. It is remarkable that the Tampere Council stated "The European Council endorses the objective that long-term legally resident third country nationals be offered the opportunity to obtain the nationality of the Member State in which they are resident." So far no measures have been taken to translate into practice this objective.

Citizenship has become a very important element as it is able to afford more protection to TCNs but measures should be focused more on the elimination of any discrimination on the grounds of race as history is full of examples of groups of people being strongly discriminated against although belonging to the dominant culture.[115]

114 According to the European Union Migrants' Forum, taking into account that the European Citizenship is a new concept aimed at complementing rather than replacing an individual's existing nationality it was argued that "Citizenship of the Union could more easily embrace TCNs resident in the Union without requiring them to possess the nationality of an individual Member State". In conclusion, acquisition of Citizenship of the Union by reason of lawful residence in the Union was proposed to be the only route available to TCNs outside the acquisition of the nationality of a Member State. The European Union Migrants' Forum, *Proposals for the Revision of the Treaty on European Union at the Intergovernmental Conference of 1996*, 1996. Also O' Leary S., *European Union Citizenship*, IPPR, 1996.

115 See Rasmussen, see note 108, 28. Also on this point Layton-Henry Z., Insiders and Outsiders in the Identity & Citizenship, in Guild E. (ed), *The Legal Framework and Social Consequences of Free Movement of Persons in the European Union*, Kluwer Law International, 1999, 49-59.

III

THE TREATY OF AMSTERDAM

III.1 The creation of an area of freedom, security and justice

The creation of an area of freedom, security and justice by the Amsterdam Treaty represents further consolidation of a process that started with the Maastricht Treaty and responded to the desire to create a safe and secure European Union close to its people,. Thanks to the Amsterdam Treaty such a desire has been codified under EC/EU law with the attempt to respect the essence of the best European traditions.

> "The challenge set out by the Amsterdam Treaty is not to reinvent democracy and the rule of law but to allow citizens to enjoy their long-standing democracies in common."[116]

Great emphasis is placed on the interdependence of three elements – freedom, security and justice. The Commission argues "these three inseparable concepts have one common denominator – people – and one cannot be achieved in full without the other two. Maintaining the right balance between them must be the guiding thread for Union action."[117] These concerns have partially included TCNs. The Commission indicates another aspect of the reform important for the creation of the area of freedom, security and justice, "the economic and social integration of lawfully established non-Union nationals, together with the principle of non-discrimination set out in the Amsterdam Treaty."[118] The creation of an area of freedom, security and justice therefore closely concerns the position of TCN migrants or would-be migrants. This was confirmed in the Tampere European Council. It was stated that"...freedom should not, however, be regarded as the exclusive preserve of the Union's own citizens".

---

116 European Commission, Communication from the Commission Towards an Area of Freedom, Security and Justice, *supra* note 64.

117 Ibidem.

118 Ibidem.

III.2 Communitarisation of immigration matters

The Amsterdam Treaty opens up the possibility of significant progress that will concern TCNs whether already within the European Union or seeking first entry.

Member States, with few exceptions, have agreed that matters related to TCNs are better dealt with on a common basis. They have decided to communitarise such matters in a new title in the revised EC Treaty and to create an area of freedom, security and justice. Therefore, TCNs and EC citizens are subject to the same legal system (Title IV EC, ex Article IIIa EC).

According to the Commission, the communitarisation responds to concerns to provide a more coherent framework, where European democratic control and judicial revision are guaranteed. It noted also that "a wider concept of freedom cannot be exclusively reserved to EC citizens. It must include the more than ten million TCNs who live lawfully and permanently in our Member States".[119]

Title IV EC (ex Title IIIa EC) covers several important areas concerning external and internal border controls, visas, conditions of entry and residence, family reunion, readmission, illegal immigration. However, "neither measures on expulsion and deportation, including the issue of transnational enforcement, nor measures relating to the prevention of migration movements are explicitly mentioned in the catalogue".[120]
Article 61 EC states:

> "In order to establish progressively an area of freedom, security and justice, the Council shall adopt (a) within a period of five years after the entry into force of the Treaty of Amsterdam, measures aimed at ensuring the free movement of persons...in conjunction with directly related flanking measures with respect to external border controls, asylum and immigration...(b) other measures in the field of asylum, immigration and safeguarding the rights of nationals of third countries...".[121]

It follows that

> "the Council...shall within a period of five years after the entry of the Amsterdam Treaty adopt (1) measures with a view to ensuring... the absence of any controls on persons, be they citizens of the Union or nationals of third countries, when crossing internal borders; (2) measures on the crossing of the external borders of the Member States which

119 Ibidem.

120 Haibronner K., "European Immigration & Asylum Law under the Amsterdam Treaty", *Common Market Law Review*, 1998, Vol. 35, 1049.

121 Article 61 EC (ex Article 73i EC).

shall establish (a) standards and procedures to be followed by Member States in carrying out checks on persons at such borders; (b) rules on visas for intended stays of no more than three months...".[122]

More specifically, Article 63 (3) EC (ex Article 73 (3)k EC) refers to measures on immigration policy as regards "conditions of entry and residence, and standards on procedures for the issue by Member States of long-term visas and residence permits, including those for the purpose of family reunion" and "illegal immigration and illegal residence, including repatriation of illegal residents". Also, Article 63(4) EC (ex Article 73 k (4) EC) includes "measures defining the rights and conditions under which nationals of third countries who are legally resident in a Member State may reside in other Member States".

However, the reform has taken place in such a way that there are severe doubts on the fact that a communitarisation of the third Pillar in this area has occurred. There is a deadline of five years from the date of entry into force of the Amsterdam Treaty before Community methods are applicable. Considering that there has not been an extension of the Community rules on majority vote in the new areas of interest, the new situation "amounts rather to introducing intergovernmental procedures under the Community framework thereby setting a disturbing precedent that stands comparison with the tactics of the Trojan Horse."[123]

It is essential to analyse the decision-making process in details in order to evaluate the impact of the new Title on TCNs.

III.3 THE DECISION MAKING-PROCESS IN THE AREA OF IMMIGRATION

The *Commission* must share its right of initiative within the first five years – *exclusive* in the Community context – with the Member States (Article 67.1 EC, ex Article 73o EC). After this period it seems that the Commission regains its exclusive right of initiative but Article 67.2 EC refers to the possibility for the Member States to make request to the Commission that this latter shall examine. Therefore, the Commission seems forced to evaluate proposals from the Member States, even though there is no an obligation to include such proposals in the final documents presented to the Council by virtue of its right of initiative. Although the Action Plan states that "what is important is not so much where the right of initiative lies, be it shared or exclusive, as the way in which this right is exer-

122 Article 62 EC (ex Article 73j EC).
123 EP, Report on the Treaty of Amsterdam, *supra* note 82.

cised",[124] it would have been advisable to follow the traditional Community system and to confer the right of initiative solely to the Commission.

For the *European Parliament* this Community Institution is highly penalised during the transitional period because its power in the legislative process is reduced to a consultative role only. Such a decision is more striking because, while it is true that there are EC law areas where the EP is only consulted, there has been, through the Maastricht and Amsterdam Treaties, a serious increase in the presence of the EP in Community legislative life and its powers have been largely reinforced. After the transitional period of five years, the Council, acting unanimously and after consulting the EP, decides whether and in which areas to apply the codecision procedure. This possibility is important from a political point of view because it indicates the willingness to proceed in that direction – towards a reinforcement of the position of the EP – but legally it was a possibility already present considering that it requires unanimity within the Council and only consultation of the EP.

The Council, mirror of the Member States' interests, keeps the greatest powers. Besides, for the transitional period, the *unanimity rule*, which is an aspect, notably, of intergovernmental cooperation, is maintained.

The legislative procedure so analysed is capable of making the elaboration and adoption of important decisions necessary in the area of immigration very difficult, for the first five years as well as after the transitional period.

It should be noted that with the exception of the area related to visas where these rules do not apply (section VII.4) the *five years deadline* does not even apply to the most important areas related to immigration, which have the greatest impact of the lives of TCNs, such as conditions of entry and residence and family reunion. These areas are left completely to the will of the Member States. It is nonetheless encouraging that the Council and the Commission have committed themselves in the Action Plan on how best to implement the provisions of the Amsterdam Treaty to adopt measures in these areas within five years from the entry into force of the Treaty.

But apart from the difficulties in the adoption of new rules in the area of immigration that can be easily anticipated due to the legislative procedure chosen, the approach for the new measures will much depend on the results that the political actors want to achieve in the EU, by means of the new legislation. As the Commission argues "the European Union needs to develop a common understanding of the extent to which TCNs and EU citizens should be treated

124 Action Plan of the Commission and the Council on how best to implement the provisions of the Amsterdam Treaty on an Area of Freedom, Security and Justice, *supra* note 84.

equally."[125] The answer to these questions will shape future legislation in this area in more restrictive or liberal terms than the present legislation.

III.4 PROTOCOLISATION UNDER THE AMSTERDAM TREATY

The major progress achieved by the Amsterdam Treaty in the area of immigration, which has been part of the Community Pillar since the entry into force of the Treaty, has been reached thanks to several concessions. Firstly, as analysed in detail above, matters related to TCNs are now part of Community competence even if for a transitional period of five years Community methods are not applicable and, after that period, it was agreed that only a few areas would be subject to full Community law, although some derogations are kept.

Most importantly, the resistance of the UK, Ireland and Denmark, to any project envisaging the communitarization of immigration issues has been overcome by accepting their opting out from these areas. The position of these Member States – the UK, Ireland and Denmark – is regulated by different Protocols, which are annexed to both the EC and the EU Treaty. The Protocols therefore have binding effects.

III.4.1 The position of the UK and Ireland

Protocol No 3[126] on the application of certain aspects of Article 14 EC (ex Article 7a EC) to the UK and Ireland codifies the reluctance of the UK to give up its powers on border controls.

It has been established that the *UK*, notwithstanding what was established in the Amsterdam Treaty, in particular, under the new Title IV EC (ex Title IIIa EC), is entitled to exercise controls on persons seeking entry in its territory at its frontiers with other Member States (Article 1 of Protocol No 3).

Ireland, being bound to the UK by the Common Travel Area (a special arrangement concerning the movement of people between these two countries) is also covered by the Protocol. Article 2 of the Protocol establishes that as long as they maintain such arrangements – relating to the movement of persons between their territories – the provisions of Article 1 of the Protocol shall apply in the same terms and conditions as for the UK. From the formulation of Article 2 of the Protocol it seems that previous obligations under the Common Travel Area is the

125 Ibidem.

126 Protocol (No 3) on the application of certain aspects of Article 14 of the Treaty establishing the European Community to the UK and Ireland annexed to the EC and EU Treaties.

justification for Ireland's opting out rather than political resistance to the Community project of eliminating border controls. This view is confirmed by a Declaration made by Ireland that the maintenance of the Common Travel Area will maximize freedom of movement into and out of Ireland.

Protocol No 3 concludes that the Member States, while forbidden to check the movements of people with the other Member States, are nonetheless entitled to exercise such rights on persons seeking entry from the territory of the UK or Ireland.

Protocol No 4 concerning again the UK and Ireland establishes that the provisions of the new Title IV EC (Title IIIa EC) are not applicable nor are the measures adopted by the other Member States for implementing that Title. But the opting out of the UK and Ireland is neither *definitive* nor *absolute*. Both Member States may opt in, accepting measures adopted under Title IV EC, before they are adopted and even after. In the first case, the UK or Ireland if they wish to take part in the adoption and application of a specific measure must communicate it to the Council within three months after the proposal or initiative has been presented (Article 3 of Protocol No 4). The UK and Ireland can also at any time after the adoption of a measure notify their intention of their wish to accept it. Again Ireland seems less reluctant than the UK to join the new Community progress and Article 8 of Protocol No 4 establishes that Ireland may notify the President of the Council in writing that it no longer wishes to be covered by the terms of the Protocol. It follows that in that case, the normal Treaty provisions will apply to Ireland.

At the time of writing, the position of these two countries has not changed and they have not availed to their powers to opt in. On the contrary, the UK has reconfirmed its opposition to the lifting of borders while accepting other JHA measures originally part of the Schengen acquis, as analysed in the next sections.

III.4.2 The position of Denmark

A third Protocol regulates the position of Denmark, which with the UK and Ireland does not take part in the Community progress under Title IV EC (ex Title III.a EC). Article 2 of the Protocol on the position of Denmark clearly states that none of the provisions of Title IV EC, no measure adopted pursuant to that Title, no provision of any international agreement concluded by the Community pursuant to that Title, and no decision of the ECJ interpreting any such provision or measure can be binding upon or applicable to Denmark, with the only exception of the area related to visas, which were already under Community competence under the Maastricht Treaty. From a legal point of view the position of Denmark does not differ from that of the UK and Ireland, however, it should be noted that politically the Danish Government was in favour of the progress made in the revision of the Treaty on the European Union, but it anticipated constitutional problems. As Ehlermann[127] argues the main difference between the Danish position on the one hand, and the British and Irish position, on the other, is that the latter is pragmatic, focusing on the substance of the measures, while the former appears to be determined by the more theoretical or dogmatic considerations of the legal quality of the measure adopted. This is why the hypothesis of opting-in is excluded for Denmark before or after measures are adopted by the other Member States. Denmark cannot opt into individual measures.

The way chosen to overcome the opposition, whether legal or political, of three important Member States to Community progress in the area of immigration, namely by means of several protocols, has only been a partial success. Progress in this area can take place only in detriment of a common evolution of the EC/EU law and this can in turn create not only political but also legal problems.

III.5 Integrating the Schengen acquis into the framework of the EU

Another important aspect of the reform brought about by the Treaty of Amsterdam is the integration of the Schengen acquis under EC/EU law. Notably, the two Schengen agreements and all the implementing measures adopted were fruit of purely intergovernmental cooperation among the majority of the Member States. Under the Amsterdam Treaty, the Schengen acquis, which is made of a substantial body of executive committee declarations, decisions and other important documents, is to be incorporated into the EC/EU Treaty and it is to be allocated partially into the first Pillar and partially into the third Pillar. The Protocol (No 2) integrating the Schengen acquis into the framework of the European Union, which is annexed to the EU and EC Treaty, establishes that: "from the date of entry into force of Amsterdam, the Schengen acquis including the decisions of the Executive Committee established by the Schengen Agreement which have been adopted before this date, shall immediately apply to the thirteen Member States...The Council, acting unanimously, shall determine, in conformity with the relevant provisions of the Treaties, the legal basis for each of the provisions or decisions which constitute the Schengen acquis".[128]

---

127 Ehlermann C., *Differentiation, Flexibility, Closer Cooperation. The New Provisions of Amsterdam*, EU Working Paper, 1997, cited in Simpson G., "Asylum and Immigration in the European Union after the Treaty of Amsterdam", *European Public Law*, 1999, Vol.5, Issue 1, 101.

128 Article 2 of the Protocol No 2.

Part of the Schengen acquis, concerned with the abolition of the internal frontiers and with the necessary flanking measures, covered immigration related issues.

The integration of the Schengen acquis is capable of ensuring better protection for TCNs because since these matters are now under EC/EU law there is more democratic and judicial control. But it must be remembered that such controls are available once the acquis has been allocated whether to the first or third Pillar. There is no Community control of what is to be moved under the Community Pillar, and what, on the contrary, continues to be subject to intergovernmental cooperation, under the third Pillar. The fear is that many measures, which, according to the new organisation of the TEU, should be placed under the first Pillar, remain under the third Pillar. The last decisions concerning the definition of the Schengen acquis and its allocation to a legal basis in the Treaty, were adopted on 20 May 1999.[129] As it was to be expected, not all the provisions of the Schengen acquis on immigration have been transferred to the Community Pillar.[130] In particular, no agreement could be reached on the allocation of the Schengen Information System (SIS), which has been, therefore, allocated provisionally to the third Pillar remaining under intergovernmental competence.

However, the incorporation of the Schengen acquis into the EU framework has been possible by resorting once again to opting out solutions for the UK, Ireland and, to some extent, Denmark.

III.5.1 The position of the UK and Ireland

Ireland and the UK were not part of the Schengen experiment, therefore, they have never been bound by the Schengen acquis. The Protocol on Schengen, annexed to the EC/EU Treaties, consolidates the cooperation of those Member States already members of the Schengen Agreements with the consequent exclusion of the UK and Ireland. It is nonetheless established that both members may at any time request to take part in some or all of the provisions of this acquis (Article 4 of the Protocol on Schengen). This possibility was also available, as discussed above, for the participation of these two countries in the progress under Title IV EC (ex

129 Council Decision concerning the definition of the Schengen acquis for the purpose of determining, in conformity with the relevant provisions of the Treaty establishing the European Community and the Treaty on European Union, the legal basis for each of the provisions or decisions which constitute the acquis, OJ 1999 L 176/1; Council Decision determining, in conformity with the relevant provisions of the Treaty establishing the European Community and the Treaty on European union, the legal basis for each of the provisions or decisions which constitute the Schengen acquis, OJ 1999 L 176/17.

130 Council Press Release 8654/99 (Presse 168).

Title IIIa EC). However, the Protocol on Schengen is more precise as regards their future participation. It was decided that request to take part in some or all of the provisions of the acquis requires the unanimity of the Schengen members. The thirteen members possess a right to veto future participation in this area for the UK and Ireland. This right of veto has been softened by a Declaration by the thirteen members reassuring the UK and Ireland that in the event that such a request is made the other members will make the best efforts with a view to allowing accession.[131]

On 20 May 1999, the UK submitted a formal application to participate in those measures of the Schengen acquis that relate to law enforcement and criminal judicial cooperation, including the SIS, by exercising the provisions of Article 4 of the Protocol on Schengen. Minister Straw underlined that this application was one part of the UK's wider intention to participate in all aspects of JHA which are consistent with its different policy on frontier controls.[132] The participation in the SIS is therefore limited and does not include areas of the SIS which are linked to the free movement title of the Schengen Convention. Ireland has declared that it would sign up to the same sections as the UK.

However, at the time of writing, the participation of these two countries in some parts of the Schengen acquis could be blocked by a Spanish veto. Spain is likely to use its power to veto the UK and Ireland from joining the Schengen acquis in order to obtain concessions over Gibraltar.

In compliance with the Treaty of Amsterdam, the Council sought the opinion of the Commission before deciding on the UK's application. On 20 July 1999, the Commission adopted a favourable opinion on the request by the UK.[133] The request is pending the decision of the other Member States.

III.5.2 The position of Denmark

The position of Denmark is also clarified in the Protocol integrating the Schengen acquis into the framework of the EU (Article 3 of Protocol No 2 on Schengen). Denmark, a member of the Schengen project, has decided that it will maintain the same rights and obligations in relation to the other signatories to the Schengen agreements but in the form prior to the incorporation of the Schengen acquis into EC/EU law. However, Article 3 of the Protocol is very unclear. On the one hand,

---

131 See on this point Simpson G., *supra* note 127.

132 See Council Press Release, *supra* note 130.

133 European Commission, Opinion on the request by the United Kingdom to take part in certain provisions of the Schengen acquis, http:// europa.eu.int/rapid/start7egi/gues...ion.getxt=gt&doc=IP/99/550/0/RAPID&lg=EN.

it seems that those parts of the Schengen acquis which are to become EC law are not applicable as such but they will maintain an international law status in Denmark. On the other hand, as some authors have argued, since Denmark has opted out of being bound by Title IV EC, Article 3 of the Protocol presumably means that the obligations are maintained in relation to the *past* Schengen *acquis* integrated into Title IV but do *not* extend to *future* decisions taken under Title IV in relation to that *acquis.*[134] However, "with regards to those parts of the Schengen acquis that are determined to have legal basis in Title VI of the Treaty on European Union, Denmark shall continue to have the same rights and obligations as the other signatories to the Schengen agreements" (Article 3 of the Protocol).

An opting in solution is foreseen for Denmark for those proposals and initiatives to build upon the Schengen acquis under the provisions of Title IV EC. According to Article 5 of the Protocol on the position of Denmark, there is a six month option for Denmark after the decision of the Council on a proposal or initiative to implement the Schengen acquis under Title IV EC, to decide whether to implement that proposal or initiative in its national law. It was agreed that if Denmark decided to do so, this decision would create an obligation under international law between Denmark and the other Member States, including the UK and Ireland if these Member States take part in the areas of cooperation in question.

Notwithstanding the major changes foreseen by the Amsterdam Treaty and its declarations, nowhere in the revised text it is possible to read the willingness to change approach as regards TCNs.[135] The conventions and regulations presently under discussion confirm the double standard approach, i.e. EC nationals *vis-à-vis* TCNs, and the willingness to keep TCN migrants as second class citizens.

It is obviously premature to make predictions on how the revised Treaty will work, but there are serious doubts that the rules regarding entry, stay, family reunion, and conditions of work which apply to EC citizens will apply to the TCN population. It is, indeed, more likely that the Community Institutions will adopt new rules introducing a different regime, not as liberal as the one regulating EC nationals, governing only TCNs.

---

134 Simpson G., *supra* note 127.

135 For an overall view of the reforms introduced by the Treaty of Amsterdam see Monar J., "Justice and Home Affairs in the Treaty of Amsterdam: Reform at the Price of Fragmentation", *European Law Review*, 1998, Vol. 23, 320-334.

It seems that the logic of exclusion, which shaped the adoption of rules under the third Pillar, will be maintained in the future, marking a great distinction between the two groups, EC nationals and TCNs.

Difficulties in the evaluation and prediction in this area are determined by the existence of a multitude of political actors, the European Institutions and the Member States, in the Community panorama.

IV

FREEDOM OF MOVEMENT PROVISIONS

One of the most important elements in the construction of the European Union is the realisation of the Common Market. The completion of the Common Market is in fact required in order to attain the objectives of the Treaty in continuous expansion. Article 2 EC Treaty states:

> "The Community shall have as its task, by *establishing a common market* (emphasis added) and an economic and monetary union and by implementing the common policies or activities referred to in Article 3 and 3a, to promote throughout the Community harmonious and balanced development of economic activities, sustainable and non-inflationary growth respecting the environment, a high degree of convergence of economic performance, a high level of employment and of social protection, the raising of the standard of living and quality of life, and economic and social cohesion and solidarity among the Member States".

The aim of the Common Market is to create an area without internal frontiers that works exactly like a domestic market. One of its main features is the freedom of movement of persons along with the other factors of production, i.e. goods and capitals. Article 14 EC, (ex Article 7a EC) clearly states "...The internal market shall comprise an area without internal frontiers in which the free movement of goods, persons, services and capital is ensured in accordance with the provisions of this Treaty". By analogy with the free movement of capital and goods, free movement of persons implies the elimination of all internal controls, shifted to the Community's common External Frontier, on any individuals whether TCNs or EC citizen. But while for goods and capital the objective of the abolition of internal barriers has nearly been achieved so that, for instance, goods from third countries, once in the Union, can circulate freely, the realisation of the freedom of movement of persons has created major difficulties.

Again, it should be remembered that the construction of the Communities responded to economic needs, therefore, the free movement of persons was an instrument to reach economic goals and it was not considered an aim in itself.

The completion of the Internal Market, as seen at the beginning of this section, still has an *instrumental* character. However, EC citizens have acquired a central position in the Community integration process. Other dimensions, such as political and social rights along with economic ones, have given other features to the Community itself. EC/EU rights granted to EC nationals are normally considered in the context of free movement rights which are the far most important, although as Guild observes "there are also other rights such as the freedom from discrimination on the basis of the sex, right to job security on transfer of undertakings and consumer protection rights".[136] EC nationals are nowadays protected in many ways under EC/EU law.

Member States have been very careful *not* to include TCNs in this process of "humanisation" of the construction of the Union. Such exclusion has strongly affected the process and, in particular, the completion of the Internal Market as far as the free movement of persons is concerned.

IV.1 THE DEBATE ON THE INTERPRETATION OF OLD ARTICLE 7A EC

The abolition of internal controls for persons within the Union has been, until the adoption of the Amsterdam compromise, a very controversial issue. Not all Member States shared the same view as regards the exact meaning of the obligation, contained in Article 14 EC (ex Article 7a EC). The UK opposed any project envisaging the elimination of internal controls on all persons, while the others, at different stages, agreed to remove barriers to allow free circulation under the Schengen Agreement (1985). The main reason that justified the delays for the complete realisation of the free movement of persons was related to the close link between the completion of the Internal Market and immigration policies.

The main concern of the UK, the fiercest opponent, was that the removal of internal border checks was to be extended to TCNs, as it was clearly impossible to eliminate controls on EC citizens and, at the same time, to keep such controls on aliens. TCNs, therefore, were to gain the right to travel freely within the European Union. But this area of law, i.e. controls on aliens' movements to and from the territory of the Member States, was considered to be a matter of national competence. This raised questions *not only* of economic concerns but also security implications.

Since 1989, when the External Borders Convention was first proposed, removing internal barriers and granting the right to travel freely to TCNs was dis-

136 See Guild E., "The Legal Framework of Citizenship of the European Union", in Cesarani D. & Fulbrook M. (eds), *supra* note 94, 31.

cussed and this attempt concerned all Member States. The Convention envisaged the possibility of abolishing visa requirements for TCNs who held a residence permit granted by a Member State. Article 8 of the External Border Convention stated that a Member State was not to require a visa of a person who wished to enter its territory for a short stay or to transit through it, provided that that person held a residence permit issued by another Member State. The Convention was never signed due to the dispute between the UK and Spain on its territorial applicability over Gibraltar.

At European institutional level, the EP frustrated with the delays in the suppression of checks at the EU internal borders, filed a complaint against the European Commission with the ECJ on 18 November 1993,[137] accusing the Commission of, inter alia, not using the powers conferred to it by the EC Treaty, to ensure the full implementation of old Article 7a. Under such pressures, in 1995, the European Commission presented, although with great delay, three proposals with a view to attaining the objective set out in Article 7a: a Directive eliminating visa requirements for family members, a Directive abolishing internal controls on persons and a Directive on the right to travel of third country nationals.[138] Accordingly, the Registrar of the Court withdrew the complaint officially, on 11 July 1996.[139] In this context it is relevant to mention the last proposal, which would have accorded the right to move freely for short stays in a Member State other than that of residence on the basis of a valid residence permit. Again, the proposal was never adopted and this right remained a dead letter.

The only legal instruments, under EU law, concerning a very limited right to travel is the Joint Action dealing with travel facilities for third country national school pupils resident in a Member State.[140] The personal scope of the Joint Action is obviously very restricted as it only covers school pupils from third countries resident in one Member State, allowed to enter without a visa into the territory of another Member State for a short stay or transit. Notwithstanding the limited scope of the Joint Action, the UK has interpreted it *restrictively*. The UK has required a visa from a TCN pupil travelling from Italy, at least on one occasion.[141]

In this context it appears relevant to mention the Joint Action concerning a uniform format for residence permits,[142] which the Council formally adopted in 1996. At first sight, one could think that this new document is directed at easing

137 Case C-65/93 *European Parliament v Council* [1995] ECR I-643.

138 COM (95) 346, 347 and 348 final, OJ 1995 C 306/5.

139 OJ 1996 C 336/15.

140 OJ 1994 L 327/1.

141 See Migrations Europe No 93/1999.

142 OJ 1997 L 7/1.

TCNs' movement within the EU. There is an increasing tendency in the European Union to adopt standard documents for TCNs, such as the above mentioned residence permits, the uniform format for visas, a specified entry in their documents for Long-term Residents, and EC service provisions cards. Unfortunately, the aim of the new documents does not seems to lessen controls on TCNs moving in the EU but *only* to ensure better controls by the competent national authorities. As far as *residence permits* are concerned, an unpublished document,[143] adopted by the Council, made clear that these documents do not substitute any valid document required to cross the frontiers, such as identity cards, passports or visa. As Peers points out "the intent of the Joint Action is therefore clearly to assist in the application of controls on third-country nationals, without in any way assisting in their movement within the Union".[144] In 1998, the Council adopted a Decision on common standards relating to filling in the uniform format for a residence permit, which only contains information on technical specifications but says nothing in respect of the effect of such documents for the holders.[145]

Securing TCN migrants the right to travel was nonetheless recognised by the great majority of the Member States. Outside the EC and EU framework, the right to travel visa-free was already accorded to TCNs in the Schengen area, which comprises almost all Member States of the EU, except the UK and Ireland .[146] Generally, TCNs are entitled to short stays, no more than three months, within the "Schengenland". Apart from a few crises, the Schengen system has proved to work perfectly and the right granted has not undermined the security of its members. This made it possible, by according the opting out solution to the UK, Ireland and Denmark, discussed in previous sections, to include the right to travel in the EC Treaty as revised in Amsterdam. Thanks to the flexibility principle, Member States, with the exception of the UK and Ireland and Denmark, finally agreed in the Amsterdam Treaty to grant the right to travel to TCNs.

The granting of this right must be welcomed as an important measure that paves the way for the integration of the extra-Community population settled in the Member States. This is a first tangible sign of a Internal Market as the European Union should be. TCNs benefit from the right to travel as they will be able to travel around Europe as tourists or consumers for periods of three months.

143 Council document, 12848/1/96.

144 Peers S., *EU Justice and Home Affairs Law*, Longmans, 2000.

145 Council document, 98/701/CFSP OJ 1998 L 333/8.

146 Italy joined the five original members, Germany, France and the three Benelux States, in 1990. Spain and Portugal signed the Convention in 1991, Greece in 1992, Austria 1995, and Denmark, Finland and Sweden in 1996.

But the economic approach when dealing with the right to travel is still evident. This right is not as *revolutionary* as it might appear at first sight. It clearly confers the right to travel for short stays (no more than three months) and not the right to free movement accorded to EC citizens. Therefore, these provisions do not represent a very significant concession, as entries for short stays, the only entries allowed, do not have drastic effect for the Member States: "a TCN admitted to a long stay in one State will be most likely to meet the lower requirements for short stay in another Member".[147]

In addition to considerations regarding the rights of TCNs to live in the host country with the same rights of nationals, some authors have strongly criticised the limitation of the right to free movement exclusively to the right to travel as they feel the objectives of the Common Market would not be reached in a market where there are around ten million TCNs, workers and consumers, whose presence is restricted to fifteen markets.[148]

Such a restriction is less acceptable for TCNs on a permanent basis, often second and third generation immigrants, with obviously strong ties to the host state.

IV.2 The position of Long-term Residents in the Union

The concession of several rights was established for TCNs legally settled into the EU for a long period by the Council Resolution on the status of TCNs residing on a long term basis in the territory of the Member States (*Long-term Residents' Resolution*).[149] Its provisions have been included, partially modified, in the Convention proposed by the Commission on rules for the admission of TCNs (*Immigration Convention*).[150] It must be noted that, as it was established in the same proposal, now that the Amsterdam Treaty is in force, the Convention's provisions will take the form of an EC Directive.

The Convention, on the basis of the Long-term Residents' Resolution, would grant a set of rights. Unfortunately, it does not accord total freedom of movement. But a few timid steps have been taken in that direction. Article 33 of the proposed Convention confers free movement rights in other Member States. It states that TCNs recognised as Long-term Residents may apply for employment in another

147 See De Jong C.D., "Cooperation in the Field of Aliens Law", in Schermers H.G. et al (eds), *Free Movement of Persons in Europe*, Martinus Nijoff Publishers, 1995, 188.

148 See Hoogemboon T., "Symposium: The Status of Non-Community Nationals in Community Law", *European Journal of International Law*, 1992, No 3, 36-52.

149 OJ 1996 C 80/2.

150 European Commission, Immigration Convention Memorandum, *supra* note 62, 136.

Member State where a job vacancy in that Member State cannot be filled in the short term by citizens of the Union or by a TCN legally resident in that State who already forms part of its regular labour market. Taking into account the greater vulnerability of TCNs compared to EC nationals in the labour market, the Convention would grant TCNs settled on a permanent basis the possibility to take advantage of a bigger market. The Convention, if approved, is an instrument that would improve their social mobility.

Such a right is important from a political point of view as it demonstrates the willingness of the Member States to guarantee TCNs the right of free movement. At the same time, it must be noted that in reality it is very unlikely that TCNs would benefit from this right. This, in fact, would presuppose a labour market as a fixed entity, offering the possibility to control vacancies and the way to fill them. While efforts can be made by the Member States in order to control the flow of workers by means of residence and work permits issued, it is doubtful that they can gain complete control of the market. In practice, therefore, the incapacity to control the real dynamics of the labour market strongly reduces the impact of this concession on TCNs.

Also, under the proposed Convention's provisions, TCNs may apply to pursue a course of study, attend preparatory courses for a specific course of study in higher education, prepare a doctoral thesis or pursue research activity in the context of basic and advanced vocational education after obtaining a degree or higher education diploma in another Member State. In the above cases, if the person obtains a work contract or enrolment in an establishment of higher education, the Member State concerned shall admit the TCN and issue him with the necessary authorisations, including those relating to residence.

The provisions analysed so far prove that a very small change in the mentality *vis-à-vis*, at least the Long-term Residents, is under discussion but the strict guarantees required to confer such few rights still demonstrate the fortress approach. It is remarkable that in the Tampere European Council it was agreed, as discussed supra, that long-term residents should be granted in the Member State where they reside "a set of uniform rights which are as near as possible to those enjoyed by EU citizens".

IV.3 THE RIGHT TO FREE MOVEMENT UNDER INTERNATIONAL AGREEMENTS

The Community has by virtue of Article 310 EC (ex Article 238 EC) the competence to conclude international agreements with third countries. Such competence was conferred when the original treaties were adopted, and since then, the Community has signed important accords with third countries. Analysis of these agreements is evidence of the evolution in the approach towards TCNs.

At the very beginning, in the first phase of migration flows towards the Community, foreign workers were more or less recruited by the Member States to move and work into their territory and the approach was very "positive".

IV.3.1 EEC/Turkey Agreement

In this context, special reference must be made to the EEC-Turkey Association Agreement,[151] signed in 1963, and its Additional Protocol,[152] signed in 1970. In the mind of the drafters of the Agreement, this was preparatory to the eventual accession of Turkey to the Community. This agreement envisaged the extension, at different stages, of EC free movement rights to Turkish workers. Notably, accession never happened and it is to be excluded in the near future.[153] The great opening towards Turkey in the early 1960s was slowed down during the intervening years. Economic difficulties along with security concerns, due to Turkish internal instability and the threat of international terrorism, blocked further steps towards the accession to the Union while all the other candidates, some of whom applied later, became members. But it should be noted that Turkey represents the most *distinct* not only from a political and economic point of view but also, *culturally*, among the European States non-members of the Union. Accordingly, although around three millions Turks are present in the Union's Member States,[154] they are often regarded with suspicion and their integration has been very difficult. Besides the economic reasons, other factors indeed seem to be evaluated as a problem. There is an alleged xenophobic incompatibility between "Christian" Europe and "Moslem" Turkey. According to Ludlow it is an unspoken assumption, which is all the more important because it is unspoken.[155] Moslems, not only Moslem Turks, comprise around 70% of all Ethnic minorities in Europe. They are often considered a threat to the identity, culture and religion of the EU

151 OJ 1976 C 113/2.

152 OJ 1972 L 293/1.

153 At the Luxembourg European Council, Member States decided to launch the overall enlargement process but they excluded Turkey from the first group of States that qualified for accession, although it formally presented its application since 1987. Turkey was however invited to participate at the Conference held in London (March 1998) for the new candidates but it refused.

154 According to EUROSTAT sources, by January 1994 there were 2 655 600 Turks legally resident in the Union. The biggest concentration, with 1 918 395 legally resident Turks is in Germany, followed by the Netherlands, 202 618, France, 197 712, Austria, 141 229, and minor concentrations in the other Member States (EUROSTAT, *supra* note 5).

155 Ludlow P., "Beyond Agenda 2000. EU Enlargement Issue", *Centre for European Policy Studies Review,* 1997/98, No 5, 1-9.

countries, worsened by the wave of anti-Islamic propaganda that has taken place in Europe in recent years.

Turkish application for membership becomes less and less attractive and will become even more so when Turkey's population rises to more than a hundred million people after the beginning of the century.[156]

Turkish workers and their families have gained only a few rights under national legislation. At European level, although foreseen in the EEC/Turkish Agreement, the right to free movement was never implemented. The opening process, started with the Ankara Agreement, has to some extent been stopped in this area. This fact is more evident if we consider the fact that in other sectors important progress has been made. For instance, the final phase of implementation of the Euro-Turkish custom union has been reached.[157]

IV.3.2 Cooperation Agreements with the Mediterranean countries

By the end of the 1970s the Community had signed cooperation accords with all the Mediterranean countries.[158] Relations with 12 Mediterranean countries with which the EU has association or cooperation agreement are being re-launched on the basis of a partnership declaration adopted by both sides in Barcelona in November 1995. The Agreements do not envisage the accession of these countries to the EU. Geographical reasons impede their membership to the Union.[159] These accords are very important as, with the exception of the oil rich states of the Arabian peninsula, many North African and the Middle Eastern countries are poor and in need of European aid. When these accords were signed, Member States had already started closing off migration channels so that, although their provisions regulate the legal position of workers in the field of labour, the right to free access and movement within the Union was denied. The new agreements recently signed

156 See Miles R. & Tränhardt D., *supra* note 29, 9.

157 Turkey is incorporating into its own laws a long list of EU Directives and Regulations relating to the removal of technical barriers to trade (OJ 1997 L 191/1).

158 A first cooperation agreement was signed between the Community and Morocco in 1976 (OJ 1978 L 264/1). In 1996, a Euro-mediterranean agreement that creates an association between the Community and Morocco was signed, COM (95) 720 final. The Community signed a first cooperation agreement with Tunisia in 1976 (OJ 1978 L 265/1) followed by a recent one OJ 1998 L 97. Other accords have been signed with Egypt OJ 1978 L 266/1, Israel OJ 1975 L 136/1, Lebanon OJ 1978 L 267/1, Syria OJ 1978 L 269/1, Cyprus OJ 1973 L 133/1 and Malta OJ 1971 L 61/1. A Euro-Mediterranean agreement was signed 24.11.1997 with Jordan. Also, an agreement was signed with Algeria in 1978, EEC/Algeria Cooperation Agreement OJ 1978 L 263/1. Negotiations to conclude a new accord were started but they stopped due to political instability of Algeria.

159 Morocco presented an application in July 1987 to join the European Community but it was immediately rejected on the grounds that Morocco was not a European country.

to renew or start new forms of cooperation with these countries confirm such a tendency of closure. Member States want to create a common area of peace and stability. In order to reach these ambitious objectives, there is general agreement for supporting the development of these countries through different means but *concessions* do not entail an opening towards labour access in the European market. On the contrary, these agreements contain repatriation clauses, as Europe strongly refuses new waves of immigrants. But it appears that "more problematic than the numbers, perhaps, are the characteristics of the migrants themselves. Because Mediterranean rim countries are racially and religiously different from Europe, South-North migration accentuates the visibility of immigration and its implications for European societies. Serious problems are arising as a result, and violence against migrants has disproportionately targeted those from less developed nations".[160] Again, there is a qualitative control in the European immigration policy.

IV.3.3 EEA Agreement and the accord with Switzerland

Under these international agreements therefore, the Community has generally restricted free movement rights to EC citizens. The only exception is the European Economic Area Agreement (EEA).[161] After the enlargement in 1995 of Austria, Finland and Sweden, it includes only the three remaining members of EFTA, Iceland, Liechtenstein and Norway (Switzerland is also an EFTA member but it has not signed the EEA Agreement). Among other things, in fact, the EEA Agreement grants the three partner countries the four freedoms of the single market. It seems that the closeness with the EEA countries and their Europeness has allowed Member States to extend EC free movement rules to EEA nationals while no other agreement grants comparable rights to TCNs. The Agreement with Switzerland,[162] recently agreed, pending for signature, envisages the same concessions to Swiss nationals to those granted to EC citizens in the area of freedom of movement. Such a great opening towards the EEA countries, on the one hand, and Switzerland, on the other, is more remarkable as it has taken place when Member States were largely closing off their borders.

---

160 Meissner D.M. et al. (eds), *International Migration Challenges in a New Era,* The Trilateral Commission, 1993, 47.

161 OJ 1994, L 1/1; OJ 1995, L 86/58 (Liechtenstein).

162 EC/Switzerland Agreement, COM (99) 229, 4 May 1999.

IV.3.4 Europe Agreements

The recent agreements concluded with Central and Eastern Europe,[163] as they now stand, although they foresee the eventual accession to the European Union of these countries, do not confer free movement rights. The only exception is the *right to establishment.* The provisions contained in the Europe Agreements, which are virtually identical, confer upon self-employed persons a right to access in the territory if they want to work in that capacity in the territory of the Union. In fact, if the right to establishment is to be interpreted in the Europe Agreements as under EC law, the right to entry is the natural consequence of that right. However, along with the restrictions to exercise that right envisaged under EC law, namely on grounds of public policy, public health or public security, there is a provision which seriously restricts the possibility to benefit from that right. It was decided that Member States maintain the right to *impose* their laws and regulations relating to entry and stay, work, labour conditions and establishment of natural persons, and supply of services, even though was also agreed that Member States will not apply such laws and regulations in such a manner as to *nullify* or to *impair* benefits accruing to any party. Such a restriction leaves great room for manoeuvre to Member States that, in practice, can affect the exercise of the same right of establishment. At the time of writing the direct effect of this right has not been tested by the ECJ. But nonetheless it is difficult to describe this right for the way it has been worded, as some authors did, "the extension of the right of establishment to nationals of Central and Eastern European countries is an extremely important development in the Community's immigration policy."[164]

Overall, the right to travel accorded to legally resident TCNs as well as a few limited rights of movement represent a first important step towards their integration into the European Union. However, TCNs will not be able to rely upon EC/EU law when moving to another Member State to reside or take up employment there. In that case they will be covered by national immigration legislation. Such exclusion is highly discriminatory as many TCNs have spent great part or all their lives in the host country but they are still subject to this double standard of rights and duties. Moreover, taking into account that the majority of the extra-Community population occupies the bottom rung of society, and that they are socially and economically marginalised, their exclusion from the benefit of the freedom of

163 Cooperation and Association Agreements have been signed with Bulgaria OJ 1994 L 358/1, Hungary OJ 1993 L 347/1, Latvia OJ 1998 L 26/1, Lithuania OJ 1992 L 403/1, Estonia 1998 L 68/1, Poland OJ 1993 L 348/1, Romania OJ 1994 L 357/1, Slovakia OJ 1994 L 358/1, Czech Republic OJ 1994 L 360/1 and Slovenia OJ 1993 L 189/1.

164 Guild E., The Europe Agreements: The Right to Establishment in the Central and Eastern European Agreements, in Guild E. (ed) *supra* note 115, 133.

movement could well increase their marginalisation. Although they are unlikely to possess the necessary Euro-skills,[165] they "*a priori*" cannot compete freely with the national population, being hostages of the state of residence. In fact, even if a TCN, wanting to emigrate from one Member State to another, complies with national immigration rules s/he is not entitled to the same advantages as EC migrants such as recognition of diplomas, social security benefits. It should be noted that the absurdity of this situation has been taken into account by the Commission in the presentation of the new package of proposals, discussed in the next sections.

IV.4 DERIVED RIGHTS UNDER FREEDOM OF MOVEMENT RULES

Notwithstanding their exclusion from the advantages of the freedom of movement provisions, TCNs, as mentioned above, were *incidentally* able to gain some derived rights by virtue of their relationship with EC citizens.

It should be remembered that the Treaty of Rome provides the right to freedom of movement for people under Title III, Articles 39-55 EC (ex Article 48-66 EC). The EEC Treaty applied to three categories: workers, Articles 39-42 EC (ex Articles 48-51 EC), the self-employed who have the right of freedom of establishment, Articles 43-48 EC (ex Articles 52-58 EC), and the providers of services, and Articles 49-55 EC (ex Articles 59-66 EC). According to the jurisprudence of the ECJ, freedom of movement is to be ensured also to the recipients of services as well.[166]

As far as *workers* are concerned, the ECJ has underlined on several occasions the role of free movement of workers as one of the fundamental principles of the Community. The most significant aspects are the right to enter and the right of residence in another Member State. However, these rights cover only EC nationals.

Articles 39-42 EC (old Article 48 to 51 EC) regulate the freedom of movement of workers without any mention of EC nationality. Historically, this can be justified by the fact that the draftsmen of the Treaty of Rome aimed to create an economic area where all the factors of production were to circulate freely, including TCN

165 On this point see Szyszczak E., "Race Discrimination: The Limits of Market Equality?", in Hepple B.A. & Szyszczak E. (eds), *supra* note 68, 126.

166 The silence of the EEC Treaty as regards recipients of service did not hinder the ECJ to interpret it in order to include this category into the freedom of movement provisions. Joined Cases 286/82 and 26/83, *Luisi and Carbone v Ministero del Tesoro* [1984] ECR 377, in keeping with its previous judgment the ECJ adopted the same position in the Case 186/87 *Cowan v. Trésor Public* [1989] ECR 195.

workers. The approach was purely economic and therefore open in the same terms to TCNs. As Plender points out the difference of the language used in the European Coal and Steel Community (ECSC) Treaty, whereby special reference is made to the nationality of workers, only Member States nationals (Article 69), and the Treaty of Rome with a general mention of workers (Article 39, ex Article 48), appears to imply that the draftspersons of the original EEC Treaty intended to establish a common policy for all workers in the Community, irrespective of their nationality.[167]

Presumably then, at least in the mind of those who drafted the Treaty of Rome, the freedom of movement guaranteed by old Article 48 was not limited to workers of the Member States. However, the secondary legislation adopted to implement the freedom of movement principle limited those rights to EC nationals. The ECJ, normally very liberal in its interpretation of EC rules when dealing with EC citizens' rights,[168] has adopted a very cautious stance where TCNs' rights are involved. In fact, it is clear that "this area is a political mine field in which Governments' reaction to judicial meddling may be particularly harsh".[169]

On the contrary, as regards the personal scope, Article 43 EC (ex Article 52 EC), *right to establishment*, and Article 49 EC (ex Article 59 EC), *right to provide services*, expressly refer to nationals of the Member States. However, Article 49 EC (ex Article 59 EC) envisaged the possible extension of the right to provide services to TCNs, from the outset.[170]

IV.4.1 TCN service providers

Although the original version of the EC Treaty envisaged the possibility of an extension of the right to provide services to TCNs, no action was taken until 10th March 1999, when the Commission formally presented a proposal, which is presently under discussion before the Council, that foresees the extension of the freedom to provide services to TCNs legally settled in one Member State.[171] The

167 Plender R., "Competence, European Community Law and Nationals of non Member States", *International and Comparative Law Quarterly*, 1990, No 39, 599-610.

168 See Kakouris C.N., "The Case Law of the Court of Justice of the European Communities on Immigration", in Korella G.D. & Twomey P.M (eds), *Towards a European Immigration Policy*, European Interuniversity Press, 1993, 155-163.

169 Weiler, *supra* note 106, 69.

170 New Article 49 EC (Old Article 59 EC), envisages the possibility that "The Council may, acting by a qualified majority on a proposal from the Commission, extended the provisions of the Chapter to nationals of a third country who provide services and who are established within the Community".

171 OJ 1999 C 76/1.

proposal only covers self-employed TCNs already working in a Member State, it does not regulate the entry of TCNs from outside the Union. The position of this category is still governed by a 1996 Council Resolution, (*infra* section VII.6.2.). The proposal represents an important step towards establishing equality of treatment between EC national and TCNs settled in the Union and towards their integration. In fact, although the proposal stresses the benefits that would derive for the Internal Market, it is undoubtedly capable of improving the position of TCNs. The proposal explicitly covers the providers of services while the *recipients* are excluded from its scope. Likewise, it excludes those TCNs seeking to settle in another Member State. In line with the well established tendency to avoid abuse by stepping up controls a new document appears: the *EC service provision card*. The Member State in which the TCN resides is obliged to issue him this document upon request. The validity cannot exceed 12 months but it can be renewed if the original conditions for its issue still exist after a year. As a guarantee for the service provider, the provision of services abroad cannot be interpreted as an interruption of the service provider's period of residence. Such a period of legal residence acquires great importance if *he* is, for instance, to *be upgraded* to the status of Long-term Resident with all the benefits that derive. *Also*, it was agreed that under no circumstances can the Member State of residence refuse the TCN readmission into its territory. This is clearly a guarantee for the service provider who is not losing his status in the original Member State as well as for the Member State in which the service is provided that TCNs are not to become permanent members of its national labour force. The EC service provision card offers to TCN service providers several advantages as it impedes the Member State where the service is to be provided from requiring entry or exit visa, residence or work permit, under any form. The only exception allowed is when the period for the service provision exceeds six months. In that case a *temporary residence permit* may be required at discretion of the Member State where the service is provided.

Finally, there is an obligation on the Member States to recognise diplomas, certificates and other qualifications, although *only when* acquired in another Member State. Notwithstanding this restriction, this is a very relevant element which will ensure greater mobility for TCNs and the overall improvement of their situation in the Union.

It is hoped that such a restriction will eventually be removed by using the same criteria for the recognition of diplomas and other certificates in force for EC nationals.

IV.4.2 Link between EC primary and secondary rights

The completion of the Internal Market has required by the European Commission and the Council to adopt several Regulations and Directives which have indirectly affected the legal position of TCNs in order to make this freedom effective. Presently, therefore, under freedom of movement provisions no *primary rights* are conferred upon TCNs. As far as the derived rights are concerned, the implementing measures have been widening the personal scope of the freedom of movement provisions, which now cover not only economic agents but also students,[172] pensioners[173] and, more generally, any EC citizen who is covered by sickness insurance and who has sufficient resources to avoid becoming a burden on the welfare system of the host Member State.[174] By means of the provisions in the Maastricht Treaty, which introduced the concept of European Citizenship for EC nationals (*supra* section II.7), the right to travel freely and reside anywhere in the Union was formalised, although this did not imply a substantial extension of the rights in the area of the freedom of movement. Major barriers still exist in the area of free movement of people within the EU for EC nationals.[175] Such a broadening of the initial scope of the freedom of movement provisions excluded TCNs. On the contrary, Member States have found several justifications of an economic and security nature, in order to exclude TCNs from enjoying such rights and to keep them as second class citizens. However, they are covered by such provisions because of their status of spouses or children, in special occasions as relatives, of the EC migrant, or because of the work relationship with an EC company which is exercising primary community rights.

In order to exercise secondary rights the existence of a primary right is as relevant as the relationship between the TCN and the EC citizen, who is entitled to exercise primary rights. In fact, in the hypothesis that the EC national does not cross any frontier, with the consequent non-existence of primary rights, EC law does not apply and national legislation on the admission and residence of aliens will apply in full.[176]

Notwithstanding, the evolution from a purely economic Community towards a more "human" Union, the ECJ's approach remains principally economic and its main objective is the correct functioning of the Internal Market. Its very liberal

172 Council Directive 90/366, replaced by Council Directive 93/96, OJ 1993 L 317/59.
173 Council Directive 90/365, OJ 1990 L 180/28.
174 Council Directive 90/364, OJ 1990 L 180/26.
175 For a critique see Moebius I. & Szyszczak E., *supra* note 69.
176 Joined Cases 35 and 36/82 *Morson and Jhanjan* [1982] ECR 3723-3743.

and extensive interpretation of the Treaties and of the secondary legislation is therefore limited to reaching that objective.

The ECJ has in fact adopted a strict stance in this area. In the *Morson and Jhanjan*[177] case, related to the free movement of workers, it held that the provisions of Treaty on the freedom of movement and the rules adopted to implement them cannot be applied to cases which have no factors linking them with any of the situations governed by Community law.[178] It concluded therefore that Community law does not prohibit a Member State from refusing to allow a relative, as referred to in Article 10 of Regulation 1612/68/EEC, of a worker employed within the territory of that State who has never exercised the right of freedom of movement within the Community to enter or reside within its territory if that worker has the nationality of that State and the relative the nationality of a non-member country. Where, however, there has been an exercise of such right, i.e. the freedom of movement right, EC law takes precedence over domestic law. In the *Surinder Singh*[179] case, the ECJ held that a couple that went to another Member State to work and then decided to return to Britain to set up a business, had exercised the right of free movement and therefore were covered by EC law, where the wife was British and the husband was a TCN. The Court, takes the view that since the EC provisions on the free movement of persons are intended to facilitate the mobility for EC citizens to work in other Member States "a national of a Member State might be deterred from leaving his country of origin in order to pursue an activity as an employee or self-employed person as envisaged by the Treaty in the territory of another Member State if, returning to the Member State of which he is a national in order to pursue an activity there as an employee or self-employed person, the conditions of his entry and residence were not at least equivalent to those which he would enjoy under the treaty or secondary law in the territory of another Member State."[180] In particular, the Court ruled that the free movement rights cannot be fully effective if the migrant may be deterred from exercising them by obstacles raised in his or her country of origin to the entry and residence of his or her spouse. It follows that the spouse must enjoy the same rights of entry and residence as would be granted to him or her under EC law if his or her spouse chose to enter and reside in another Member State.[181]

In 1997, the Commission proposed a Convention on rules for the Admission of third country nationals to the Member States,[182] which as said above must

177 Ibidem.
178 Ibidem.
179 Case C-370/90 *Surinder Singh* [1992] ECR I-4265.
180 Ibidem, para 19.
181 Ibidem, para 23.
182 Convention on Rules for the Admission of TCNs to the Member States, *supra* note 62.

now take the form of an EC directive. It proposes to put an end to the ambiguous situation whereby a national of a Member State must move to another Member State in order to exercise his/her Community rights. The proposal, presented under old Article K.3(2)c TEU and, therefore, outside the Community framework, governs the admission of TCN family members of EU citizens who have not exercised the right of freedom of movement. As the Commission explained in its memorandum, there is a need to fill the lacuna as regards family reunification. As Union Citizenship is a single Citizenship, the gaps in the current situation should be filled by a provision for equal treatment of all Union citizens. Therefore, Article 23a of the proposal extends the conditions as they are imposed by Articles 10 and 12 of 1612/60 Regulation to TCN members of the family of a Union citizen who resides in the Member State of which he is national.

IV.4.3 Derived rights for EC migrants' family members

Several Regulations and Directives grant non EC nationals some rights as family members of an EU migrant. The Internal Market requirements impose the removal of any barrier which can hinder mobility of EC nationals and, consequently, in order to ensure such a mobility, secondary legislation facilitates movement within the Community of family members of employees, self-employed persons, and more recently of non economic categories such as students and retirees.[183]

EC law appears very liberal when dealing with family reunification, especially when we compare such legislation with the regulation of TCN family members under intergovernmental co-operation (*infra* section VIII.3). In general, the scope of EC law does not cover all relatives but it does include the migrant's spouse, his/her children under 21 and dependant relatives in the ascending and descending line of the migrant or of the spouse, regardless of their nationality.[184] However, Regulation 1612/68/EEC states that "Member States shall facilitate the admission of any member of the family... dependent on the worker... or living under the same

183 The most important secondary legislation related to these matters is the following: Regulation 1612/68/EEC JO 1968 L 257/2; Directive 68/360 JO 1968 L 257/13; Regulation 1251/70 OJ Sp. Ed. 1970 L 142/24; Directive 73/148 OJ 1973 L 172/4; Directive 75/34 OJ 1975 L 14/10; Directive 90/364 OJ 1990 L 180/26; Directive 90/365 OJ 1990 L 180/28; Directive 93/96 OJ 1993 L 317/59.

184 Article 10(1) of Regulation 1612/68/EEC grants rights to the EC migrant's spouse, their descendant who are under the age of 21 years or are dependant and their dependant relatives in the ascending line; Article 1(1) of Directive 73/148 states the abolishment of restrictions on the movement of residence of the migrant's spouse, their children under the age of 21 years and their dependant relatives in the ascending and descending line; Article 1(2) of Directive 90/364 and Article 1(2) of Directive 90/365 recognise rights to the migrant's spouse, their children only if they are dependant and dependant relatives in the ascending line; finally, Article 1 of Directive 93/60 includes in its personal scope only the spouse and their dependant children.

roof in the country whence he comes". In principle, therefore, if these conditions are met, every relative, no matter what degree of relationship with the EC worker, falls within the scope of the Regulation.

Notwithstanding the wide range of categories included in its personal scope, the Regulation has been subject to criticism, on the basis that "there are no valid grounds for denying non-dependent children over 21 years of age or relatives in the ascending line who are not dependent, the right to join their family in another Member State".[185]

EC law is concerned with the realisation of the freedom of movement of workers, which cannot be ensured if the worker is impeded by the existence of barriers to install himself/herself in the host country with his/her family, regardless of their nationality. However, equal rights are not granted to TCN family members as Member States may demand entry visas or equivalent documents from them even though it is stated that Member States "shall accord such persons every facility to obtain any necessary visas" (Article 3 of Directive 68/360 and Article 3 of Directive 73/148). Such an obligation is uncertain and it allows Member States to discriminate against TCN family members on grounds of race. It should be remembered that as EC law now stands, TCNs belonging to minority groups are already disadvantaged as the great majority of third countries whose nationals are required to have a visa are "Black" countries (*infra* section VII.5.3.). In fact, presently, the visa requirements are a source of difficulties.

The personal scope of secondary legislation has been defined by the ECJ on several occasions.

First of all, EC law covers the *spouse* of the EC migrant. The term "spouse" as included in the secondary legislation must be interpreted as covering a legal marital relationship. Unmarried partners are therefore excluded from its scope. The ECJ nonetheless in the *Reed*[186] case, has contemplated the possibility that even an EC unmarried companion can be covered by EC law. It, indeed, held that if a Member State grants certain advantages to unmarried companions of its nationals, following the non-discrimination principle, it cannot refuse to grant them to the companions, regardless their nationality, of workers who are nationals of other Member States. Such static interpretation of EC law has been criticised as "failure to adopt a broad interpretation would have the effect of restricting the free movement of persons on the grounds that many couples who live together today would, in 1968, when the Regulation was drafted, have been married. Changes in social circumstances would, therefore, result in a more limited applica-

185 European Commission, Report of High Level Panel on Free Movement of People, 1997.
186 Case 59/85 *Reed* [1986] ECR 1283.

tion of the principle contained within Regulation 1612/68/EEC than it had a number of years ago".[187] Also, there is an increasing number of gay couple who are recognised some rights under a few Member States' national legislation but they are completely neglected under EC law.

In the hypothesis that the marital relationship breaks down, as the spouse's derived rights follow the EC migrant, in principle, the spouse loses his/her rights. However, the ECJ held that, in the case of a marital relationship, spouses only lose their rights in case of divorce but not separation. Separation, therefore, cannot justify the Member States measures to expel third country spouses.[188] Two Commission's proposals, the first presented in 1989[189] and the second in 1998[190] have been presented to amend Regulation 1612/68/EEC in order to protect family members of EC workers who are TCNs. It was proposed that TCN family members *retain* the right of residence in the Member State of residence if the marriage is dissolved on condition that they have lived in that country for a period of three consecutive years.

Another exception to the above mentioned principle is the case of *death* of the EC migrant. EC secondary legislation guarantees that the beneficiaries keep their derived rights, if certain conditions are met.[191]

Secondly, all *descendants who are under the age of 21 years or are dependant* are covered by Regulation 1612/68/EEC.

The Court in the *Lebon* case[192] ruled out clearly the possibility to rely on the Regulation when the children of the worker have reached the age of 21 and who are no longer dependent on the worker.

Finally, in order to ensure the realisation of the free movement of people, Regulation 1612/68/EEC includes in its personal scope several categories of relatives. EC law appears to be very generous when dealing with family reunion. However, a comprehensive analysis shows that EC law does not benefit TCNs as

---

187 Ackers L., "Women, Citizenship and European Community Law: The Gender Implications of the Free Movement Provisions", *Journal of Social Welfare of Family Law*, 1994, 398-399.

188 Case 267/83 *Diatta* [1983] ECR 567 and case C-370-90 *Surinder Singh supra* note 179. In both cases the ECJ dealt with separation situations and it held that a marital relationship cannot be regarded as dissolved so long as it has not been terminated by the competent authority (*Diatta*, para 20).

189 OJ 1989 C 100/6.

190 Proposal for a European Parliament and Council Regulation amending Council Regulation (EEC) No 1612/68/EEC on freedom of movement for workers within the Community COM (98) 394 final, OJ 1998 C 344/9.

191 Article 3 of Regulation 1251/70 and Article 3 of Directive 75/34.

192 Case 316/85 *Lebon* [1987] ECR 2811.

it might seem at first sight. In particular TCN women can be strongly affected by EC legislation as it now stands.

IV.4.4 Spouses' rights, women's rights

In the family reunion scheme spouses' rights are, in general, women's rights as the majority of migrant workers are males who bring their family to the host state.[193] "The high masculinity ratio (in the non-national population) can be explained by the nature of successive waves of migration: more men emigrate".[194]

The female partner is also a migrant but she is dependent on the husband. Such general considerations are applicable to all women whether EC nationals or TCNs but the particular position of TCN spouses makes them more vulnerable. It has already been remarked that the rights conferred are derived rights so that they always follow the EC citizen's rights. However, EC spouses can decide to exercise their primary rights thanks to their nationality, while TCNs, apart from a few exceptions, in cases of divorce face expulsion, under this legislation.

The uncertainty of women's position has been strongly criticised. As the European Commission argued in the *Diatta* case, this EC law lacuna gives great power to partners and "it would be contrary to fundamental rights if a migrant worker could remove, unilaterally and arbitrarily, the protection accorded by Community law to the Members of his/her family".[195] It was argued that:

> "The precariousness of this situation is hard to accept, in particular as it may be used to the disadvantage of such persons. It is not rare for them to be subjected during marriage to the threat of divorce. Even in the event of the marriage being dissolved, Community law should continue to offer some legal protection to the spouse who is a third country national, in particular with regard to her right of residence. The fact that the third country national may have exercised certain rights in the Community during her marriage creates objective ties whose effects exceed the duration of the marriage. Such is the case in particular where there are common children or where the spouse has exercised her right to pursue a profession".[196]

193 See Social Europe, Strategies for Gender Democracy: Women and the European Social Dialogue, Supplement 4, 1995.

194 EUROSTAT source, see note 7.

195 Case *Diatta*, *supra* note 188.

196 European Commission, Report of High Level Panel on Free Movement of People, *supra* note 185.

Often, wives live under the threat of divorce and are forced to endure unpleasant situations, for instance domestic violence.[197] Indirectly, the lack of independent rights can more seriously affect them. Notwithstanding the absence of statistical evidence it is probable that migrant wives would rather stay with their husbands under threat of deportation. For many women a return back to their countries of origin where life for separated or divorced women is intolerable can be a trauma. Consequently, it is very likely that they would prefer to be subjected to physical and sexual violence, abuse and desertion than to go back. Such construction neglects the recent acquired "human rights" dimension of the Union, in particular, the right to family life, which seems to be subordinate to economic logic. The ECJ jurisprudence, as seen in the *Kadiman* case discussed in detail in section VI.2.4, is in fact in contrast with the position of the European Court of Human Rights where such a right is widely recognised. In the *Berrehab* case, a Moroccan migrant in the Netherlands successfully argued that deportation after the breakdown of his marriage would deny him the right to see his child and would therefore be an infringement of the right of respect for family life contained in Article 8 ECHR.[198] This tendency has been confirmed in other cases.[199] EC law, as it now stands, therefore, prevent could result in preventing TCN women from seeking protection from violence and abuse.

The Commission's proposal has reached a compromising solution as the right for the divorced or widowed spouse to maintain her right to stay in the host country is only available after three years. As a first step it is encouraging that finally spouses are receiving some protection but surely the *three years period* should be removed. Each situation should be analysed on a case by case basis in order to avoid abuse.

IV.4.5 Material scope of Regulation 1612/68/EEC

EC law is also very liberal as far as the *material scope* is concerned. Under Community law, family members, and therefore also TCNs, dispose of several

197 The EP adopted several Resolutions and Reports wherein it focused its attention on the position of women, given the special discrimination they suffer. EP, Resolution on violence against women, A2-44/86; EP, Report on discrimination against immigrants women in Community legislation and regulations, A2-133/87; EP, Report on the 1992 Single Market and its implications for migrant women in the EC, A3-0358/90/PART A. Many MEPs insisted on the importance of granting an independent right of residence to EC migrant family members to strengthen women position in the EU and presented written questions to the European Commission (Written Question No 1336/89).

198 See on this point Chalmers D. & Szyszczak E., *European Union Law, Volume II , Towards a European Polity?,* Ashgate, 1998, 459.

199 For further information on this point Moebius I. & Szyszczak E., *supra* note 69.

important rights: the rights to entry, residence, work, social security benefits, education and other social and fiscal advantages.

As far as the right to work is concerned, the ECJ in the case of *Gul*[200] has confirmed that non-Community spouses and children are exempt from requiring a work permit in the host country: they may do any job, even those subject to special administrative procedure or specific professional rules.

The spouse and the children who are under the age of 21 years or dependent have the right to take up any activity as an employed person throughout the territory of that same State, even if they are not nationals of any Member State. Analogous rights are not conferred upon the other categories of family members.[201] This is another form of discrimination against TCN family members. This exception, indeed, must be interpreted as a restriction on TCN family members, as EC family members have the right to free movement and can therefore decide to work in another Member State. In that case, EC workers by virtue of their nationality are immediately and directly covered by EC law, but TCNs must rely upon national rules. Proposals, presently under discussion, envisage the possibility of granting family members the right to pursue a professional activity also as a self-employed person.[202]

IV.4.6 Derived rights: Posted workers

TCNs benefit from freedom of the movement provisions not only as family members but also thanks to the working relationship with EC firms that exercise their right to the freedom of movement of services.

Old Article 59 EC stated that restrictions on the freedom to provide services within the Community were to be progressively abolished during the transitional period in respect of nationals of Member States who were established in a State of the Community other than that of the person for whom the services were intended. Since the early 1980s the freedom to provide services has shown its complexity as regards the position of TCNs employed in the undertaking which provide the service in another Member State. In Joined Cases *Seco & Desquenne & Giral SA*,[203] the ECJ was asked whether Community law was able to preclude a Member State from requiring an employer, who is established in its territory in order to provide services, to pay a special contribution for those employees who are not nationals of any of the Member States. The argument that "since the

200 Case 131/85 *Gul* [1986] ECR 1573, 1 CMLR 501.
201 Article 11 of Regulation 1612/68/EEC.
202 European Commission, Report of High Level Panel, *supra* note 185, 75.
203 Joined Cases 62 and 63/81 *Seco & Desquenne* [1982] ECR 223.

Member States may completely refuse to allow workers who are nationals of non-member countries to enter their territory or to undertake paid employment there, they may *a fortiori* attach to any work permit which they choose to grant conditions or restrictions..."[204] was considered unacceptable. The ECJ held that "a Member State's power to control the employment of nationals from a non-member country may not be used in order to impose a discriminatory burden on an undertaking from another Member State enjoying the freedom under Articles 59 and 60 of the EC Treaty to provide services".[205] In the *Rush Portuguese*[206] case, the ECJ has made it clear that the freedom to provide services involves that an undertaking established in a Member State must be allowed to provide services in another Member State under the same conditions as national firms. Consequently, an undertaking must be enabled to use its own staff, regardless of their nationality. In that case, a Portuguese undertaking arranged for Portuguese workers to come to France for the purpose of carrying out a job which it had subcontracted in that country. The problem was that while all the freedoms were directly applicable, freedom of movement of persons was made object of an exception until 1 January 1993. When those facts occurred therefore the Portuguese were not covered by freedom of movement provisions and they were classified as TCNs. The ECJ further developed this reasoning in the *Vander Elst*[207] case, which represents clear progress in the strengthening of social integration of TCNs.[208] In this latter case, a Belgian firm transferred TCN workers to France in order to carry out its assignment in that country. The French Government, supported by the governments of some other Member States, tried to make a distinction between the two cases, i.e. *Rush Portugue SA* and *Vander Elst* cases, arguing that even if Portuguese workers at the time the facts occurred were not entitled to free movement, they nevertheless belonged to a Member State, and this could justify a wider legal protection to free movement for the firm which employed them. The Advocate General not only considered this argument to be completely without foundation, but also raised the essential point of the ECJ ruling: "the question here is not the rights of the workers themselves, but the rights of firms

204 Ibidem para 11.

205 Ibidem para 12.

206 Case C-119/89 *Rush Portuguesa* [1990] ECR 1439.

207 Case C-43/93 *Vander Elst* [1993] ECR I-3803.

208 On this judgment see Peers S., "Towards Equality: Actual and Potential Rights of Third-Country Nationals in the European Union", *Common Market Law Review*, 1996, Vol. 33, 7-50. Also, see Cremona M., "Citizens of Third Countries: Movement and Employment of Migrant Workers within the European Union", *Legal Issues of European Integration*, 1995/2, 87-113, and Castillo de la Torre F., "La libre Circulation des Services et les Ressortissants des Pays Tiers: Quelques Réflexions au Sujet de l' Arrêt Vander Elst", *Revue du Marché Unique Europeén*, 1995/2, 131-158.

on which the workers are dependent".[209] The ECJ nonetheless restricted the right to the transfer of legally and habitually employed staff and placed emphasis on the *temporary* nature of the provision of the service.

IV.4.7 TCN posted workers

Important progress has been made for posted TCN workers, considering the growing number of firms exercising their right to supply services in another Member State and the fact that they often send (temporarily) members of their staff, both EC nationals and TCNs to work in the Member States. First of all, in 1996, Directive 96/71[210] on the *posting of workers* for provision of services was adopted. The Directive ensures a minimum level of statutory protection for posted workers regardless of the law applicable to their employment contract. This represents a guarantee for the receiving States against unfair competition *but also* for the posted workers, who are better protected against exploitation. Secondly, the Commission presented a Directive on the posting of workers who are TCNs for the provision of cross-border services.[211] This proposal was presented simultaneously with the Directive on extending the right to provide service to TCNs (*supra* section IV.4.1.) with which it has important similarities. In this case, as well, there is an obligation for the Member State in which the TCN resides to issue, at his/her request, the document known as EC service provision card. The conditions for the issue and renewal of this document are the same as under the other Directive. The card is issued for a period not exceeding 12 months with the possibility of renewal if the initial conditions persist after a year. Article 2.4 of the proposal establishes that the EC service provision card is a separate document belonging to the service provider which he puts at the disposal of the posted employee. Analogue guarantees, with the other proposed Directive, are granted against the interruption of the posted worker's period of legal residence, in the Member State of residence, and against the refusal of readmission by the country of residence. Moreover, posted TCN workers for the provision of the services in another Member State *cannot* be required to have entry or exit visas, residence or work permits. Again, only one exception is admitted. If the total period required for the service provision or provisions in question exceeds 6 months out of a period of one year, the Member State shall issue, after entry of the posted worker, a temporary

209 Opinion of Advocate-General in *Vander Elst* (Case C-43/93 [1994] ECR I-3803).

210 Directive 96/71 of the European Parliament and the Council relating to the secondment of workers within the framework of provision of services, OJ 1997 L 18/1.

211 Proposal for a Council Directive extending the freedom to provide cross-border services to third-country nationals established within the Community, OJ 1999 C 76/17.

residence permit showing that residence is authorised (Article 3.3 of the proposal). Finally, Member States must recognise the TCN's diplomas, certificates and other qualifications, if they were acquired in the Union, and must ensure equality of treatment between TCNs and EC nationals posted as workers.

IV.4.8 Freedom of establishment: Lack of progress

In the context of the freedom of establishment, Articles 43-48 EC (Articles 52-58 EC), the working relationship between a TCN worker and an EC firm does not confer any right upon the TCN worker. Such rights are limited to EC citizens. In the light of the *Vander Elst* judgment it is hard to understand the justification of such restriction as the impossibility for a firm wanting to establish itself in another Member State to hire workers freely, whether EC nationals or TCNs, in the new branch represents a clear obstacle to the freedom of establishment. In order to ensure the completion of the Internal Market, a firm should be able to hire TCNs, lawfully resident within the Union not only when providing services but also when establishing in another Member State. But the ECJ rejected the possibility of extending those rights to TCNs. In the case of *Vander Elst*, indeed, it held that TCNs in the ambit of the freedom of movement of services are allowed to work in another Member State but it stressed the temporary character of the work and therefore it implicitly refused the hypothesis of establishment. At the time of writing no case law on the freedom of establishment had been brought before the Court but it is arguable that an EC company can post TCN managers.

Also the Directive on posting service providers emphasised the temporary character in the provision of the service *implicitly* excluding the possibility of establishment.

V

THE SOCIAL RIGHTS OF TCNs

All Member States have a historical basis as welfare states and they have developed advanced social systems in order to protect their nationals. Although across Western Europe the privatisation of social security is taking place, national social security systems offer important protection for their national.

The construction of the welfare state implies the creation of boundaries in order to define those who are entitled to the welfare privileges and those who are excluded. Entitlement to such privileges is generally restricted by nationality: such systems are based therefore on the exclusion of foreigners and inclusion of only the national population. But "welfare States bring a dual dimension into the migration context: on the one hand, it becomes pertinent to control the limited goods of the welfare societies, yet, on the other hand, the welfare aspect makes it more attractive to enter from the other side".[212] One of the major fears of Western governments, widely used in political propaganda against "economic refugees" is that welfare privileges are abused by poor TCN immigrants and that they can become a burden on Member States' national welfare systems with social disruptive effects for the host society. Again, the protection of social security systems has been *instrumentalised* to discriminate against TCNs legally resident in the Union. Nevertheless, it should be remarked that a few social rights are accorded by national systems to the extra-Community population legally living in their territory.

The exclusionary idea on which the national welfare model is based in Western Europe is reflected in the European Union which works as a welfare state itself. The entitlement to social rights is limited to nationals, to some extent, to EC citizens, while the extra-Community population is generally outside EC scope.

212 Brochmann G., "Control on Migration Policies: a Closed Europe in the Making", in King R. (ed), *supra* note 6, 102-103.

V.1 THE EVOLUTION OF SOCIAL REGULATION UNDER EC LAW

It should be remembered that defining EC social policy is a difficult task. Even nowadays, according to Chalmers and Szyszczak:

> "The provisions relating to social policy in the EC Treaty are geographically scattered and conceptually diffuse. As a result social policy could be said to embrace socio-economic rights such as the free movement of persons provisions, human rights, Citizenship rights, general principles such the principle of non-discrimination in relation to nationality, rights to education, vocational training, public health. Consumer protection as well as general programmes relating to poverty, social exclusion and racism".[213]

Originally, EC regulation of the social field was very limited.[214] Although not explicitly, EC social policy was subordinated to the achievement of economic integration. According to Hervey, while at national level, "social policy goals tend to be expressed as concerned with social justice and a political aspiration…In the EC context, on the other hand, the dominant explanation for social policy provisions has tended to be economic."[215] Therefore, action in the social field becomes instrumental to reach an "integrated and efficient market" and not a specific tool to ensure the welfare of individuals.[216] It was, in fact, assumed that economic growth, generated by economic integration, would be able *per se* to improve living and working conditions throughout the European Union. One of the main areas that were originally linked to EC social policy was the elimination of any obstacle to the freedom of movement provisions which was and still is largely restricted to EC nationals. Nowadays, social provisions are mainly the competence of the Member States, although they are affected by EC law.

Such a strict economic approach left the single Member States the task of ensuring social protection. Therefore, under Community law, EC nationals were barely protected while TCNs were totally neglected. In the first phase of immigration, once again, TCNs were only considered guests and their social protection was not considered a problem.

The restricted competence in regulating social matters, which was left to the individual Member States, proved to be inappropriate and since the 1970s, the

---

213 Chalmers D. & Szyszczak E., *supra* note 198, 482.

214 Originally, social policy matters were included in Title VIII, chapter 1, Articles 117-122. Under this section the European Community had competence to promote close co-operation between Member States to improve working conditions and a standard of living for workers. A clear mention of TCN workers was absent.

215 Hervey T., *European Social Law*, Longman, 1998, 3.

216 For further comment, Hervey T., ibidem.

European Institutions have intervened in this area more actively. Accordingly, several measures to improve living and working conditions of EC citizens under European co-ordination were taken. As far as the TCNs were concerned, the relevance of the presence of an increasing extra-Community population on the labour market within the Union and the necessity to adopt measures to regulate such a presence was addressed by means of several declarations and proposals. Since then, many Member States, principally the Northern industrialised countries of the Community, were experiencing similar situations in the immigration patterns, namely the change from *immigration* to *settlement*. The guest worker system was a failure and the extra-Community populations were becoming ethnic minorities within the host societies. But, despite the urgency to adopt a common answer no binding measures were adopted in this area.

Since the Social Action Programme of 1973, the co-ordination of immigration policies of the Member States *vis-à-vis* immigration from third countries was the object of European interest but time were not ready for a political and legal commitment in this area. Member States were particularly reluctant to cede powers in this field and to adopt binding measures on immigration. Such hostility was openly shown when the European Commission decided to resort to the implicit powers conferred by old Article 118[217] to regulate this field. In 1985, the Commission adopted a Decision setting out a procedure for prior communication and consultation on migration policies in relation to non-member countries.[218] Several Member States immediately reacted and brought legal action against the Commission before the ECJ, in order to annul the Decision. They considered that the Commission was not empowered under old Article 118 EC to adopt a decision or any binding instruments and they argued Community law did not have competence to regulate the area concerning migration issues, an area wherein Member States had full sovereignty. As Ugur points out "the concerns of the Member States were about maintaining national control on immigration policy and not about whether or not policy harmonization is necessary or desirable".[219]

217 Old Article 118 EC Treaty in its original version stated that "without prejudice to the other provisions of this Treaty and in conformity with its general objectives, the Commission shall have the task of promoting close cooperation between Member States in the social field...To this end, the Commission shall act in close contact with Member States by making studies, delivering opinions and arranging consultations both on problems arising at national level and on those of concern to international organisations".

218 European Commission, Decision 85/381 OJ 1985 L 217/25.

219 Ugur M., "Freedom of Movement vs. Exclusion: A Reinterpretation of the 'Insider'-'Outsider' Divide in the European Union", *International Migration Review*, 1995, Vol. 29, 985.

The ECJ, in a very impressive judgment,[220] analysed and interpreted old Article 118 EC in a teleological way. It reasoned that this Article gives the Commission the task of promoting close co-operation between Member States in the social field, particularly in matters relating to employment and working conditions. Migration policy in relation to non-member countries is part of the social field within the meaning of old Article 118. Therefore, the ECJ held that the employment situation and, more generally, the improvement of living and working conditions within the Community are liable to be affected by the policy pursued by the Member States with regard to workers from non-member countries. As regards the competence of the Commission under Article 118 to adopt binding decisions, the ECJ interpreted the aforementioned Article as conferring such powers upon the Commission. It affirmed that where an Article of the EEC Treaty confers a specific task on the Commission, it must be accepted, if that Article is not to be rendered wholly ineffective, that it confers on the Commission necessarily and *per se* powers which are indispensable in order to carry out that task. However, the ECJ annulled the Decision because the Court considered that promotion of cultural integration as a whole fell outside the scope of old Article 118 EC. What was remarkable, despite the annulment of the Decision by the Court, was the recognition of EC competence deriving from old Article 118 EC to regulate some immigration related issues.

The position of TCNs was therefore governed by national immigration rules until the late 1980s when some Member States agreed that legally resident workers from non-member countries and members of their family should enjoy comparable treatment to Community workers as regards living and working conditions. Such commitment was formalised with the adoption of the *Social Charter* but, as the responsibility to implement its provisions was shared between the Member States and the Community, and due to the hostility of the UK, it remained a dead letter, as far as migration was concerned.

V.1.1 Maastricht and beyond

The Treaty on European Union included an Agreement on Social policy annexed to Protocol 14 which conferred clear powers upon the EC Council to take decisions on conditions of employment for TCNs, regularly established in the EC territory.[221] Such power was never used. The Agreement was one of the first examples of the flexibility principle that was widely used during the revision of the TEU and

220 Joined Cases 281, 283, 285 and 287/85, *Germany and others v. Commission* [1987] ECR 3203-3258.

221 Article 2(3) of the Agreement attached to the Protocol attached to the EC Treaty. Now Article 137 EC.

the adoption of the Treaty of Amsterdam. In fact, all Members approved the Agreement but the UK opted out. In practice, eleven members agreed to rewrite the EC social Chapter, old Articles 117-122 EC, in the Social Protocol, so that this Chapter was principally valid for the UK. By means of the Amsterdam Treaty, the political adhesion of the UK to the social agreement made its insertion into the EC social provisions possible. The provisions contained in the Social Protocol, partially modified, have replaced old Articles 117-122 EC.

The revised Article 137.3 gives the competence to the Community to regulate "the conditions of employment for third-country nationals legally residing in Community territory". Unfortunately, as in other areas moved into EC law related to TCNs, the unanimity rule has been kept. This element by itself can slow down progress on areas sensitive as this one.

Another element, which was introduced in the new text, is the decision to fight social exclusion by supporting activities to integrate persons excluded from the labour market (Article 137.1). This can be used as the legal basis to combat discrimination and the marginalisation of TCNs in the host States. Remarkably, the measures in this area can be adopted by qualified majority. The European Commission has attributed great importance to the fight against social exclusion in the building up of the Union's social dimension. In the action programme for 1998-2000 it states: "As far as promoting a society based on the integration principle is concerned, the focus will be on developing policies designed to modernise and improve social protection, promote social inclusion and combat discrimination and inequalities". However, to what extent the extra-Community population is to be included is not known. Refugees are surely included. Proposals are presently under discussion to adopt action in favour of the social and economic integration of refugees as they represent a particularly vulnerable group "whose integration requires specific action and measures".[222] At the time of writing, no action has been taken or proposed in such general terms to target the category of TCN migrants in order to ensure their integration in the host countries.

V.2 DERIVED SOCIAL RIGHTS

As discussed above, TCNs were directly excluded from EC social protection but they were nevertheless granted rights as family members of EC migrants. One major concern of EC social policy since the creation of the Community was to ensure the freedom of movement of workers within the Union. It was evident that

222 See Proposal for a Council Decision establishing a Community Action programme to promote the integration of refugees, COM (98) 731 final, OJ 1999 C 36/70.

the lack of co-ordination of social security systems was capable of hindering migrants' mobility in Europe. To achieve such a condition, the Council adopted Regulation 1408/71[223], in May 1971, which represents the first important regulation in this area. This Regulation, amended several times, is directed at coordinating national social security legislation with a view to ensuring all workers who are nationals of the Member States and their dependants equality of treatment and entitlement to social security benefits, irrespective of their place of employment and residence. The Regulation applies to all legislation relating to social branches concerning sickness and maternity benefits, invalidity benefits, old age benefits, survivor's benefits, benefits in respect of accident at work and occupational diseases, unemployment benefits, family benefits and death grants. It applies to general and special contributory and non-contributory social security schemes.

TCNs, except refugees and stateless persons, are outside the personal scope of the Regulation but they are covered as family members.

As with family members' rights under the free movement provisions, social protection rights accorded to the EC migrant's family members under the Regulation are derived or "parasitic" rights.[224] As discussed above, this means that the members of the migrant's family enjoy EC social rights, with few exceptions, as long as they keep their relationship with the holder of the primary rights, i.e. the EC migrant. In particular, according to ECJ judgments,[225] the spouse in the case of divorce can be deprived of these rights. Since spouse's rights are mainly women's rights, as discussed in the previous sections, this results as being highly discriminatory on the grounds of sex. The TCN spouse, under the freedom of movement provisions, can lose her residence right but even in the hypothesis that national legislation grants her a right to stay she loses social protection under EC law. Social benefits are often the main source of income for many women not undertaking paid work and therefore the lack of an independent entitlement to social benefits is likely to disadvantage them strongly. The construction of EC law again disregards the special position of women in the Union. Although in a neutral fashion, such legislation is capable of perpetuating the dependence of women on their husbands. However, the vulnerability of TCN spouses is greater as they must face more serious obstacles. They must face hostility and discrimination not only as women but also as members of minority groups. "For Black women, the status of being both a woman and a Black is not regarded as additive

223 Regulation 1408/71 OJ 1971 L 149/1.

224 See Moebius I. & Szyszczak E., *supra* note 69.

225 Cases *Diatta,* see note188, and *Surinder Singh, supra* note 179.

but synergistic".[226] Their position very often differs from their White European counterparts. They occupy the lowest level of the social hierarchy not only in comparison to the national population but also within their group as "they entered a labour market which is not only gender-segregated but is simultaneously racialised".[227] Their vulnerability puts women in a greater need of protecting under social security schemes.

More generally, considering minority groups as a whole, women and men, data available related to type and conditions of work, housing, education,[228] show that they face wider discrimination in the host societies as they occupy the very bottom of the social rung. They are excluded from the *social cohesion* idea that underlines the social welfare system in the Member States. EC law, as it now stands, is capable not only of perpetuating their exclusion but also of *exacerbating* it. Their lack of skills often combined with racial discrimination, impede them from competing fairly in the national market but their exclusion from the scope of EC free movement provisions and related social provisions imprisons them in the country of residence, depriving them of the benefits of the wider European market. As noted above, although it is doubtful that TCNs and female migrants possess the Euro-skills to take advantage of the Common Market, they must face enormous obstacles to move within the European Union. In fact, even if admitted to migrate within the Union, according to national immigration rules, they cannot benefit from the coordination of Member States' social security systems (only specific of TCNs are covered, such as stateless persons or refugees).

V.2.1 Progress for the social protection for TCNs

The exclusion of the extra-Community population from the scope of the Regulation 1408/71 has been severely criticised. In the perspective of the declared commitment of the European Union to integrate TCNs into the host societies and the Union as a whole, to respect fundamental human rights and to fight against racism, accepting their exclusion is seriously questioned.[229]

---

226 See Fredman S. & Szyszczak E., *supra* note 68, 215.

227 Brah A., "Black Women and 1992", in Ward A., Gregory J. (eds), *Women and Citizenship in Europe. Borders, Rights and Duties*, Trentham Books, 1992, 13.

228 On the social position of immigrants see Wrochno-Stanke K., "Immigrant Workers in Western Europe and European Integration", in De Marchi B. & Boileau A.M. (eds), *Boundaries and Minorities in Western Europe*, Franco Angeli Editore, 1982.

229 See Verschueren H., "EC Social Security Coordination excluding Third Country Nationals: Still in Line With Fundamental Rights After the Gaygusuz Judgment?", *Common Market Law Review*,

Moreover, the exclusion of TCNs from the scope of the Regulation cannot be justified by their exclusion from free movement rights as the social protection accorded by the Regulation has a wider scope. It seems that the main criterion for the applicability of the Regulation is to be insured in one of the Member State under a social security system. Accordingly, as Verschueren points out:

> "There is no objective and reasonable justification for excluding some categories of persons on the basis of their nationality, as long as they fulfil the central criterion, i.e. being insured by a scheme of a Member State".[230]

Currently, the European Commission, aware of inappropriateness of the Regulation, presented a proposal aimed at extending the application of social security schemes under Regulation 1408/71 to TCNs.[231] The regulation should therefore apply to persons who are or have been subject to the social security legislation of one or more Member States, as well as to the members of their family and to their survivors.

The Commission, considering that the lack of social protection afforded by the Regulation, as it now stands, could put TCNs concerned at a disadvantage, proposes to remove the restriction of nationality. However, the proposal does not grant the persons concerned any entitlement to enter, stay and work in a Member State. In line with the criticism advanced, the Commission in proposing the amendment of the Regulation is not only concerned with the administrative confusion[232] that TCNs' exclusion from the scope of the Regulation produces but, more importantly, by the fact that it "heightens discrimination in terms of

---

1997, 34, 991-1017. Also see Commission, Report of High Level Panel on Free Movement of People, *supra* note 185.

230 Verschueren, ibidem, 1014-1015.

231 Proposal for a Council Regulation to extend to non-EU nationals Regulation (EEC) No 1408/71 on the application of social security schemes to employed persons, to self-employed persons and to members of their family moving within the Community, COM (97) 561 final. Also, Proposal for a Council Regulation on coordination of social security systems, COM (98) 779 final.

232 As matters stand, there are a multitude of instruments applicable to non-EU nationals. The Commission identifies seven categories: non-EU nationals already covered by the Regulation, i.e. stateless persons and refugees; TCNs partially covered as family members of an EC migrant; TCNs covered by Agreements concluded between the Community and third countries containing provisions relating to social security, i.e. agreements with Turkey, Morocco, Algeria and Tunisia; TCNs covered by bilateral agreements concluded between one or two Member States; TCNs covered by the Council of Europe's European Interim Agreement of 11 December 1953 or by other multilateral agreements; TCNs who do not fit into any of the above categories and therefore do not benefit from any protection in relation to social security when they move within the Community, not even qualifying for equal treatment. Ibidem.

legal status, which would scarcely be compatible with the principles of equal treatment based on respect for human rights and the fight against racism".[233]

Furthermore, from a purely economic standpoint, omitting other social and political considerations, the lack of protection under EC law can easily result in discriminating against such categories and to a "social" dumping situation, favouring only some Member States.[234]

In an integrated market which is supposed to function as a national market, without internal frontiers and one single external border, the lack of such harmonisation could influence TCN workers' choice to enter in one State instead of another, and, consequently, the migration flows towards them. Indeed, once the conditions of entry are completely harmonised, TCNs' decision to apply for entry in one Member State may be influenced by social policy considerations: the Member State with the most *generous* social policy is likely to receive the biggest flow of TCN workers.[235] These economic implications, more than other considerations, will enable a further reform of the present regulation in a sense more open towards TCNs with a higher level of harmonisation of national laws.

However, the principle of equality of treatment limited to social security is guaranteed in many international agreements signed by the Community with third countries.

V.3 Social security: Right to equal treatment

It is evident that the right to equal treatment is the only way towards the complete integration of the extra-Community population settled within the European Union and the best way to combat racism and xenophobia. Although the Community has in different occasions declared its willingness to guarantee the equality of treatment for TCNs, from a legal point of view, this objective has not been achieved under either EU or EC law. The non-discriminatory principle is ensured only in few specific areas. Many agreements signed by the Community with third countries contain, indeed, a non discriminatory clause in matters of *employment* and *social security.*

Non-discrimination in social security is another sensitive area for the migrant worker. The possibility to aggregate periods of insurance accrued in various Member States, to benefit from family allowance scheme for family members

233 Ibidem, 8.
234 See Evans A., *supra* note 16.
235 Hailbronner K., "Visa Regulations and Third-country Nationals in EC law", *Common Market Law Review*, 1994, 31, 969-995.

and, in particular, the right to transfer old-age, invalidity and death benefits to the country of origin without discrimination, represents an essential element in the decision to migrate. Under EC provisions this area is regulated for EC citizens and, specific categories of TCNs, by means of Regulation 1408/71. Again, the strict economic approach which shaped this regulation at the origin of the Communities is evident. Such an economic approach has been maintained in the several modifications of the Regulation. The granting of social security rights enabled secure movement between the Member States. But TCNs, being excluded from the free movement provisions, were also excluded from protection afforded by the Regulation 1408/71, with the exception of TCN family members of an EC migrant, refugees and stateless persons. The absurdity of the situation for the TCNs legally settled in the Union who cannot enjoy the protection granted by this Regulation has forced the Commission to present a proposal under EC law to extend the personal ambit of application in order to include the extra-Community population[236] (*supra* section V.1). At the time of writing, no measure has been formally adopted and TCN workers gain some protection against discrimination under international agreements. The great majority of these agreements, in fact, contain a non discriminatory clause in this field.

V.3.1 EEA and Swiss Agreements

EEA nationals are the best protected as they are accorded the same protection as EC nationals.[237] The accord signed, pending for ratification between Switzerland, on the one hand, and the Member States and the Community, on the other, establishes the coordination of social security systems between the Contracting Parties to ensure among other objectives equality of treatment.

V.3.2 EEC/Turkey Agreement

Turkish nationals are protected by Decision 3/80 which incorporates the main provisions of Regulation 1401/71 as it was in 1980. However, in the *Taflan-Met* case,[238] the Court ruled that since the supplementary measures essential for implementing Decision 3/80 had not been adopted, the Decision does not have direct effect. Therefore, individuals cannot rely on it before the national courts. But,

236 Proposal for a Council Regulation to extend to non-EU nationals Regulation 1408/71, *supra* note 231.

237 Article 29 of the EEA Agreement.

238 Case C-277/4 *Taflan-Met* [1996] ECR I-4085.

in 1999, in the case of *Sürül*,[239] the Court while affirming the need to implement measures for the application of the provisions contained in Decision 3/80, nevertheless reasoned that the *non-discrimination* principle contained in Article 3 (1) of Decision 3/80, on the contrary, *does not*, as it is not affected by other provisions. This was a very difficult judgment[240] and it required two Opinions by the Advocate General.[241] The first is the one that the Court eventually followed. The second concentrated more on Article 9 of the EEC/Turkey Agreement. That Article contained a non-discrimination obligation on the Contracting Parties and the effect on that provision was questioned. But the Court in its ruling decided to limit its judgement on the interpretation of Article 3(1) of Decision 3/80 without reference to Article 9 of the Agreement. Concretely, the Court, contrary to its ruling in the *Taflan-Met* case, and to some extent overturning its previous judgment, held that a provision of the Decision *can* have *direct effect* and it concluded:

> "It follows from the foregoing considerations that Article 3(1) of Decision 3/80 establishes, in the area in which that decision applies, a precise and unconditional principle such as is capable of being applied by a national court and, therefore, of governing the legal situation of individuals. The direct effect which must therefore be accorded to that provision means that the persons to whom it applies are entitled to rely on it before the courts of the Member States."[242]

According to the ECJ ruling on the *Sürül* case, Turkish workers are now better protected.

V.3.3 Cooperation Agreements with the Maghreb countries

Among the international agreements signed by the Community with third countries, reference must be made to the cooperation agreements with the Maghreb countries (Morocco, Tunisia and Algeria). Such Agreements impose equality of treatment in the field of social security. The provisions of the agreements in this area are identical[243] and they have required the interpretation of the ECJ on several oc-

239 Case C-262/96 *Sürül* judgment delivered on 4 May 1999, not published yet.

240 For a comment of the judgment see Peers S., "Social Security Equality for Turkish Nationals" forthcoming.

241 The first Opinion was delivered on 12 February 1998 and the second on 17 December 1998, not published yet.

242 *Supra* note 239, para 74.

243 Article 39 Algeria, 41 Morocco and 40 Tunisia agreements state "...Workers of Algerian/Moroccan/ Tunisian nationality and any members of their families living with them shall enjoy, in the field of social security, treatment free from any discrimination based on nationality in relation to nationals of the Member States in which they are employed".

casions. First of all, the ECJ, in the *Kziber*[244] case, in keeping with its judgment in the *Demirel*[245] case, stated that a provision of an agreement concluded by the Community with non-member countries must be considered as being directly applicable when, having regard to its wording and to the purpose and nature of the agreement itself, the provision contains a clear and precise obligation which is not subject, in its implementation or effects, to the adoption of any subsequent measure.

The ECJ, in the context of the Morocco Agreement, considered that the provisions related to social security (Article 40 and 41) far from being purely programmatic in nature, establish a principle capable of governing the legal situation of individuals,[246] where these are not already covered by Regulation 1408/71.

The ECJ has in several judgments defined the personal and objective scope of the equality principle. Thanks to the teleological interpretation of the Court, important rights are derived for workers and in particular for their family members. In the *Kziber*[247] case, the ECJ pointed out that the agreement covers family members and retired persons and it interpreted as precluding a Member State from refusing to grant and therefore discriminate on grounds of nationality a special family benefit, "allocation d'attente", to a member of the family of a worker of Moroccan nationality. In *Yousfi*[248], again in the ambit of the Morocco Agreement, the ECJ held that these provisions must be interpreted as precluding a Member State from refusing to grant a disability allowance to a Moroccan national suffering permanent incapacity for work following an industrial accident occurring in that State who has resided on that State's territory on the grounds that the person concerned is of Moroccan nationality.

In the *Krid*[249] case, in the ambit of the Algerian Agreement the widow of an Algerian migrant worker who satisfies all the conditions, save that of nationality, must be considered as eligible for a special contributory benefit paid by a national solidarity fund, which is provided for recipients of a survivor's pension.

In the *Hallouzi-Chocho*[250] case, it held that Article 41(1) of the Cooperation Agreement with Morocco is to be interpreted as precluding a Member State from refusing, on the grounds that the person concerned is of Moroccan nationality, to grant benefits such as the transitional benefits established by the AOW, which

244 Case C-18/90 *Kziber* [1991] ECR I-199, para 15.
245 *Demirel supra* note 66.
246 *Kziber supra* note 244, para 21.
247 *Kziber* ibidem.
248 Case C-58/93 *Zoubir Yousfi* [1994] ECR I-1353.
249 Case C-103/94 *Zoulika Krid* [1995] ECR I-719.
250 Case C-126/95 *Hallouzi- Chocho* [1996] ECR I-4807.

are provided for by its legislation in the case of nationals who satisfy certain residence conditions in that State, to the spouse of a Moroccan worker who fulfils such residence conditions.

In the *Babahenini*[251] case, the ECJ held that the non discriminatory clause contained in the Algerian Agreement is to be interpreted as precluding a Member State from refusing to grant a benefit, such as disability allowance, to the disabled spouse of a retired Algerian worker on the ground that she is of Algerian nationality and has never been engaged in a trade or profession.

The migrant's family members have benefited the most from the wider interpretation of the ECJ of the Maghreb Agreements. The majority of the cases in fact involved family members but it should be noted that "in respect of family benefits, discrimination is only prohibited where the family members are in the Community. There is no requirement that these benefits be payable for family members in the country of origin."[252]

It seems that, after these important judgments, the equality principle in the social field, contained in the agreements, has been gradually accepted by Member States that no longer dispute its objective and personal scope.[253] It is doubtful that Member States wanted to ensure such levels of protection for Maghreb nationals whether workers or family members.

In the context of the EC/Morocco Agreement, special mention must be made to the *Mesbah* case,[254] pending before the Court, which raises problems related to the possession of dual nationality for workers from third countries. There is an increasing number of TCNs settled within the EU who acquire the nationality of the host State. Often, the foreign migrant becomes a national of one Member State without renouncing to his/her original nationality. In the case of dual nationality problems arise about the applicability of which agreement. This is particularly important for the migrant's TCN family members because, paradoxically, under some accords, such as the EC/Morocco Agreement, they are better protected than the family members of national workers. Until the proposal from the Commission to abolish cases of reverse discrimination is adopted (*supra* in section IV.4.2), TCN family members lose important rights if the foreign worker,

251 Case C-113/97 *Henia Babahenini* [1998] ECR I-0183.

252 Guild E., "Protecting Migrants' Rights and Community Law: the Co-operation Agreements with Algeria, Morocco and Tunisia", *Immigration & Nationality Law & Practice*, 1993, Vol. 7, No 1, 17.

253 In the recent case of *Djabali* the dispute on whether the spouse of an Algerian worker has the right to an allowance for disabled adults was solved without the intervention of the ECJ as the authority competent finally decided the granting of this benefit (Case C-314/96 *Djabali* [1998] ECR I-1149).

254 Case C-179/98 *Belgium v Mesbah*, pending. Advocate General Opinion, presented 18 May 1999, not published yet.

in this case Moroccan, acquires the nationality of the host state. Complications may occur in cases of dual nationality. The Advocate General,[255] in the *Mesbah* case, pointed out that in the light of the *Micheletti* case (*supra* section II.6), the concession of the nationality is of exclusive competence of the Member States but its loss must comply with EC law. He concluded that once it is ascertained that the migrant concerned has a double nationality, the host Member State cannot deprive him or his family members of the rights they are accorded by virtue of a valid international accord, such as the EC/Morocco Agreement.

V.3.4 Other Agreements covering social security

Non discriminatory treatment in social security is guaranteed by other agreements signed by the Community but with less effective formulas. The Agreements with *Russia* and the *ex-Soviet Republics* have nothing or just a reference to Treaties between the Member States and these countries. The *ACP* countries, by means of the Lomè Convention, all contain a non-discriminatory clause in the field of social security. This is not in the main text of the Agreement but in the annex. Finally, the *Europe Agreements* do not contain any *express* reference to non-discrimination in the social field.

V.3.5 Final remarks

It will be interesting to see the ECJ's position in this area after the European Court of Human Rights' judgment in the *Gaygusuz*[256] case. This represents the first judgment of the Court in Strasbourg in which the object discussed was related to non-discrimination regarding nationality and social rights. The Strasbourg Court considered social security rights as property rights and, accordingly, it held that the right to social security and social protection must be considered as a fundamental right to be protected under the Human Rights Convention. Any discrimination in this field, based on the nationality of the worker concerned, represents a breach of human rights. This judgment will probably pave the way towards the equal treatment in the field of social security of all TCNs, no matter what the current protection accorded by each agreement is, and hopefully between TCNs and EC citizens by the inclusion of TCNs in the scope of Regulation 1408/71.[257]

255 Advocate General Opinion, delivered 18 May 1999.
256 European Court of Human Rights Case 39/199/545/631 *Gaygusuz v Austria*.
257 On this point see Verschueren, *supra* note 229.

Whilst waiting for new developments in this area, it should be remembered that this is a very delicate field for TCNs. Securing social protection can have great significance for the extra-Community population settled in the Union. As seen above, TCNs are generally situated at the bottom of the society in which they live, and their flexibility and capability to adjust is less effective than that of EC nationals, so they are therefore more affected by permanent poverty. Considering that all the Member States are welfare states, based on social solidarity, even though, as said above, major restructuring of social security systems is presently under process, they must ensure minimum protection to their members in order to avoid social marginalisation and exclusion. But this raises the problem of *who* are the members of that State. The granting of social rights, as seen in other areas, imposes the creation of boundaries to define those covered and those excluded.[258] At EU level, important statements have been made to fight the marginalisation and discrimination of their members. But TCNs are often not considered as *proper members*. Statistically, many immigrants, in particular women, are in need of protection, although those who actually benefit from social security system are very limited.

Under the Maastricht Treaty, ensuring proper social protection and combating social exclusion[259] were areas to be dealt with in the Social Protocol. As discussed in section V.1.1, Member States agreed to insert, the partially modified provisions of the Social Protocol in the main EC Treaty during the IGC. Therefore, under the Amsterdam Treaty, EC law is competent to fight social exclusion in the labour market (Article 137 EC, ex Article 118 EC). Although the fight against social exclusion is restricted to the labour market, this represents an important step toward rescuing those marginalised into the mainstream society.

TCNs might face other types of discrimination and exclusion, for instance in education or housing, but their presence in the labour market is surely one of the tools in the the fight against their marginalisation. European societies should improve their social security systems with a more liberal approach towards those most marginalised and discriminated against. This is a very unlikely scenario as Member States, throughout Europe, are making great efforts to modify and rationalise their domestic systems and to reduce the categories protected to meet the strict requirements imposed by the Maastricht Treaty and by the agreements that followed. Also, there is a widespread siege and racist mentality misused by

---

258 As regards the different categories of rights in the social field see Schnapper D., *L' Europe des Immigrés, Essai sur les Politiques d' Immigration*, Éditions François Bourin, 1992.

259 Article 2 of the Agreement on Social Policy attached to the Social Protocol.

the competent authorities that are concerned by the abuses of the welfare systems by immigrants. According to Eurobarometer a majority (75%) of those interviewed considered that minorities pay less than they claim, and 59% said that they abuse the systems of social benefits.[260]

260 Eurobarometer Opinion Poll No 47.1, Racism and Xenophobia in Europe, 1997.

VI

TCNs' RIGHT TO NON-DISCRIMINATION AS REGARDS WORKING CONDITIONS AND THE RIGHT TO RESIDENCE

VI.1 THE RIGHT TO NON-DISCRIMINATION AS REGARDS WORKING CONDITIONS

This section covers the right to non-discrimination in working conditions. TCNs have not gained this right under EC/EU law but under many agreements signed by the Community and the Member States with third countries. Development in this direction has not, in fact, been adopted under the Amsterdam Treaty and EC nationals maintain a priority right in the labour market. However, the non-discrimination provision in Article 13 EC, which prohibits race discrimination, may lessen their discrimination in access to employment and in working conditions.

The rights conferred upon TCNs under the several agreements signed by the Community with third countries responded to economic needs rather than to improving their integration in the host societies. Employers must respect the same labour conditions when hiring employees regardless of the nationality of the worker, whether they are EC nationals or TCNs. This excludes unfair competition in the labour market and, at the same time, the exploitation of foreign labour. Most of these agreements were signed in the first or second phase of immigration when Member States were concerned more with by the beneficial economic impact of foreign labour in their countries than its social and cultural consequences.

The strict economic approach which was, it is presumed, in the mind of the draftspersons of the international agreements, has been partially extended by several judgments of the ECJ in this area. The ECJ has maintained an economic approach and an economic interpretation of these agreements but it has expanded the economic "requirements" of the market which eventually have benefited TCNs.

VI.1.1. EEC/Turkey Agreement

Under the EEC/Turkish Agreement, Turkish workers and their family members are partially protected under Article 6 and Article 7 of Decision 1/80. Turkish workers and their family members gain, if certain conditions are met, the right to equal treatment in access to employment. But also, as in the majority of the Agreements signed by the Community, the right to equal treatment in employment covers non-discrimination as regards *remuneration* and *other conditions of work*. Although limited, this right is extremely important as it impedes EU employers from hiring TCNs on less favourable labour conditions than those which they are obliged to observe for EC citizens.

VI.1.2 Cooperation Agreements with Maghreb countries

During the 1970s the Community signed cooperation accords with its neighbouring Mediterranean countries. These do not envisage accession to the Community for obvious geographical reasons and they have, therefore, very limited regulation concerning labour. However, they do contain a general obligation on the Contracting Parties not to discriminate against workers on grounds of nationality as regards working conditions or remuneration. Among these accords, special mention must be made to the cooperation agreements with some Maghreb countries, Algeria, Morocco and Tunisia, in which the *non-discriminatory principle* as regards *working conditions* is formulated to have direct effect. These agreements, signed in the late 1970s, contain very similar not to say identical provisions as regards non-discrimination in working conditions and remuneration:

> "The treatment accorded by each Member State to workers of Algerian/Moroccan/ Tunisian nationality employed in its territory shall be free from any discrimination based on nationality, as regards working conditions or remuneration, in relation to its own nationals".[262]

The wording of these Articles is almost identical to Article 48 (2) EC. The extent to which they must be interpreted in the same way has not yet been tested before the ECJ. At the time of writing just one case had been brought before the Court to test the real extent of the non-discrimination principle contained in the Morocco Agreement. In the *El Yassini*[263] case, the ECJ was asked whether the protection guaranteed by the non-discrimination principle contained in the agreements could impede expulsion measures of a Moroccan worker while legally working in a Member State. By analogy with the ECJ's progressive interpretation of Decision 1/80, where the ECJ derived the right to residence from the right to work for Turkish workers (*infra* section VI.2.3), the right to non-discrimination accorded to Moroccan nationals should be interpreted as conferring a right to stay for the

262 Article 38 Algeria, 40 Morocco and 39 Morocco agreements.
263 Case C-416/96 *El Yassini* [1999] ECR I-1209.

duration of the worker's lawful employment. But the ECJ, in its ruling which followed the Conclusions of the Advocate General,[264] ruled that the right not to be discriminated against as regards working conditions contained in Article 40, taking into account that the EC/Morocco Agreement contrary to the EEC/Turkey Agreement does not envisage the realisation of the freedom of movement of workers, cannot be interpreted as conferring the right to residence to Moroccan workers. The Court refused to acknowledge that, as some authors have highlighted, the precariousness of their residence status can result in discriminatory treatment. Guild observes:

> "If they have less security in the labour market than 'own nationals' or EC nationals, then discrimination in working conditions must result. For example, uncertainty of residence will be a disincentive to employers considering the promotion of workers. It is also a disincentive for the workers to upgrade their skills and qualifications which may be of use to them in their country of origin. Discrimination in promotion and training resulting from the uncertain position of the workers in the labour force must inevitably be reflected in their wages. Workers whose position is insecure are likely to remain in the lowest paid and least skilled posts as these are the easiest to fill in the event that the worker is expelled".[265]

The Court only admitted one exception, which is to be evaluated by national courts. The ECJ ruled that there is an obligation on the Member States to extend the right of residence when the competent national authorities have granted a work permit with longer validity than the residence leave. But in the event, as the present one, where *only the working contract* has been freely established for a longer period between the employer and the employee there is no obligation for the national authorities to grant such an extension of the worker's right to stay in the host country. This will require more coherence in the issuing of work and residence permits by national authorities. The exception does not have great consequences in those Member States, such as the UK, where the residence permit is, as a general rule, of the same length of the work permit. In other Member States, on the contrary, this exception could have a great impact on TCNs who would be able to obtain a right of residence for the same length of a valid work permit issued by national authorities. The exception established by the ECJ in the *El Yassini* case is a general rule, which is not limited to Moroccan workers, but must be interpreted as concerning all the TCNs covered by similar provisions.

264 Opinion of Advocate General in the *El Yassini* case, ibidem.
265 Guild E., *supra* note 252, 15-18.

VI.1.3 EEA Agreement and the Accord with Switzerland

By far the most important agreement is, once again, the EEA Agreement since EEA nationals are accorded the same protection granted to EC citizens.[266] Again, it seems that closeness with Europe and its population has allowed the accession of EEA nationals to the EC privileges in a period of great closure towards foreigners. Also, the Agreement recently signed with *Switzerland* grants the same protection to the nationals of the Contracting Parties.

VI.1.4 Europe Agreements and the Agreements with the ex-Soviet Republics

The Europe Agreements signed by the Community with ten Central and Eastern European States after the collapse of the Soviet Empire mark a great opening towards these countries even though the approach is more cautious with respect to labour. The Europe agreements contain similar not to say identical provisions and they recognise the accession to the European Union as the final objective. However, they include only limited provisions relating to the free movement of workers. In practice, these agreements do not regulate the right of workers to enter the territory or their access to the labour market of a Member State. They only aimed at ensuring that once in employment they cannot be discriminated against in their working conditions and pay.

After the fall of the Berlin wall and the disintegration of the Communist empire, the Community concluded partnership and cooperation agreements with the majority of the ex-Soviet Republics.[267] These agreements mark an important step in the road to cooperation with the Community but they represent a lower level of relationship: accession to the Union is not foreseen and not foreseeable in the near future. Nonetheless, all the agreements contain an obligation to ensure equal treatment as regards remuneration and working conditions. However, such an obligation is clear only in the agreement with Russia.

266 Article 28.2 of the EEA Agreement forbids any discrimination based on nationality between EEA citizens and EC nationals.

267 Partnerships and Cooperation Agreements have been concluded with Armenia OJ 1999 L 205; Azerbaijan OJ 1999 L 246; Belarus signed 06.03.1995, not published yet; Georgia OJ 1999 L 205/1; Kazakhstan OJ C 319/94; Kyrgystan OJ C 326/94; Moldova OJ 1998 L 181/1; Uzbekistan OJ 1999 L 229; Russia OJ 1997 L 327, and Ukraine OJ 1998 L 49/1.

VI.1.5 ACP Agreement

Finally, as regards non discriminatory treatment in employment, the Community signed an agreement with around 70 African, Caribbean and Pacific States. This agreement also recognises equality of treatment in working conditions of migrants from these countries. However, there is no enforcement system as efficient as in other agreements as, for instance, in the Maghreb Agreements.

VI.1.6 Non-discrimination as regards working conditions: Impact on TCNs

Although very restricted, the right to equal treatment as regards working conditions and remuneration is very important because, as seen above, TCNs are generally at the bottom of the social ladder. The overall situation of foreigners in the Community's labour market has not changed much from year to year. Their structural vulnerability remains higher than that of EC nationals. They have to face greater difficulties to improve their economic and social conditions. Although TCNs movements have changed in 40 years of migration, in many countries their presence is still considered temporary. Foreign workers were, at the origin of the Communities, seen as additional and replacement labour. Castles clearly defines this concept in the German context in the 1950s:

> "Foreign workers were *additional labour*; they allowed expansion of the labour force at a time when the number of German workers was stagnating or declining. The need for additional workers was especially great in the growth industries...which were the driving force in expansion. Foreign workers were also *replacement labour;* they entered the labour market at the bottom, where they replaced West German workers who were able to benefit from growing employment and training opportunities to move into better paid and pleasanter skilled and white-collar jobs".[268]

Obviously, nowadays, TCNs are no longer needed as *additional labour* as Western Europe is facing serious unemployment problems. But foreign labour is still needed for *replacement*. Although there is a declining demand for unskilled workers, there are still important sectors of the economy in which workers are required to do low-skilled, low-paid and low-status jobs. Normally, EC nationals refuse to take these kind of jobs which are now largely taken by TCNs. Their presence allows the upward social mobility of national workers. But TCNs must stay at the bottom. Indeed, very little has been done to integrate them in the labour market or to

---

268 Castles S. et al (eds), *Here for Good. Western Europe's New Ethnic Minorities*, Pluto Press, 1984, 127.

ensure their social mobility. On the contrary they are often discriminated against. Their precarious presence – they are in fact always treated as temporary workers – has worked as a hampering factor in their integration and it has worsened discrimination against them.

It is known that it is very difficult to prove to be the victim of discrimination in access to employment and in the place of work. However, it has been demonstrated that their greater vulnerability is caused by several factors and race is often a relevant factor. Their difference – the majority of TCNs belong to a minority group – becomes a decisive factor for employers when deciding who to hire.

VI.1.7 Special position of TCN female migrants in the market

Among the extra-Community population special attention must be paid to the specific position held by TCN migrant women.

Their situation among their community group is generally worse than men. Many migrant women do not even enter the labour market and they rely completely upon their men, husbands or fathers.[269] Women as a group suffer from stereotypes and discrimination. Important measures are being discussed under EC and EU law to combat and prohibit the spread of this situation. But female migrants, if they enter the labour market, must face more obstacles because in the labour market they suffer from the cumulative effect of their sex and minority group status. Often they are the instruments for the emancipation of their white counterparts. Female workers as a whole must enter a gendered labour market. Their position in the labour market is made more difficult by the presumption that women although working outside the house, still have the responsibility of child caring and in more general terms of the private dimension of the house and family. Many white female workers have been able to reach high status jobs because they were able to reduce their presence in the home sphere thanks to a massive recourse to cheap foreign labour, such as housemaids or nannies. There is in fact a strong presence of female migrants in these sectors.[270] The absence of skills requirements ensures easy accession of migrants in these sectors but, at the same time, it blocks their social mobility as they do not acquire new skills and often they are not even recognised as labour.

---

269 According to EUROSTAT sources, when available, migrant women are less present than men in the labour market. EUROSTAT, *supra* note 7.

270 See Anthias F., "Connecting Ethnicity, 'Race', Gender and Class in Ethnic Relations Research", in Joly D. (ed), *Scapegoats and Social Actors, The Exclusion and Integration of Minorities in Western and Eastern Europe*, MacMillan Press LTD, 1998, 173-192.

Notwithstanding several declarations made at EU level in the fight against discrimination, marginalisation and social exclusion, the situation of these invisible female migrants has barely improved and in many cases has worsened.

VI.2 THE RIGHT TO RESIDENCE IN THE HOST STATE

Originally, the right to residence of TCNs was not covered by EC law. This right was subordinate to their right to work in the host State. Taking into account that they were only considered as guest workers, their right to stay was never considered *independently* from the right to work. But, since it was clear that migration was taking the form of settlement during the 1970s, the right to stay for TCNs was increasingly on the political agenda in the Member States regardless of their position in the labour market.

At EU level, since the adoption of the Maastricht Treaty, the conditions of residence by nationals of third countries in the territory of the Member States have been considered a matter of common interest (old Article K(1)(3)(b)TEU). This area was mainly governed by national rules. Securing residence rights to TCNs legally resident in the Union is an important method of ensuring their integration in the host countries which requires a concerted effort at European level.

The European Union presents itself as a common space without internal frontiers but great differences exist among national regulations in this area. It is absurd that in one country it takes five years to secure residence rights, while in another it takes ten, if a minimum level of integration is to be achieved. In the meantime, before the TCN migrant has reached the period necessary to allow automatic renewal of the permit, short permits are issued, according to national priorities. It is obvious that once such a permit expires TCNs can be expelled. Generally, TCNs admitted by Member States into the Union are not protected under EU or EC law against deportation.[271] Their status is regulated under national legislation, which governs the residence status of foreigners.

Action was taken under the Maastricht Treaty in respect of a specific category of TCNs, notably long term Residents, also known as Denizens.

271 On the contrary Member States have elaborated under the third Pillar several important measures aimed at harmonising measures of expulsion discussed in the next sections.

VI.2.1 Special position of denizens under EC/EU law

In 1996, the Council adopted the Long-term Residents' Resolution[272] which accords the automatic right of residence to certain categories of TCNs. On the basis of the Resolution, the Commission has elaborated the Immigration Convention that also envisages the right for TCNs settled on a permanent basis to the automatic renewal of the residence permits.[273] The proposed Convention would reduce Member States' discretion compared to the Resolution: Long-term Residents are defined as those who have been legally resident on a regular basis in a Member States for at least five years and when they hold an authorisation which permits residence for a total period of at least ten years from their first admission. The Resolution is more vague as it defines Long-term Resident as those who have been legally resident for a period specified in the legislation of that Member State, although such period could not exceed ten years' legal residence.

According to the Commission's proposal, which is to be reworded to be a Directive now that the Amsterdam Treaty is in force, "persons recognised as long-term residents no longer need to show good cause for admission for a specific purpose as their legal status automatically entitles them to work in an employed or a self-employed capacity, or to engage in studies, or to reside for family reunification or other purposes."[274] In order to *physically* recognise their status based on a uniform approach, "once TCNs acquire recognition as long-term residents, this shall be shown by a specific entry on their residence authorisation document".[275] As noted above, there is a great effort to rationalise the controls and to make them more efficient on a European basis. TCNs must be recognisable throughout the Union by a uniform visa, uniform residence permit and for long-term residents, a uniform specific entry in their documents, also, EC service provision cards for service providers are under discussion.

In the perspective of the equality of treatment between TCNs and EC citizens, TCNs enjoy greater protection as regards the circumstances in which they can be expelled. The privileges connected to the status of Long-term Resident can also be exported to other Member States. According to the Commission since those Long-term Residents are allowed to take up employment in another Member State and, therefore, also to remain there, it would be somewhat illogical to regard them as new arrivals there. Consequently, they must be allowed to have their rights

272 Long-term Resident Resolution, *supra* note 149.

273 Article 31 and Article 32 of the Immigration Convention, *supra* note 62.

274 European Commission, Explanatory Memorandum of the Convention on Rules for Admission of TCNs, *supra* note 62.

275 Article 31 of Immigration Convention.

as Long-term residents recognised in the new Member State of residence. Such recognition would become effective only after a *two-year probationary* period, allowing those in question to take a clear decision about whether they wish to settle in the new Member State on a long-term basis and have the benefit of long-term Residents' rights transferred".[276] It is evident that TCNs can be recognised as Long-term Residents, and therefore enjoy the privileges connected with that status, only in one Member State. However, proposals aimed at reducing these rights are currently under discussion. Proposals[277] forwarded by the Council to amend the Convention suggest a limitation on the right against expulsion. It is proposed that "third country nationals who are recognised as Long-term Residents in a Member State may (despite being lawfully resident) be transferred at any time for reasons of public order or internal security to the Member State which previously recognised them as Long-term Residents".[278] The possibility of being expelled is also a measure foreseen for EC nationals, available under EC law when specific circumstances occur.[279] It remains to be seen what meaning is attributed to this amendment, if ever approved. Anyway, it is difficult to imagine a willingness to interpret such an exception in strict terms as the proposed Article 35a continues "third country nationals who have been recognised by another Member State as long-term third country residents may (despite being lawfully resident) be transferred to that Member State for other reasons" which leaves a great margin of discretion to the Member States. This last exception should be considering as unacceptable considered the gravity of the consequences on the TCN in question, namely the expulsion from the State of new residence. EC citizens *as well* can be subject to an expulsion order but according to EC legislation and, in particular the ECJ jurisprudence, such interference in their right to free movement must be strictly interpreted.

The right to the automatic renewal of the right of residence would be limited to those TCNs settled in the Member States on a permanent basis which implies, according to Article 30 of the proposed Convention, a legal residence on a regular basis in the host State for at least ten years and, at the same time, an authorisation which permits residence for a total period of at least ten years from their first admission. Although TCNs covered by the proposal are an increasing number of

276 European Commission, Explanatory Memorandum on the Convention, *supra* note 62.

277 Council document, Draft Supplementing the Convention on rules for the Admission of third-country nationals to the Member States of the European Union, 9584/98.

278 Article 35a, ibidem.

279 Council Directive 64/221 on the co-ordination of special measures concerning the movement and residence of foreign nationals which are justified on grounds of public policy, public security or public health, OJ 1964 L Sp. ED. 850/64.

the extra-Community population, many new arrivals are nonetheless outside its personal ambit of application.

VI.2.2 EC progress under the Amsterdam Treaty

The Amsterdam Treaty represents a step forward as this area has been communitarised. Article 62 (4) EC (ex Article 73 j (4) EC) confers the competence to the Council to adopt measures defining the rights and conditions under which nationals of third countries who are legally resident in a Member States may reside in other Member States. But here there is an exception to the five years deadline as Article 63 (4) EC (ex Article 73 j (4) EC) establishes that when adopting the new measures the Council is not subject to that deadline. The consequences of that exception are clear. While in the other areas of the new Title IV EC (ex Title IIIa EC) there is an obligation for the Council to adopt new measures within five years from the entry into force of the Amsterdam Treaty, regulation of this area is left to the will of the Council as any deadline is lacking. The Commission or the EP will not be able to stimulate the Council to adopt necessary legislation through recourse before the Court under Article 232 EC (ex Article 175 EC). It is evident that during the negotiations of the Amsterdam Treaty the integration of the foreign population, and the securing of residence rights is an important way to reach that aim, was not considered a high priority matter requiring immediate action.

However, it is to be noted that the Council and the Commission on how best to implement the provisions have committed themselves to the Action Plan establishing an area of freedom, security and justice,[280] to adopt such measures within five years after the entry into force of the Amsterdam Treaty. This does not represent a legal obligation but it is nonetheless important from a political point of view as it shows the willingness of the Member States to legislate in this area.

TCNs may, also, gain some residence rights by means of the international agreements signed by the Community and third countries.

VI.2.3 The right to residence under international agreements: EEC/Turkey Agreement

Turkish workers and their family members may gain some residence rights under the EEC/Turkish Agreement.

The EEC-Turkey Council of Association adopted two significant decisions related to the free movement of workers, based on Article 12 of the Ankara

280 Action Plan of the Commission and the Council on how best to implement the provisions of the Amsterdam, see note 84.

Agreement: Decision 2/76 and Decision 1/80. The first Decision is no longer valid. The provisions related to free movement of workers are only those contained in Decision 1/80. In particular those of Article 6 and 7 of the Decision confer, if certain conditions are met, residence and working rights to Turkish nationals. The ECJ has repeatedly pointed out that the Decision 1/80 does not encroach upon the competence retained by the Member States to regulate both the entry into their territory of Turkish nationals and the conditions under which they may take up their first employment, but it merely regulates, in Article 6, the situation of Turkish workers already integrated into the labour force of the host Member State and in Article 7 that of the Turkish worker's family members.

Article 6 states that Turkish workers duly registered as belonging to the labour force of Member State are entitled, according to procedures established under national rules: (a) after one year's legal employment, to renewal of a permit for the same employer; (b) after three years' legal employment and subject to priority of Community workers, to take up another offer of employment for the same occupation; and (c) after four years' legal employment, to enjoy free access in that Member State to any paid employment. Article 6 of Decision 1/80 covers only workers and it excludes Turkish nationals who are self-employed, although obviously if they then become employed they are covered. The ECJ has interpreted the Decision on several occasions. In terms of the right to settlement, the most important finding is that by means of the recognised right to work conferred by Article 6 of Decision 1/80, Turkish workers gain the right of residence. In the *Sevince*[281]case, the ECJ held that Article 6 of the Decision contains in *clear, precise* and *unconditional* terms, the obligation for Member States to recognise the right of residence after a number of years' legal employment in its territory, to enjoy free access to any paid employment of his choice.

The Decision only expressly grants the right to work, but the ECJ was nevertheless able to rule that there is a close relation between this right and the right of residence.

> "The fact nevertheless remains that those two aspects of the personal situation of the Turkish worker are closely linked and that by granting to such a worker, after a specified period of legal employment in the Member State, access to any paid employment of his choice, the provisions in question necessarily imply, since otherwise the right granted by them to the Turkish worker would be deprived of any effect, the existence, at least at that time, of a right of residence for the person concerned".[282]

---

281 Case C-192/89 *Sevince*, *supra* note 67.

282 *Sevince*, ibidem.

This is a very important finding as Turkish workers are protected against expulsion after only one year of employment, when the above conditions are met.

It is important to recall that such a right is derived from the right to work and it is, therefore, based on periods of legal employment. The ECJ has been called upon to define the *meaning of the legal employment* concept. It pointed out that the legality of employment presupposes a *stable and secure situation* as a member of the labour force.[283] Therefore, the expression legal employment cannot cover a situation of a Turkish worker who has been legally able to continue in employment only by reason of the suspensory effect deriving from his appeal pending a final decision by the national court, when the court dismisses his appeal.[284]

The Court obviously refused to be moved by humanitarian considerations when giving its ruling, *contrary* to the interpretation of the same provisions under Article 48 EC. It should be considered, as O'Leary argues, that "when Mr Sevince was expelled he had been in the Netherlands for 8 years and 8 months and that the Dutch authorities had taken more than 5 years to decide that he had to leave."[285]

In the recent *Nazli* case,[286] still pending before the Court, case the ECJ was asked whether a Turkish worker who is covered by Article 6(1) of Decision 1/80 loses the rights accorded thereunder due to the fact that he has been condemned.

The stable and secure situation as a member of the labour force is irrelevant of whether or not the competent authorities have issued administrative documents. Moreover, in the *Kus*[287] case, the ECJ stated that periods of legal employment completed while the decision refusing the person concerned the right of residence was suspended as a consequence of the proceedings brought by him against that decision were not periods of "legal employment". The ECJ, in *Kus*, also pointed out that a Turkish worker can rely upon the Decision directly in order to obtain the renewal not only of the work permit but also of the residence permit, regardless of the original reason of entry, in this case marriage.[288] Furthermore, in the *Suat Kol*[289] case, the ECJ held that Article 6(1) is to be interpreted as meaning that a Turkish worker does not satisfy the condition of having been in legal employment within the meaning of that provision, in the host Member State, where he

283 *Sevince*, ibidem para 30.
284 *Sevince* ibidem para 32.
285 O' Leary S., Employment and Residence for Turkish Workers and Their Families: Analogies with Case-Law of the Court of Justice on Article 48 EC, in *Scritti in onore di Giuseppe Federico Mancini, Vol. II, Diritto dell' Unione Europea*, Giuffrè Editore, 1998, 739.
286 Case C-340/97 *Nazli* pending.
287 Case C-237/91 *Kus* 1992 ECR 1-6781.
288 Ibidem para 15.
289 Case C-285/95 *Stuat Kol* [1997] ECR I-3069.

has been employed there under a residence permit which was issued to him only as a result of fraudulent conduct for which he has been convicted. In the *Eker*[290] case, the ECJ held that a TCN worker in order to rely upon Article 6(1) to obtain an extension of the right to residence in the host state must have been legally employed continuously for one year with the same employer. Once the conditions contained in Article 6 of the Decision are met, the discretion of the Member States as regards the decision to renew the work or residence permit is strongly reduced. Therefore, Article 6 of the Decision cannot be construed as reserving the Member States the power to adapt as they please the rules governing Turkish workers already integrated in their labour force, permitting them to adopt unilateral measures preventing certain categories of workers who already satisfy the conditions contained in Article 6 from benefiting from the progressively more extensive rights enshrined in it. In the *Ertanir*[291] case, the ECJ reaffirmed that the wording of Article 6 is general and unconditional and it does not permit Member States to deprive certain categories of Turkish workers, in this case specialist chefs, of the rights to directly rely on the provisions of the Decision. Moreover, in the *Günaydin*[292] case, the ECJ affirmed that the Decision's provisions cannot be interpreted by the Member States as limiting the rights of the Turkish worker who qualifies under the terms contained in the Decision. In this case, a Turkish national may seek the renewal of his residence permit in the host Member State notwithstanding the fact that he was permitted to take up paid employment there only temporarily with a specific employer for the purpose of acquainting himself with and preparing for employment in one of its subsidiaries in Turkey, and obtained work and residence permits for that purpose only.

In the case of *Birden*,[293] the Court was once again asked to interpret Article 6(1) of Decision 1/80. In this case, Mr Birden, as a result of the marriage to a German national, was granted a residence permit in Germany, valid until June 1995, and, at the same time, he was granted an *unconditional* work permit of unlimited duration. When his marriage was dissolved and his residence permit expired, he was refused an extension of this permit. The reason was that he was not "duly registered as belonging to the labour force" in the host state. In fact, since Mr Birden was unable to find a job, he was first offered social assistance and then he entered into a contract relationship wholly funded with public funds.

290 Case C-386/95 *Eker* [1997] ECR I-2707.

291 Case C-98/96 *Kasim Ertamir* [1997] ECR I-5179, para 33.

292 Case C-36/96 *Faik Günaydin, Hatice Günaydin, Günes Günaydin and Seda Günaydin v Freistaat Bayern* [1997] ECR I-5179.

293 Case C-1/97 *Birden* [1998] ECR I-7747.

But the Court, in keeping with its previous jurisprudence,[294] held that the *nature* of the legal relationship is not relevant so long as this is not purely marginal or ancillary. It concluded that Mr Birden was entitled to an extension of his residence permit. In the light of the *El Yassini* case (*supra* section V.3.3), the sole existence of a valid work permit, as in this case, granted by the competent national authority should have been able to guarantee the holder an extension of his residence permit so long as work was available.

As mentioned above, the right of residence is a derived right and it depends on the right to work. However, in the *Bozkurt*[295] case, the ECJ, interpreting Article 6(2) of Decision 1/80, pointed out that annual holidays and absences or reasons of maternity or an accident at work or short periods of sickness shall be treated as periods of legal employment. Periods of involuntary employment duly certified by the relevant authorities and long absences on account of sickness shall not be treated as periods of legal employment, but shall not affect rights acquired as a result of the precedent period of employment. In 1997, in the *Tetik*[296] case, the ECJ was called to interpret the case of voluntary unemployment. By analogy with EC jurisprudence,[297] the ECJ held that the third indent of Article 6(1) must be interpreted as meaning that a Turkish worker who has been legally employed for more than four years in a Member State, who decides voluntarily to leave his employment in order to seek new work in the same Member State and who is unable *immediately* to enter into a new employment relationship, enjoys in that State, for a reasonable period, a right of residence for the purpose of seeking new paid employment there, provided the he continues to be duly registered as belonging to the labour force of the Member State concerned, complying where appropriate with the requirements of the legislation in force in that State, for instance by registering as a person seeking employment and making himself available to the employment authorities. It is for national courts to decide the length of what must be considered as a reasonable period. By analogy with the *Antonissen*[298] case, it is assumed that the period accorded to the worker to seek a new occupation shall be of minimum 3 months. After that period it must likewise assume that the impossibility for the migrant worker to find a job justifies his

294 The concept of "worker" and "working relationship" under Article 48 EC has been the object of several ECJ's judgments see Case 53/81 *Levin* [1982] ECR 1035, Case 139/85 *Kempf* [1986] ECR 1741, Case 66/85 *Lawrie-Blum* [1986] ECR 2121, Case 344/87 *Bettray* [1989] ECR 1621. For a commentary see Chalmers D. & Szyzsczak E., *supra* note 177, 425-431. See also Moebius I. & Szyszczak E., *supra* note 69.

295 Case C-434/93 *Bozkurt* [1995] ECR I-1475..

296 Case C-171/95 *Tetik* [1997] ECR I-0329.

297 Case C-292/89 *Antonissen* [1991] ECR I-745.

298 Ibidem.

expulsion from the host Member State.[299] However, when a Turkish worker has definitively *ceased* to belong to the labour force of a Member State because s/he has reached the *retirement age* or become totally and *permanently incapacitated to work* it must be assumed that s/he is no longer covered by Decision 1/80, although s/he might be covered by other provisions.[300]

In this context, the case of *Ergat*[301] pending before the Court is to be mentioned. In this case the ECJ is questioned whether a late request for the renewal of the residence permit can be the basis for the expulsion of the Turkish worker, who has nonetheless acquired that right under Article 7(1) of Decision 1/80. According to the Opinion of the Advocate General,[302] the right of residence accorded to the Turkish workers under Decision 1/80 is neither *unlimited* nor *unconditional*. There is no absolute obligation upon the Member States to renew the permit, it is always necessary to evaluate if the conditions for the granting of that right still exist. However, as the Court already ruled in the *Sevince* case, if the Turkish worker met the conditions required under Decision 1/80 and his situation is therefore regular, the host Member State is obliged to issue the residence permit. When, on the contrary, the worker is not in a regular situation, Member States are not under such an obligation, *strictu sensu*. The Advocate General in his Opinion follows a liberal interpretation of the Agreement and he takes into account the effects on the migrant concerned of a strict interpretation of the Agreement. He, indeed, considers that the consequences, i.e. expulsion from the host State, are disproportionate since in the present case the irregular situation is caused by a late request for renewal. The Advocate General concludes that controls must be carried out to check whether the conditions for the granting of the right to stay still exist because what is important is that the rights acquired under the Decision still exist substantially, regardless of the issue of a formal document.

The analysis of the ECJ jurisprudence shows that Turks have benefited greatly from the extensive interpretation of the Court. But Member States, although initially moved by the desire to prepare Turkey to accede to the Communities, had always tried to limit such a broadening of the scope of the Agreement. The ECJ has been guided in the interpretation of Decision 1/80 by the aim of the Accord which envisaged, in its origin, the free movement of workers who are nationals of the Contracting Parties. But, it must be noted that its liberal stance is strictly connected to the economic position held by the Turkish migrant in the

299 Case C-171/91 *Tsiotras* [1993] ECR I-2925.
300 *Bozkurt*, *supra* note 294.
301 Case C-329/97 *Ergat*, pending. Advocate General, presented 3 June 1999, not published yet.
302 Advocate General Opinion, *Ergat* case, delivered 3 June 1999, not published yet.

labour market. When Turkish workers are economically active in the host state they deserve protection under the Agreement but when they cease their activity they are forced to leave the host state if not otherwise foreseen under national legislation. The ECJ has, over the years, widely interpreted the Decision moved by market logic but, as has been argued,[303] it has neglected the human rights dimension of the Union. The Turkish community settled within the Union represents the largest group among TCNs. Turkish migrants might have lived most of their lives, or in the case of second and third generation, all their lives in a Member State, so that they have stronger ties with the host state than with the country of origin. This makes such restrictions less acceptable. Turkish nationals may always rely upon the Long-term Residents' Resolution for protection against expulsion but its legal force is obviously not comparable to that of the Agreement. This strict economic approach has strong effects on the integration of the Turkish community. Obviously, the ECJ interpretation of the Agreement could have been modified by the Community legislator, but the presence of a large Turkish population within the Union has blocked any opening towards Turkey.

Besides, since Turkish society is in many ways sexist, the Agreements' provisions in certain circumstances could have a stronger impact on female migrants. Decision 1/8 does not take into due account the specific position held by Turkish women who must often face domestic responsibilities which impede them from working continuously and, therefore, to qualify under its provisions in order to acquire the right of residence. Many of them however can benefit from the Decision and they acquire the right to stay by virtue of their status of spouse of a Turkish migrant.

VI.2.4 Turkish workers' family members

Article 7 of the Decision 1/80 provides that the members of a Turkish worker's family who have been authorised to join him are entitled (a) to respond to employment offers after three years' lawful residence in the Member State and (b) to free access to any paid employment after five years of lawful residence. Moreover, the children of Turkish workers who have completed a course of vocational training in the host country may, irrespective of their period of residence, respond to an offer of employment, where one of their parents has been legally employed there for at least three years. Again, it is evident that *no* right of entry is conferred. Those provisions apply to family members who have already been admitted under national legislation. Moreover, the Decision does not define who must be con-

303 Peers S., "Aliens, Workers or Humans? Judicial Activism and Turkish Nationals in the EU", Paper delivered at the Sociology of Law Symposium, Onati, Spain, September 1997.

sidered as family members. According to Cremona "although the Decision does not, surprisingly, define "members of the family" there must be a strong presumption that in the absence of any restrictive provision the term will be defined in accordance with Article 10 of Regulation 1612/68/EEC".[304]

These provisions are very important as they grant the spouse and the children of the Turkish migrant the right to work and the right to stay in the host State. However, the ECJ, although generally guided by EC rules and its jurisprudence, in the interpretation of Decision 1/80 has adopted a more restrictive approach than under EC rules when dealing with the right of residence of Turkish workers' spouses.

In the *Kadiman*[305] case, the Court held that since the aim of Article 7 is the reunion of the spouse with the Turkish worker, such a provision "cannot therefore be interpreted as merely requiring the host Member State to have authorised a family member to enter its territory without at the same time requiring that person to actually continue to reside there with the migrant".[306] The ECJ, therefore, held that Article 7 of the Decision does not in principle preclude the competent authorities of a Member State from requiring that the family members of the Turkish migrant live with him for the period of three years required in order to gain the right of residence in the host state. It seems that in this case not just on the divorce of the couple but merely on their separation spouses will lose their rights.

The Court consistently transposed the principles contained in Article 48 of EC Treaty and its implementing measures when interpreting the EEC/Turkey Agreement and the decisions that followed. But in the *Kadiman* case the ECJ has interpreted that Agreement in a much more restrictive way than under EC law. Such a strict interpretation of the decision is less understandable considering that measure are presently under discussion in order to grant independent rights to widowed and divorced spouses (*supra* section IV.4.4).

Once the amendments to Regulation 1612/68/EEC are, if ever, approved, great protection is afforded to divorced or widowed spouses against expulsion.

In the family reunion scheme, TCN women could hold a very weak position in respect of their husbands and they could be subject to domestic violence, partly due to the sexist culture of the country of origin and also due to the fact that they reside in a foreign country. In this case, Mrs Kadiman accused her husband of having mistreated and deceived her.[307] Also she declared that her extended stay

---

304 Cremona, *supra* note 208.
305 Case C-351/95 *Kadiman* [1997] ECR I-2133.
306 Ibidem para 37.
307 Ibidem para 13.

in Turkey was involuntary, and it was due to her husband who took her passport away. The image is that of an authoritarian and violent husband but, as EC law now stands, he still has the power over his wife's fate as regards her possibility of staying in the host state. Although the ECJ pointed out in the judgment that there may be *objective reasons* to justify the family member concerned living apart from the migrant worker, it has not, unfortunately, considered in clear terms such evident violation of the rights of the spouse as an objective reason. Again, therefore the threat of divorce and in this case of only separation can keep spouses and, therefore, many women under the power of violent husbands. But amazingly, under EU law few measures have been taken or elaborated and generally this problem is neglected.

Finally, Article 7 of Decision 1/80 grants a set of rights the *children* of the Turkish migrant. In particular, as discussed above, Article 7 (2) is intended to provide specific treatment for children as opposed to other members of the family of the Turkish worker with a view to facilitating their entry into the labour market following completion of a course of vocational training. In the case of *Akman*,[308] the Court ruled that for the Turkish worker's children to enjoy the rights granted by Article 7 (2) it is not necessary that their parent is still working or s/he is resident in the Member State concerned *at the time* when they wish to gain access to the employment market.

As Peers argues there is a great difference between the protection accorded to the children of an EC migrant to that accorded to the children of the Turkish worker.

> "The family provisions of Regulation 1612/68 are thus (rightly or wrongly) designed to assist the *worker's* integration, while Article 7(2) of Decision 1/80 is an independent right designed to assist the *graduate's* integration, not the parent's...It thus follows that the rights of Turkish graduates are distinct and independent rights which lack an explicit parallel in EC free movement law."[309]

VI.2.5 EEA and Swiss Agreement

Once again, among the international agreements signed by the Community with third countries, the most relevant is the EEA Agreement, which confers the same rights of free movement as those accorded to EC citizens and, therefore, the right of settlement.

---

308 Case C-210/97 *Akman* [1998] ECR I-7519.

309 Peers S., Akman case note, *Common Market Law Review*, 1999, forthcoming.

Also, the recent agreement signed with Switzerland by the Community extends EC rights to Swiss nationals.

VI.2.6 Conclusions

Waiting for the Immigration Convention to be signed, only EEA and Turkish workers and their family members are granted some residence rights. The Long-term Residents' Resolution with its doubtful legal effect, does not seem to be an appropriate instrument for regulating this area.

As things now stand, after years of residence within the Union, TCNs' situation can still be completely precarious. In the perspective of integration such precariousness is unbearable as it impedes TCNs legally settled in the Community from planning their future in the host States. According to the Commission, residence rights "represent a source of stability for those concerned and therefore serve as an effective integration factor".[310] Whether there is the willingness to facilitate TCNs' settlement is doubtful. Throughout Europe the Member States are elaborating voluntary repatriation programmes for TCNs. At EU level, in 1997, the Council adopted a Decision on the exchange of information concerning assistance for the voluntary repatriation of TCNs[311] by which, although great emphasis is put on the fact that in "the case of legal residents, Member States' policies should aim at their integration and assistance for voluntary repatriation should not be interpreted as reflecting a policy of actively encouraging such return", in practice, Member States try to facilitate such return more than integrate TCNs in the host society. They facilitate the return of foreigners to their original countries by several means, especially economic. Racist and xenophobic attitudes underlie these policies. It is difficult to imagine nationals from Canada or the USA being the target of these policies. More often, TCNs from developing countries are chosen in these programmes.

VI.3 FINAL REMARKS

The measures that regulate the position of TCNs within the European Union analysed so far, whether under EC/EU law or under international agreements, have far from achieved the actual integration of the foreign communities in the Member States.

---

310 COM (97) 387 final.
311 OJ 1992 L 147/7.

After years of total inactivity the European Commission, backed by the European Parliament, has elaborated important proposals. The measures proposed, motivated also by the obligations imposed to implement the provisions of the Treaty of Amsterdam, are likely, if approved, to partially reduce the gap between EC citizens and TCNs in key sectors, such as social protection and freedom to provide services.

The proposals are drawn to regulate specific situations in the life of the extra-Community population but it seems that they are not part of a more forward-looking project concerned with the integration of TCNs in the host States.

As discussed above, it is necessary "to develop a common understanding" on how this area is to be regulated. This should be the first step to be taken in the direction of ensuring great economic and social solidarity for TCNs lawfully settled against any temptation of discrimination and exclusion in the European Union. Only after this is decided will it be possible to adopt a common approach in the elaboration of a European migration policy.

PART 3

IMMIGRATION POLICIES IN THE EUROPEAN UNION

VII

ADMISSION POLICIES AND RULES

VII.1 General remarks

The adoption of a common approach in the elaboration of immigration rules at European level has been very difficult. However, nowadays, the need to adopt a common approach in this area is no longer questionable. The draft strategy Paper submitted under the Austrian Presidency (July 1998), clearly stated:

> "National interests still dominate the process of decision-making in the European Union's migration policy. This is as anachronism insofar as it has in any case become clear in the decade now ending that migration policy challenges always concerned the Union as a whole and did not refer exclusively to one country...It is therefore essential for a uniform European policy concept to be developed. The European Union should devise its future immigration policy as an entity and cannot expect such a policy to develop, so to speak, from the product of national decisions."[314]

This view has been confirmed by the European Council held in Brussels (June 1999): "The European Council is convinced of the need for a European migration strategy, since migration and asylum issues are not only concerned with justice and home affairs policy but also require an approach covering other policy areas as well."[315] By this passage, it is evident that this area requires a common approach and it is also the proof of the complexity of doing so. One year after the Strategy Paper was elaborated, Member States are still looking for a European migration strategy.

As regards *immigrant policies and rules*, as discussed in the previous Chapters, many measures were not directed at regulating the legal status of TCNs but they eventually affected them, in the elaboration and adoption of rules in the area of

314 Council document, Draft Strategy Paper on Immigration and Asylum Policy, 9809/2/98.
315 Finnish Presidency's draft Report, "Guidelines for a European Migration Strategy", ASIM 23.

immigration, *strictu sensu,* Member States have especially targeted the regulation of their entry. In this sense this area is more coherent than the previous one.

The great tension between the two tendencies of *inclusion/integration* v. *exclusion* is always present but it seems that the exclusionary trend has prevailed. Some moves towards the integration and recognition of rights have been made to improve the position of TCNs lawfully settled within the EU, but Member States have clearly preferred to adopt an *exclusionary stance* vis-à-vis first-entry-TCNs arriving in the EU.

The study of the immigration rules shows the restrictive approach of the Member States in this area more clearly.

Until the late eighties, Member States responded to all matters related to immigration individually and in a reactive way. However, the internationalisation of the character of the immigration flows and the pressure in the final completion of the International Market have imposed the elaboration of rules common to all Member States.

Member States have been very reluctant to give up powers in this area since this was considered as the core of their sovereignty. The power to control who the *members* belonging to a State are and *who* are *not* and the control over the movement of population in and out of the national territory of the State have been traditionally considered as fundamental powers of a country since the creation of the modern "nation-state" entity. As some authors have pointed out:

> "Frontiers...are part of political beliefs and myths about the unity of the people and sometimes myths about the 'natural' unity of the territory."[316]

The adoption of common rules implies that a Member State is no longer the solely responsible in deciding who belongs to that State and who does not and who can enter its territory and who, *on the contrary*, must stay out. Entry permits are accorded by one member but they will be nonetheless valid throughout the Union. This requires a great level of trust of each member on the part of the Others, which unfortunately has not been completely achieved.

Internal and external pressures have partly overtaken these fears only recently. Accordingly, despite strong opposition from a few Member States, in particular the UK, very important steps have been taken in the last decade (1989-1999) in the area of immigration.

---

316 Anderson M., European Frontiers at the End of the Twentieth Century: An Introduction, in Anderson M. & Bort E.(eds), *supra* note 14, 5.

It should be noted that Member States in the elaboration of the Maastricht Treaty agreed to consider matters related to the entry of TCNs into the territory of the Union, as matters of common interest but, at the same time, they decided, apart from a few aspects related to visas (old Article 100c EC), not to extend Community competence in these areas.

The third Pillar of the European Union represented a reinforced intergovernmental cooperation but outside the EC legal system. Besides, it represented the weakest of the three Pillars of the Union as it did not even foresee a common policy, contrary to the second Pillar (Common Foreign and Security Policy).

Therefore, the measures to regulate this area were not adopted by means of the instruments provided for under the Community Pillar in old Article 189 EC.

Until the Amsterdam Treaty entered into force (1 May 1999) such instruments[317] were not available to regulate immigration matters as *these* were largely dealt with under the third Pillar.

As regards the JHA instruments previous to the Treaty of Amsterdam, many authors[318] have already written about such instruments and commonly criticised their inappropriateness to deal with issues related to immigration. This area of study is outside the scope of the present research but since the object of the research is the analysis of legal basis of the European immigration policy, an examination of the legal instruments under the third Pillar is significant to observe what the approach of the Member States on these matters has been.

VII.2 Legal instruments under the Maastricht Treaty

Old Article K.3 listed the specific[319] instruments of JHA cooperation: joint actions, joint positions and conventions. Also traditional instruments as resolutions, recommendations and conclusions were available.

317 Old Article 189 EC (new Article 249 EC) stated that "In order to carry out their task and in accordance with the provisions of this Treaty, the European Parliament acting jointly with the Council, the Council and the Commission shall make regulations and issue directives, take decisions, make recommendations or deliver opinions".

318 Just to name but a few, see: Haibronner K., "Migration Law and Policy within the Third Pillar of the Union Treaty", in Bieber R. & Monar J., *Justice and Home Affairs in the European Union. The Development of the Third Pillar,* European Interuniversity Press, The Bruges Conference, 1995, 102-108. See also Lepoivre M., "Le Domaine de la Justice et des Affaires Intérieures dans la Perspective de la Conference Intergouvernamentale de 1996", *Cahier de Droit Européen*, 1995, Vol. 3, 332-337.

319 The term specific is referred to the JHA as regards the first Pillar (EC Pillar), indeed, joint actions and common positions already existed under the second intergovernmental Pillar and the conventions are traditional instruments of international law.

Although migration was increasingly considered as a prominent issue Member States have, until recently, regulated this field giving preference to the lightest form of regulation, namely resolutions, recommendations or conclusions. Member States privileged these instruments given their features: they are not legally binding on Member States and they do not afford a ground for action by individuals.[320] These latter instruments had the evident advantage that *while*, their provisions generally were observed and implemented by national law, their non-binding intergovernmental character prevented substantial parliamentary influence, at both national and Community level, and judicial supervision and control. Besides, although deprived of any legal effect, Member States were expected to implement their provisions. The Council, in fact, monitored the implementation of the measures adopted by the Member States in different areas by means of questionnaires.[321]

By means of joint actions and joint positions, Member States have regulated several aspects of immigration.[322] The only clear legal binding instruments under the third Pillar were therefore the conventions. But, although they ensure parliamentary control and judicial supervision, the time generally required to draw up, sign and ratify a convention did not make them a suitable instrument to regulate an area in continuous evolution.[323]

320 Resolutions, Recommendations and Conclusions are instruments of international law unable to produce legal effect on national legal system. However within the first Pillar, the ECJ in the *Grimaldi* case, held that a Community recommendation which specifically has no binding force nonetheless still has some legal effects. National courts are bound to take such measures into considerations in order to decide disputes submitted to them (Case C-233/88 *Grimaldi* [1989] ECR 4407).

321 So far two Decisions have been adopted by the Council: Decision on monitoring the implementation of instruments already adopted concerning admission of third-country nationals, OJ 1996 C 11/5 and Decision on monitoring the implementation of instruments adopted by the Council concerning illegal immigration, readmission, the unlawful employment of third country nationals and cooperation in the implementation of expulsion orders, OJ 1996 L 342/5.

322 The most relevant are Joint Action 96/197 on airport transit arrangements OJ 1996 L 63/8; Joint Action 96/443 concerning action to combat racism and xenophobia OJ 1996 L 185/5; Joint position 96/622 on pre-frontier assistance and training assignments OJ 1996 L 281/5; Joint Action 96/636 on a programmeme of incentives and exchanges for legal practitioners ("Grotius") OJ 1996 L 287/3; Joint Action 96/637 introducing a programmeme of training, exchanges and cooperation in the field of identity documents ("Sherlock") OJ 1996 L 287/7; Joint Action 96/700 establishing an incentive and exchange programmeme for persons responsible for combating trade in human beings and the sexual exploitation of children OJ 1996 L 322/7; Joint Action 97/11 concerning a uniform format for residence permits OJ 1997 L 7/1; Joint Action 97/154 concerning action to combat trafficking in human beings and sexual exploitation of children OJ 1997 L 63/2.

323 Member States have elaborated in the area of immigration only the External Border Convention that, for a dispute between the UK and Spain, was never signed COM (93) 684 final, OJ 1994 C 11/15, and the Convention on Rules for the Admission of TCNs to Member States of the European Union, pending for signature, *supra* note 62.

Under the Amsterdam Treaty, the large majority of matters related to the area of immigration are to be regulated in the new Title IV EC (ex Title IIIa EC). The instruments available within the first Pillar will be those contained in Article 249 EC, (ex Article 189 EC), namely regulations, directives or decisions. These instruments are more appropriate to ensure the legal effects of new legislation and its common implementation.

It should be noted that a problem arises as regards rules adopted under the Maastricht Treaty in the form of soft law. Immigration matters under the Amsterdam Treaty have been moved from third Pillar to the Community Pillar therefore their regulation must now take the form of EC law. Contrary to what was agreed in relation to the Schengen acquis (*infra* section III.5), for the measures adopted under the third Pillar there is no obligation for their reallocation under the new system. This evidently creates legal uncertainty. The Council being aware of the need for major reform in this area, stated: "In legislative work, account has also had to be taken of the existing third-Pillar 'acquis'; making it necessary to decide which, if any, of the present provisions should be replaced by more effective ones. Those classifiable as 'soft law' formed the prime candidates for this purpose."[324]

Under the Maastricht Treaty matters related to immigration were considered of common interest under the third Pillar.[325] Old Article K.1 TEU stated that:

> "For the purposes of achieving the objectives of the Union, in particular the free movement of persons, and without prejudice to the powers of the European Community, Member States shall regard the following areas as matters of common interest: rules governing the crossing by persons of the external borders or the Member States and the exercise of controls thereon; immigration policy and policy regarding nationals of third countries: conditions of entry and movement by nationals of third countries on the territory of Member States; conditions of residence by nationals of third countries on the territory of Member States, including family reunion and access to employment; combating unauthorised immigration, residence and work by nationals of third countries on the territory of Member States; ...".

Notwithstanding the limits of the Pillar structure, Member States were able to adopt several measures, mainly in the form of resolutions and recommendations, that regulated important aspects of the field of immigration.

This new area of law had to reconcile the often opposite interests of Member States' internal and foreign policies and that has made the adoption of immigration rules very controversial.

324 Council document, 12028/1/98.

325 Few aspects connected to visas are regulated under EC law, *infra* section VII.5.1.

However, presently *none* of the Member States is pursuing an active policy as regards new migration. At EU level, it has been easier therefore, to adopt measures aimed at reducing the flows, which have generally prevailed over policies directed at integrating the extra-Community population legally settled within the European Union. Migratory concerns have shaped both domestic and foreign policies.

VII.3 External aspects of the immigration policy

"The reduction of migratory pressures calls for a coordinated policy which extends far beyond the narrow field of policy on aliens, asylum, immigration and border controls, and also covers international relations and development aid".[326] The European Council held in Brussels (1 June 1999) insists on the fact that "a consistent asylum and migration policy by the European Union and its Member States needs to address the root causes of asylum-seeking and migration and the human rights situation in countries of origin.[327]" Migration matters are increasingly becoming a central topic in the EU's external relations with third countries.

Member States have in recent decades signed several agreements with developing countries in order to tackle the root causes of migration and to encourage immigrants to stay in their countries of origin. Such agreements envisage the concession of "generous" development aid to support their growth. In the elaboration of these accords, great emphasis has been placed on the respect of human rights and fundamental freedoms.[328] It is in fact believed that a serious improvement in the economic and political conditions of a country as well as in respect of its human rights record will deter its nationals from emigrating. This scheme has worked for Southern Europe so that, in a few decades, it has changed from a region of emigration into a region of immigration. There is an obvious assumption that, despite some exceptions, in the greatest majority of cases people are not happy to leave their own country. This is also confirmed in the European

326 See draft Strategy Paper, *supra* note 311.

327 *Supra* note 312.

328 See Council Regulation 1484/97 on aid for population policies and programmes in the developing countries, OJ 1997 L 202/1; Council Regulation 975/99 laying down the requirements for the implementation of development cooperation operations which contribute to the general objective of developing and consolidating democracy and the rule of law and to that of respecting human rights and fundamental freedoms OJ 1999 L 120/1; Council Regulation 976/99 laying down the requirements for the implementation of Community operations, other than those of development cooperation, which, within the framework of Community cooperation policy, contribute to the general objective of developing and consolidating democracy and the rule of law and to that of respecting human rights and fundamental freedoms in third countries OJ 1999 L 120/8.

Union context, where EC citizens who benefit from the freedom of movement provisions, which make the cross border mobility for some categories of EC migrants easier than for others, in particular for TCNs, who are still very reluctant to leave their home countries. According to EUROSTAT sources, the percentage of EC nationals who have actually taken advantage of these provisions is relatively a small number.[329]

The great majority of immigrants from developing countries who arrive in Western Europe want to escape political instability, extreme poverty and lack of professional opportunities. But, at European Union level "no illusion can be entertained with regard to the huge volume of such a project: this aspect of the strategy must incorporate all the main regions of origin of immigrants world-wide. In view of the breadth of this field, slow progress will have to be accepted, since the possibilities of – for example – eliminating the economic causes of migration from the Third World are undoubtedly very limited. The same applies to demographic and environmental facts and to durable change in the human rights situation.".[330] Already some authors have criticised such a lack of commitment in all the areas mentioned in the Strategy Paper.[331]

The close link between migration and human rights and development issues was highlighted in the Tampere European Council: "The European Union needs a comprehensive approach to migration addressing political, human rights and development issues in countries and regions of origin and transit. This requires combating poverty, improving living conditions and job opportunities, preventing conflicts and consolidating democratic states and ensuring respect for human rights, in particular rights of minorities, women and children. To that end, the Union as well as Member States are invited to contribute, within their respective competence under the Treaties, to a greater coherence of internal and external policies of the Union. Partnership with third countries concerned will also be a key element for the success of such a policy; with a view to promoting co-development." Remarkably, there is no mention of how to reach those objectives.

Moreover, there are discordant opinions that an *improvement* of the conditions of developing countries will stop the flows immediately. The counter effect could be that with more means TCNs would be more likely to travel and they would be able to reach Europe easily. According to Overbeck:

329 Only 1.5% of EC citizens reside in a country other than their own while 95.2% are citizens of the country in which they are resident, EUROSTAT sources, *supra* note 7.

330 See draft Strategy Paper, *supra* note 311.

331 ILPA, "The European Presidency's Draft Strategy Paper on Immigration and Asylum Policy and the European Commission's Memo 98/55 on the Implementation of the Amsterdam Treaty in Immigration and Asylum", September 1998.

> "Migration is explained in terms of the interaction of push and pull effects originating from environmental, and socio-economic disparities. The 'demographic transitional model' predicts that countries in the second and third stages of modernisation (with a rapidly declining death rate and a continued high birth rate) will display a high mass emigration potential. Countries in the youth stage of modernisation, with a stagnant population will become immigration countries. When looked from this perspective the recent explosion in the third world is extrapolated into the future and from combining the resulting graph with data about the structural poverty of the region in question it is then concluded that migration pressures will continue to rise unless something drastic is done."[332]

However, by means of these accords, Member States try to find a medium/long-term solution to the pressures of migration and, in particular, to illegal immigration. Again, the draft Strategy Paper recalls that "an expansion of development aid and economic cooperation with the main regions of emigration is essential. There can however be no illusions that such efforts will result in curbing emigration in the short term; the opposite may in fact be the case: initially, an economic boom potentially leads to increased emigration from the urban areas of the Third World. However, in the medium term – and this by means of only a few years – emigration figures fall considerably".[333]

Accordingly, these agreements envisage the granting of development aid, sometimes in the form of trade agreements, but they *never* include labour. It is noteworthy that the globalisation process has produced the "elimination of national barriers in trade and investment; rapid development in transportation systems and in information and communication technologies which have transformed the ordering of time and space in our lives...Set against the massive internationalisation of capital flows and subsequent economic interdependence, however, the international flow of labour remains under the jurisdiction of individual nation-states which jealously protect their right to decide who is allowed entry and on what terms."[334] The international community has not adopted any international agreement which protects international movement of labour unlike in other areas concerning factors of production, such as goods or services. According to Luciani:

332 Overbeek H., "Towards a New International Migration Regime" in Miles R. &Tränhardt D (eds)., *supra* note 115, 18-19.

333 See draft Strategy Paper, *supra* note 311.

334 Phizacklea A., "Migration and Globalisation: a Feminist Perspective", in Koser K. & Lutz H. (eds), *The New Migration in Europe, Social Construction and Social Realities,* Macmillan Press LTD, 1998, 31.

> "In the case of international migration, there is no international agreement or guideline due to the fact that there is no widely shared ideological point of view with respect to the phenomenon itself. If anything, the implicit consensus appears to be that migration is intrinsically undesirable, and can only be accepted under special circumstances...but there is no rule which protects international movements of individuals in general, in the same way that international movements of goods and capital are protected."[335]

The European Union in this sense works as a national state. It opens towards its nationals and closes towards foreigners. In the short-term the need to face migratory flows from non-Community countries has forced Member States to find alternative solutions as well. In the near future, the strategy adopted is to keep potential TCN migrants away from the Union's frontiers and to develop repatriation programmes, whether forced or voluntary, to send illegal immigrants back to their countries of origin or to other countries of their choice.

VII.4 Internal dimension

In their domestic policies, Member States are principally concerned, in the immediate future, with how to stop and control migratory flows for both economic and security reasons. Since the 1970s Member States have faced very high and persistent unemployment rates and therefore there has been a serious attempt to regulate new migration towards any European countries strictly since then.

Also, security reasons justify the adoption of increasingly restrictive and repressive measures. The removal of internal frontiers could increase international crime and illegal immigration. A common market for people could also be a common market for criminal and illegal activities. A vast number, which is difficult to estimate, of the TCNs within the territory of the Union are in an illegal position. Many of them entered legally, thanks to a work permit or a short-stay visa, and then overstayed, others entered illegally *directly*. It seems that the more difficult access to the European Union is, the larger the number of illegal migrants. The toughening in the conditions of admission is aimed at avoiding these situations.

However, there is a process of "ethnicisation" or "racialisation", sometimes more overt and others more hidden,in the elaboration of these measures.

The ban on new immigration seems to target *some areas* of immigration, in particular Black developing countries. Again, Black has become an elastic political

335 Luciani G., "Migration: A Global Phenomenon calling for Common Solutions", in Luciani G. (ed), *Migration Policies in Europe and the United States,* Kluwer Academic Publishers 1993, 2.

term that covers many shades of skin but the essential distinction is between White (European) and non-white".[336] Apart from economic/security reasons for refusing entry to immigrants from poor developing countries, there are racial factors which are relevant. As Den Boer points out:

> "In the re-conceptualisation of European security and identity, immigrants have emerged as the enemy number one. The external antagonist of communism has been substituted by that of immigration. This discursive replacement coincides with a glowing European culture and political cohesion which in turns is coalesced by reinforcing the discourse of 'Otherness' and by specifying the internal community in antithesis to external threat".[337]

There is an assumption that the larger the immigrant community the more difficult it is to integrate them in the host society and that the degree of "assimilation" is directly proportional to the closeness of the foreign community to the "European" standard. After years of family reunion and, also, family formation to which migrants' high fertility rates should be added, migrant communities have grown at a very fast pace.[338] The new reality, it is felt, is menacing the national identity of the host countries. These fears could provoke *internal instability*, as is shown by the increase of xenophobic and racist attitudes of nationals towards migrants. "There are also xenophobic elements within States that tend to perceive a significant presence of foreign nationals on their territory as a threat to social cohesion or public order *per se*."[339]

Consequently, policies on admission for TCNs have become increasingly restrictive. As Achermann remarks "all the concrete measures have concerned restrictive measures so that restriction is the objective."[340] The paradox of this situation is clearly shown by Räthzel who points out that:

> "Although none of us would openly declare that a growing number of migrants leads to a growth of racism, I daresay that many of us believe secretly that there is some truth in it. At least many of us think that Europe does not have the resources to feed 'all the poor of the world'. If one argues that we do not have as many refugees in Europe as in Africa and Asia, one is staying precisely within same logic. After all, it seems so

336 On this point see Dummett A., "Racial Equality and '1992'", *Feminist Review*, 1991, Vol. 39, 88.
337 Anderson M. & Den Boer M., *Policing across National Boundaries*, Pinter, 1994, 189.
338 EUROSTAT, *supra* note 7.
339 Beyani C., *Human Rights Standards and Freedom of Movement of Peoples within States*, Oxford University Press, 1999, forthcoming.
340 Achermann A., Asylum and Immigration Policies: From Cooperation to Harmonisation, in Bieber R. & Monar J., (eds) *supra* note 315, 134.

> reasonable no object of racism, no racism. Of course, no one would propose to reduce the number of women in order to reduce sexism".[341]

Presently, access to the territory for first entry migrants must be considered a privilege or an exception that can be revoked at any moment with a full discretionary powers and Member States maintain great discretion to encourage or discourage the entry of particular types of migrants by visa policies and admission rules. According to the draft Strategy Paper "an effective entry control concept cannot be based simply on controls at the border but must cover every step taken by a third country national from the time he begins his journey to the time he reaches his destination. Management begins in the country of origin when a visa is granted".[342] Although the draft Strategy Paper was never adopted, this very short passage is the perfect example of the fortress mentality in the elaboration of a system of controls and barriers against entry into the Union by TCNs. Getting a visa represents the first barrier or filter for certain TCNs wanting to enter the European Union.

VII.5 Visa policy

Until the signature of the Maastricht Treaty all matters related to visas were considered to be national matters and, accordingly, they were governed by domestic law and no regulation was explicitly foreseen under the EC Treaty, although the Commission originally suggested it would propose measures under old Articles 100 and 235 EC (new Articles 94 and 308 EC). Each Member State was free to decide any formal and substantial aspect for issuing national visas to foreigners. However, since 1985, some Member States have decided to coordinate their visa policies within the Schengen framework.

The completion of the Internal Market (Article 14 EC, ex Article 7A EC) and *specifically* the realisation of the free movement of people foreseen by the SEA, forced Member States to consider the area related to visas as matters of common interest requiring some form of harmonisation: it was made clear that progress to achieve this freedom was closely connected with progress on the way to a common European visa and entry policy.

Under EC/EU law, once Member States finally do away with internal frontiers, the only controls permitted will be those at the external borders. Controls that

341 Räthzel N., "Racism in Europe, a case for Socialist Feminists?", in Ward A. et al (eds), *Women and Citizenship in Europe*, Trentham Books, 1992, 31.

342 See draft Strategy Paper, *supra* note 311.

presently Member States carry out according to their national immigration legislation. As in the near future, permits for short stays issued by a Member State are to be considered as valid throughout the EU, harmonisation of conditions of entry have become extremely important for they must be the same at each point of entry, if Member States want to control commonly the flows. Not all Member States share this view, namely the UK that does not interpret Article 14 EC (ex Article 7A EC), as imposing an obligation upon the Member States to remove controls at internal frontiers, which accordingly the UK has kept (*supra* section III.4).

VII.5.1 Visa Regulation under the Maastricht Treaty and beyond

The Maastricht Treaty introduced Article 100c EC, which is now included in Title IV EC (ex Title IIIa EC), which brought certain aspects of visa regulation under Community competence.

During the negotiations of the Treaty on the European Union, harmonising visa policies had been a matter of great complexity because of the various aspects involved, such as historical factors, security considerations, and national immigration and asylum policies. The end result was therefore that, under the Maastricht Treaty, Member States regulated visa matters, instead of resorting to a single framework, in two different sections of the TEU. Visa issues were, indeed, dealt with in old Article 100c EC but also by the newly introduced third Pillar. Certain aspects, only the formal ones, of harmonisation of visas were under Community competence and all substantial and therefore relevant aspects were governed by intergovernmental co-operation under old Title VI TEU.

During the intergovernmental conference (IGC) for the revision of the TEU which led to the Amsterdam Treaty, many delegations underlined the ambiguity of this situation.

The Treaty of Amsterdam communitarised all aspects related to short term visas. Article 62.2.b EC, (ex Article 73j EC), states "the Council shall adopt rules on visas for intended stays of no more than three months, including: i. the list of third countries whose nationals must be in possession of visas when crossing the external borders and those whose nationals are exempt from that requirement; ii. the procedures and conditions for issuing visas by Member States; iii. a uniform format for visas; iv. rules on a uniform visa".

The implementing measures referred to the visa list and the uniform format for visas require a qualified majority in the Council from the entry into force of the Treaty. These measures were already under EC competence under the Maastricht Treaty. Old Article 100c EC stated:

> "1.The Council, acting unanimously on a proposal from the Commission and after consulting the European Parliament, shall determine the third countries whose nationals must be in possession of a visa when crossing the external borders of the Member States". "3. From 1 January 1996 the Council shall adopt the decisions referred to in paragraph 1 by a qualified majority. The Council shall, before that date, acting by a qualified majority on a proposal from the Commission and after consulting the European Parliament, adopt measures relating to a uniform format for visas".

Therefore, the measures related to a uniform format for visas were to be adopted by the Council by a qualified majority since the entry into force of the Maastricht Treaty. The adoption of an EU visa list was to be adopted by the Council acting unanimously until 1 January 1996. After that date, measures concerning the adoption of a visa list required a qualified majority vote in the Council.

The other two areas require a unanimous vote in the Council for a transitional period of five years and the codecision procedure from then onwards.

At the time of writing, visas are not required for all TCNs and they do not confer *immediate* right to enter the issuing country, as they only represent one of the various conditions that must be met. However, when required, they represent a *conditio sine qua non* to entry. This justifies the importance of harmonising national policies in this field. In 1995, the Council on a proposal from the Commission adopted two regulations implementing old Article 100c EC: Regulation 1683/95,[343] laying down a uniform format of visa, and Regulation 2317/95,[344] determining the third countries whose nationals must be in possession of visas when crossing the external borders of the Member States. This last Regulation was annulled by the ECJ,[345] after an action brought before the Court by the EP against the Council, and it was replaced by Regulation 574/99.[346]

VII.5.2 Format visa

Regulation 1683/95 does not regulate any legal aspect regarding conditions for the issuing of such visas. These matters were confined to intergovernmental cooperation under old Title VI TEU. The Regulation only deals with technical specifications in order to lay down a uniform format that would be difficult to counterfeit or falsify (Articles 1 and 2). As Community law now stands, taking into account that no further measures have been taken to adopt a common visa policy, such

343 Council Regulation 1683/95 OJ 1995 L 164/1.
344 Council Regulation 2317/95 OJ 1995 L 234/1.
345 Case C-392/95 *Parliament v Council* [1997] ECR I- 3213.
346 Council Regulation 574/99 OJ 1999 L 72/2.

visas have only national validity. Nonetheless the Member States who are also members of the Schengen Agreements should, at least in principle, mutually recognise such visas. It should be noted that the Commission proposed in the original version of the visa list Regulation,[347] which is analysed in the next section, the mutual recognition of visas issued by the Member States but the final version abandoned such requirements.

VII.5.3 Visa lists

As far as the visa list is concerned, it was hoped that the annulment by the ECJ of Regulation 2317/95 could be followed by two definitive visa lists. One including those countries whose nationals require a visa to enter the Union, and the other containing all the other countries, whose nationals would not. This would have excluded any discretion of the Member States and it would have abolished national visa lists. This was the original project of the Commission, which interpreted old Article 100c EC as limited to draw up two lists. In its original proposal, submitted to the Council in 1993, the Commission only proposed a negative list of countries whose nationals were required to possess a visa to enter any Member State. The proposal likewise established a transitional period, until 30 June 1996, by when the Council should have adopted a positive list of countries whose nationals were exempted from having a visa when entering the EU. In the final version, no mention of that deadline was made, allowing the Member States to maintain national visa lists for an indefinite period. However, Member States started co-operating to establish two lists, one negative and one positive, but they were able to agree to the drawing up of only the negative list which, not being definitive, did not in itself imply a positive or white list. Soon it was clear three lists existed: the negative, positive and a "grey list", which contained those third countries whose nationals are required to possess a visa but only in some Member States.[348] The EP considered that these changes, as well as the ones mentioned above of mutual recognition of visas, were substantial amendments of the original proposal, in particular, the European Parliament argued that they undermined the principal objective of the Regulation, which was the *harmonisation of visas*.

The EP brought an action before the ECJ because of the lack of consultation in the final version of the Regulation. The ECJ therefore annulled it and ruled that Regulation 2317/95 be in force until it was replaced by a new one.[349]

347 OJ 1994 C 11/15.

348 See annexes for the different visa lists.

349 Case C-392/95 *European Parliament v Council* [1997] ECR I-3213.

In the light of the developments under the Amsterdam Treaty,[350] which clarifies any doubts and specifies that only *two* definitive lists are admitted, some progress in that direction was expected. But, amazingly, the new Regulation 574/99 has reproduced the same text with just a few irrelevant changes, ignoring the position of the EP.[351] However, the abolition of the grey list should be the next step, according to the Action Plan proposed by the Council and the Commission.[352]

Regulation 574/99 has maintained the number of countries included by Regulation 2317/95, 101 third countries are listed plus Taiwan as a territorial entity not recognised as a State by all Member States. The original proposal for Regulation 2317/95 presented by the Commission contained 129 countries whose nationals required a visa and it was based on the list used by the Schengen countries, but 28 states were taken off. Until the signature of the Treaty of Amsterdam, there were two separate lists in the EU: the Schengen visa list and EU visa list.

Four categories of countries existed. The first group was of countries whose nationals were not required to possess a visa to enter the European Union in any Member State, the second made of countries such as Libya or Iraq whose nationals were required a visa to enter any State in the Union, the third included countries whose nationals required a visa only in certain member countries, such as Australia, and finally, there are 28 countries which were in the Schengen visa list but not in the EU list.

The incorporation of the Schengen acquis into the framework of the European Union by the Amsterdam Treaty partially solved this chaotic situation where for a TCN seeking entry, the Union appears all but a unified area. According to the 1997 Schengen Annual Report "the Executive Committee decided to abolish the list of third countries subject to different visa regulations by 1 January 1999 on the understanding that for three countries, the Schengen States undertook to adopt the solution pursuant to Article 100c of the Treaty of the European Union".[353] Presently, there are 101 states and territorial entities whose nationals require visas,

---

350 Article 62.2.b.i EC refers to two lists, the list of third countries whose nationals must be in possession of visas when crossing the external borders and those whose nationals are exempt from that requirement.

351 Migrations Europe, No 92/1999-4.

352 Action Plan of the Council and the Commission on how best to implement the provisions of the Treaty of Amsterdam on an area of Freedom, Security and Justice, *supra* note 84.

353 See Statewatch, 1998, Vol. 8, No 3 & 4.

twenty one states whose nationals do not require a visa and fifty six in the grey list, so that their nationals require a visa in one or more Member States.[354]

The criteria, if any, followed in the list do not seem clear or rigid. In fact, the list takes into account mainly the risks related to immigration or security represented by sending immigration countries.

Race factors, more than objective criteria,[355] seem to have played an important role in the choice of countries in the different lists.

The willingness of the EU to restrict the entry of TCNs into its territory is reflected in this Regulation. But more importantly, it seems that in the drafting of the Regulation, race factors were taken into account in the decision leading to the inclusion or exclusion in the list of certain third countries. There is, in fact, an overwhelmingly majority of Black countries in the negative list, the majority poor developing countries with enormous reserve on potential emigrants, not only due to their poverty and political instability but also because of the extremely high birth rate, especially in comparison to Western Europe.

As Bhabha and Shutter remark:

> "The nationals of all but a handful of rich, white countries, will need a visa before entering the European Fortress. The list of countries for which visas will be required is being formulated on a lowest common denominator basis, the siege mentality having taken a firm hold. Race and wealth are the defining criteria for the exclusion from the visa list, not historical ties, or humanitarian desperation".[356]

The inclusion of several countries where severe conflicts, civil wars or grave human rights violations are presently taking place has the effect of making it virtually impossible for people escaping from those situations to find a refuge in the EU, for without a visa they will find it impossible or, at least, extremely difficult to board flights or ships taking them to the EU,[357] especially considering that throughout the Union Member States are toughening sanctions against carriers in cases of illegal entry of TCNs.

---

354 European Commission, Commission Communication in pursuance of Council Regulation 574/99 determining the third countries whose nationals must be in possession of visas when crossing the external borders of the Member States, OJ 1999 C 133/19.

355 Migration News Sheet, 151/95.

356 Bhabha J., & Shutter S., *Women's Movement, Women under Immigration, Nationality and Refugee Law*, Trentham Books, 1994, 218.

357 Statewatch, 1995, Vol. 5, No. 5.

VII.5.4 Emergency situation: Restoration of visa

The Fortress mentality is also shown by the possibility envisaged in old Article 100c.2 EC to require a visa for nationals of a third country in which an emergency situation has occurred and there is a threat of a sudden inflow of nationals from that country into the Community. This provision has been kept in the revised text of EC Treaty, although partially modified. New Article 64.2 EC does not expressly foresee the requirement of a visa but of "provisional measures" to confront an emergency situation in a third country characterised, and therefore it is not just a *threat*, by a sudden inflow of nationals from that country.

VII.5.5 The proposed External Border Convention: Paving the way for the Amsterdam Treaty

The importance given to visas was recognised by Member States that included visa regulations in several Conventions.[358] Visa regulations were included in other agreements even before the adoption of the Maastricht Treaty. In particular, the External Border Convention, which was virtually agreed in June 1991 and then reproduced almost unchanged after the ratification of the TEU in November 1993, although never signed, stated "Member States undertake to harmonise their visa policies progressively" (Article 17). The proposed Convention dealt with several aspects of uniform and short-stay visas. Article 19 included uniform visas as only one among other conditions to enter the Union. Among the other conditions, it was necessary to possess a travel document which had to be valid and recognised in the other Member States, and allowing for the return of the traveller to the country of origin or his entry into a third country. Common visas were normally short-stay visas that could not exceed three months in a six month period starting on the date of entry (Article 22). Accordingly, visas for stays of more than three months were to be national visas issued by each Member State in accordance with its national law.

The External Border Convention was based on the Schengen Agreements signed in 1985 and 1990. The first Agreement (1985) established that the Parties endeavoured to approximate their visa possibly in order to avoid adverse consequences that could result from the easing of controls at the common frontiers in the field of immigration and security (Article 7). Accordingly, Chapter 3 of the Implementing Schengen Convention, signed five years later, was dedicated to

358 Matters regarding visas were included in the Dublin Convention, the External Border Convention and the Schengen Agreements.

matters concerning visas. Its provisions regulated the area of common, short-stay or transit visas while long-stay visas remained within national competence. The conditions for issuing visas were also agreed.

The External Border Convention like the Schengen Agreements were not conferred competence to deal with long-term visas exceeding a three month period, because that competence would have had great impact on national immigration policies on which the Member States were not prepared to cede powers. Such reluctance was finally overtaken in the new text of the TEU. Article 63 (3) (a) EC provides the legal basis to adopt measures on "procedures for the issue by Member States, of long-term visas..." This is great progress towards the harmonisation of national visa policies but the impact of the newly introduced provision has been limited by the lack of the 5 year deadline imposed, on the contrary, in other new areas of Community competence. Once again, the Council and the Commission in the Action Plan on how best to implement the provisions of the Treaty of Amsterdam on an area of freedom, security and justice have committed themselves from a political point of view to take action in this area within five years of the entry into force of the AmsterdamTreaty.

VII.5.6 Remaining areas of visa regulation

In the context of visas, two other EU measures must be mentioned that reflect the concern of the Member States about immigration issues: the Recommendation relating to local consular cooperation regarding visas[359] and the Joint Action on airport transit arrangements[360] both adopted on 4 March 1996. The Recommendation states that consular services should strengthen, inter alia by way of an exchange of information, their cooperation on the issuing of visas so as to take account of the interests of other Member States, in particular, the protection of national security and the prevention of clandestine immigration. The siege mentality is clear in the Recommendation as the consular services should exchange information to help determine the *good faith* of visa applicants as well as their *reputation*. Again, there is the introduction of very subjective elements about what a good reputation is and how the good faith of the applicant can be demonstrated. It is very likely that Blacks are discriminated against given the wide discretionary powers of the authorities and due to their *visibility*.

The Joint Action imposes more rules on TCNs belonging to some countries. In fact, they must not only possess a visa to enter the Union but also an *airport transit visa* for access to the international areas of the airports of the Member

359 OJ 1996 C 80/1.
360 OJ 1996 L 63/8.

States. Such measures have raised doubts about the meaning of the "crossing of the external borders of the Member States". The different interpretations that the Commission and the Council held, led the Commission, to bring an action[361] to annul the Joint Action. According to the Commission "crossing the external borders" means physical entry onto the territory of the Member State concerned, while the Council would restrict it to the crossing of a border control point. In the view of the Court the interpretation of the Council is the one that must be upheld. Accordingly, "the airport transit visa is concerned with the situation of a passenger arriving on a flight from a third country and remaining in the airport of the Member State in which the aircraft landed in order to take off in the same or another aircraft bound to another third country". The holder of an airport transit visa is not entitled to cross any external border of the Union. As declared by the Council the objective of the Joint Action was to avoid the risk that nationals of certain third countries taking advantage of their presence in the international zone of a Member State airport in order to submit abusive requests for asylum, or even enter the territory illegally by avoiding immigration control at a border post. Nationals of certain countries must therefore *not only* acquire a visa from the country of their final destination *but also* from the country they may transit through, even though it has been made clear that an international waiting lounge is not to be considered the territory of a Member State. It is *again* evident that the Member States have a siege mentality and co-operate in order to make it extremely difficult for TCNs to reach the Union. The countries included in the transit visa list confirm suspicions of racial discrimination (see annex VI).

A common policy on visas has not yet been reached at European level. But the few rules so far examined, related to the negative list and the other recommendations made by the Member States, could make it much more difficult for TCNs to gain access to the Union. Nonetheless, "visas" are only the first obstacle for a TCN wanting to emigrate to or, at least, reach one of the Union's Member States. In fact, at the same time that visa rules have become more and more restrictive, conditions for admission have become stricter.

VII.6 ADMISSION POLICY

As repeatedly discussed in the above sections, the first phase of immigration, where migrants were encouraged to come and work in Western Europe, is over. Since the 1970s, when the recession started there has been a U-turn as regards

361 Case C-170/96 *Commission v Council* [1998] ECR I-2763.

recruitment of foreign labour in the main industrialised European countries. Obviously, with a high level of unemployment among the national population there was no longer need to hire workers from abroad. All Member States are, individually, banning on new entries. Such policies were reinforced when Member States realised that the majority of TCNs settled within their boundaries were not simple guests but that they were there for good. The measures adopted over the years ensure that the external border is severely protected in order to avoid illegal immigration and, at the same time, to help the "sealing off borders" policy to be respected.

Since the late eighties and early nineties, Member States have decided to cooperate in this area in order to ensure that the desired goal of rigidly regulating the migratory flows could be reached. All the measures are directed at reducing the flows.

However, the ban is not as rigid as it might seem at first sight. Member States have agreed, indeed, that some level of immigration is necessary as it could benefit both the sending and receiving countries. "The European Council is aware of Europe's position as a continent marked by migratory movements and highlights the crucial positive impact of immigration into Europe on the continent's cultural, demographic and economic development."[362] Nonetheless accepting large numbers of immigrants leads to problems in the short as well as in the long-term. Some degree of restriction on migration has been considered therefore *necessary*.

Accordingly, legislation adopted by Member States has been largely directed at stopping new entries, but the *ban* is not strictly respected and some categories are still allowed. Apart from those migrants permitted entry on humanitarian grounds, such as asylum seekers and migrants' family members, other categories are allowed entry under specific conditions.

This area is regulated by means of three Resolutions, adopted in 1994,[363] and a proposed Joint Position,[364] whose content has been partially resumed in the recent Commission's proposal of the TCNs Admission Rules Convention. By means of these instruments Member States supposedly want to harmonise the area at European level.

362 *Supra* note 312.

363 Workers' Resolution, OJ 1996 C 274/3, Self-employed persons' Resolution, OJ 199 C 274/7, and Students' Resolution, OJ 1996 C 274/10.

364 Council document, Proposal for a Joint Position on the admission as residents to the territory of the Member States of TCNs who do not wish to engage in gainful activity or to study, 8630/95. According to Peers "three subsequent drafts were produced during the Spanish Presidency, although the Council has refused to disclose any of these". Peers S., "Building Fortress Europe: The Developing of EU Migration Law, *supra* note 28.

As far as the personal scope is concerned, the proposed Convention covers virtually all TCNs, namely employees, the self-employed, students, trainees and others and it has the advantage of dealing with them in a single text. The proposed Convention maintains a strict approach as regards new entries.

None of the Member States is pursuing a policy of active immigration, consequently, it is evident that, in the Convention as well as in the Resolutions, the approach is directed at restricting or stopping migratory movements towards the Union.

As discussed above, the predilection of resolutions, as a legislative instrument to harmonise national policies in the area related to TCNs does not seem to be the most adequate.

First of all, while it is agreed that "national policies in the areas covered by the resolution should be governed by the principles set out ... which may not be relaxed by Member States in their national legislation", it follows that "the principles are not legally binding on the Member States and do not afford a ground for action by individuals". The end result is far from the originally declared aim, i.e. reaching a common harmonised approach in the treatment of TCNs. On the contrary, Member States normally choose the principles of the Resolutions that they consider most convenient, given their national situation and immigration channels and they disregard the others. Secondly, as has been remarked,[365] there is a serious democratic deficit in this area as Member States' governments may pick out and choose among the "principles" but *apparently* they are not responsible to their Parliaments for the measures taken as they are politically and morally obliged to amend national legislation in accordance with the principles of the Resolutions.

Therefore, once implemented into national law, the measures discussed are legally binding *de facto* on individuals but they have escaped democratic control and are not subject to judicial supervision.

The Commission's proposal for the Convention must therefore be welcomed as it represents a legally binding instrument. However, a more generous approach was expected, since the text was elaborated by this Institution. As often happen, due to the hostility of some Member States, efforts to harmonise national rules in the area of immigration result in the elaboration and eventually adoption of "lowest common denominator" measures. These measures if, on the one hand,

365 Groenendijk C.A. & Guild E., "Admission for Employment", in Meijers M. et al (eds), *A New Immigration Law for Europe? The 1992 London and 1993 Copenhagen Rules on Immigration*, Standing Committee of Experts in International Immigration, Refugee and Criminal Law, 1993.

do not ensure harmonisation, on the other, could lower the minimum guarantees granted to TCNs.

The Convention would establish minimum standards based on a very restrictive approach for the admission of TCNs which nonetheless do not impose an obligation on the Member States to admit those TCNs who meet the requirements needed. This led the EP to criticise the Commission's proposal because, as it now stands, it represents a political rather than a legal text.[366] The merit of the proposed Convention lies in the discussion that followed that will possibly pave the way for more liberal measures under the Amsterdam Treaty.

Member States maintain wide discretionary powers. This, in practice, means that national authorities can favour the entry of certain migrants and refuse others on a completely discriminatory basis. Immigrants are generally a source of fear and irritation in the host countries. They are often held responsible for several problems in European societies, i.e. unemployment, crime, etc. While, sometimes, these are rational concerns, immigrants are often merely *scapegoats*. Black migrants due to their visibility are the most affected by these xenophobic and racist attitudes in Western Europe and they are therefore the most targeted by the restrictive admission policies.

VII.6.1 Workers

As regards TCN workers, the high level of unemployment reached in Western Europe seems to justify the adoption of very restrictive measures concerning the entry of foreign workers. The Convention would maintain the ban on new entries for employment reasons, but in clearer terms than the Resolution.
As Peers points out:

> "The Resolution established three general principles governing admission for employment, without making clear the hierarchy between them. Member States should refuse admission; they should admit only for vacancies that could not be filled by EC nationals or third country nationals with permanent residence in that State; and without prejudice to the first two principles, they could admit a worker temporarily for a specific period if the worker fit into a specified category....The Convention would replace this awkwardly drafted list with one general rule: third country nationals could only be admitted to employment if a vacancy could not be filled by EC nationals, third country nationals

366 EP, Report on the Proposal for a Council Act establishing the Convention on rules for the Admission of third-country nationals to the Member States, A4-0266/98.

already in the labour market in that Member State or persons qualified as long-term resident, presumably in any Member State".[367]

The proposed Convention seems softer than the Resolution as it does not impose a ban on new entries but it makes it conditional upon vacancies in the labour market. But taking into account that all Member States are experiencing high unemployment rates, the new formula also amounts to a ban. More importantly, the fact that it is extremely difficult to control the dynamics of the labour market, which is not a fixed entity, can be instrumentalised to admit certain migrants and to refuse entry to others.

It should be noted that many Member States, especially the Southern countries, notwithstanding the high level of unemployment, still demand TCN workers as nationals are not willing to perform the manual and low-status jobs, on the one hand, and national employers look for a cheap, non demanding labour force, on the other.

In principle, this policy is able to benefit both racial and ethnic minorities, especially women, generally unskilled or low-skilled *ready* therefore to work in any sector for a low salary. But this Member States' "benevolence" to admit them has the effect to hamper their social mobility, already difficult, in the host society. This approach is likely to keep them at the bottom rung of the society and perpetuate their marginalisation.

Nonetheless, admission must be considered as an exception. Member States seem to privilege temporary, seasonal and trainee workers as their admission is, at least in principle, short and for a specific duration. Restrictions to the period of admission for employment attempt to avoid migrant workers admitted for "temporary" employment to settle *permanently* in the country of immigration. Accordingly, applications to extend a stay for the purpose of employment is in principle not permitted. There is a clear attempt to reintroduce a guest-workers system, even though it proved to be a failure in the past. Such a system as happened in the 1970s is likely to encounter the opposition of the employers because of the costs it would impose on them. A rotation system implies that the newcomers must be recruited and trained and this is very expensive.

More limitations are foreseen in respect to initial authorisations that are normally restricted to employment for a specific job with a specific employer. A TCN admitted under the category of worker cannot switch to other categories such as self-employed, student, trainee, etc.

---

367 Peers S., Raising Minimum Standards or Racing for the Bottom? The Commission's Proposed Migration Convention, in Guild E. (ed), *supra* note 115, 156.

As regards the maximum length of the permit, both the Resolution and the Convention provide a four year permit.

The economic and political reasons are evident. Member States look for a disposable work-force to improve the competitiveness of their economies but they do not want any more settlement of foreigners within their boundaries. In this sense, TCNs from poor developing countries are encouraged to come to do the dirty jobs when needed but always in a "wave system" in order to prevent their settlement in the host societies and to allow for a peaceful integration of those already resident. This is the most recent approach. It has not always been this way. In the past, Member States were much more open towards TCNs coming to work in Western Europe. For instance, Decision 1/80 adopted to implement the EEC/ Turkey Agreement still allows Turkish workers or their family members to remain in the country after a short period of time, if certain conditions are met (*supra* section VI.2.3).

The doors are closed to migrants looking for a better life but wide open to those who are prepared to do the worst jobs in terms of salary, status and flexibility, etc. Although indirectly, Blacks will be targeted by this approach for two main reasons. The great reserve of work-force with these characteristics is to be found in the developing countries. But, in terms of settlement, Blacks are the most unwanted as they represent a threat to European identity and culture.

The system so created affects Black populations but among them special attention must be paid to female migrants. Unfortunately, data do not give information on the reasons for admission of TCNs. But there is a growing demand for admission by TCN female migrants which seems to imply, considering that the great wave of family reunification is almost completed (*infra* section VIII.1), that an increasing number of women are emigrating on their own. They are generally unskilled and they work in specific sectors in the host country, mainly *domestic service, hotels* and the *catering sector.*

The jobs available to women are often not even given a clear definition which makes it even more difficult to get entry and work permits.

Overall, these restrictive rules could affect their integration. But impeding their settlement and integration seems to be the final goal of these rules.

VII.6.2 Self-employed workers

As far as the self-employed Resolution is concerned, the approach seems more generous with respect to admission. The Council takes the view that to a certain extent, the question of the admission of persons for the purpose of pursuing a salaried activity and that of the admission of self-employed persons can be treated distinctly. The Convention has also adopted this stance. Therefore, while there is an implicit ban on salaried workers, the admission of persons for the purpose of an independent economic activity who add value to the economy of the host country is considered a benefit for the host country. Since this is the reason for a more liberal regime regarding admission of self-employed aliens, it was decided, consequently, that care must be taken to ensure that persons admitted to pursue activities as self-employed persons do not eventually enter into a paid employment relationship. In particular, severe controls are foreseen to make sure that the TCN seeking entry into the Union has sufficient resources to set up the business and contribute to the improvement of the economy of the receiving country.

Article 12 of the proposed Convention in fact establishes that TCNs may be admitted into the territory of a Member State under two conditions. They must have sufficient resources to undertake, in the relevant Member State, activity for which they submit their admission application and, secondly, that the business generated by the person admitted will have, during the period of validity of the initial residence authorisation, a beneficial effect on employment in the Member State in which he resides.

Obviously, Member States dispose of their wide discretionary powers because there are no guidelines in the Convention to define concepts such as "sufficient resources" or when a business is a benefit from the receiving country but, in particular, as noted above, there is no *obligation* to admit TCNs although they meet all requirements.

Again, Member States may use such discretionary powers to discriminate against TCNs coming from certain countries.

VII.6.3 Students

The last Resolution, concerning admission for students, is also directed at restricting the conditions of entry for TCNs. Its content has been mainly reprised in the Convention. The main concern of Member States is that TCNs, admitted for study purposes, *settle*, as frequently happens, on a *permanent basis* in the host country. Therefore, it was agreed that the residence permit would expire with conclusion or interruption of the studies. Moreover, in order to avoid their entry into the labour market and the strengthening of their position in the host country, all students have to dispose of sufficient resources and sickness insurance to prevent them from becoming a burden of the public funds on the Member State concerned. Relationship with the labour market is in fact restricted as they may not engage in any gainful employment, either in a self-employed or employed capacity. Member States may allow short-term or subsidiary jobs so long as these jobs do not represent a vital income for the subsistence of the student nor do they affect the continuation of the student's studies.

Again the "siege" mentality is present in the elaboration of immigration rules which *evidently* try to prevent students from settling in the Union. Even in the event that students, after completing their studies, get a concrete offer of job in the host State they must go back to their original country and make a new application for the category of worker or self-employed person. *Here* economic considerations cannot justify such a closure. If foreign students after completing their education cycle in the host country are able to find a job even in times of recession they are surely improving competition and this will eventually benefit the economy of the host country. But, it appears that through this system of controls, discrimination against certain migrants finds a legal cover.

VII.6.4 TCNs who do not wish to engage in gainful activities

In 1995, a proposal was advanced for a Joint Position on the admission of TCNs who do not wish to engage in gainful activity or study[368] but, although three versions were drafted, it never became law. The proposed Convention also includes these categories of migrants. Apart from a few irrelevant differences, the two proposals agree that this category of TCNs must fulfil all the requirements demanded of TCNs for entry and their admission must in no case represent a burden on the State in which they wish to reside. Indeed, they must have sufficient economic resources to live in the host State. The Member States in which they want to reside will consider such resources when granting the residence permit, which period of validity will be initially restricted to one year with the possibility of a subsequent extension. The original proposal was mainly directed at rich TCNs, a small percentage of TCNs wanting to enter the EU. The great majority of TCNs belongs to developing countries and arrives in Europe in search of a better life and better opportunities.

---

368 Joint Position on the Admission of TCNs who do not wish to engage in gainful activity or study, see note 326. See for a comment Peers S., *supra* note 28.

The proposed Convention has, according to the Commission,[369] a wider target. The proposal refers not only to rich TCNs but also to pensioners, writers receiving royalties and young people with *au pair* status, and the list does not seem to be exhaustive.

Considering the broad personal scope, it is very likely that TCNs that otherwise enter in the other categories, as workers for instance, may try this channel to escape the new restrictive rules. In particular, special attention must be paid to the fact that this may be a privileged channel for criminal networks to smuggle in immigrants under a legal cover. The trafficking in human beings especially for sexual exploitation but also slavery in a more wider sense is a growing business. In many cases the victims are kidnapped in their original countries or deceived about their final destination, but others arrive legally. Women and children are obviously the target of this ignominious trade which has increased in terms of *quantity* and *quality*. Although it is difficult to give exact data, it seems that an increasing number of women are involved and the criminal networks are better organised. After the fall of the Iron Curtain, mainly women from Central and Eastern Europe, but also from Africa and Asia, are brought into the Union as artists or *au pairs*, than deprived of their passports and, more importantly, of their freedom and forced into prostitution or to work in conditions near to slavery.[370] Only recently, have the European institutions started discussing it in order to provide a Union-wide solution which is discussed in the next sections in more detail (*infra* section IX.5).

VII.7 ADMISSION UNDER INTERNATIONAL AGREEMENTS

When considering the conditions of entry, special mention must be made to the various Agreements signed by the Community, by virtue of old Article 228 and 238 EC (new Articles 300 and 310 EC), with several third countries.

As noted above, these agreements are mixed agreements in which the Community shares its competence with the Member States, in most cases.

Most of these agreements accord some rights to TCNs.

---

369 See Explanatory Memorandum of the Convention, XV, *supra* note 62.

370 This danger has been highlighted by the EP that denounced that there should be greater controls over issuing residence and work permits to folk artists, au pairs and chambermaids to avoid entry of girls and women brought into the Union as slaves. EP, Resolution on trafficking in human beings, OJ 1996 C 32/88.

VII.7.1 EEA and Swiss Agreements

Apart from the European Economic Area (EEA) Agreement that grants free movement rights to EEA citizens, and, recently, the accord signed by the Community and the Member States with Switzerland that grants important rights of entry to the nationals of the Contracting Parties, the other Agreements do not grant entry rights nor have they been automatically transposed into the legislation of the associated countries. The choice to grant the rights to free movement only to EEA citizens and Swiss citizens on the same basis as EC citizens only seems to be justified by *race* and *wealth* considerations. The other Agreements vary widely as regards the rights conferred upon nationals.

VII.7.2 EEC/Turkey Agreement

The EEC-Turkey Agreement has included, since its signature in 1963, provisions referring to the possibility to grant free movement rights to Turkish nationals, but these provisions have never been implemented. Important rights are conferred once Turkish migrants have already been admitted into the Union (see section VI.2.3).

VII.7.3 The Europe Agreements

As regards the agreements signed with Central and Eastern European countries in the perspective of their accession to the Union, the Commission is presently evaluating their legislation and their progress to accede to EC law in order to confer on them the privileges of the freedom of movement as soon as possible.

As far as *Bulgaria* is concerned "the European Commission considers that in relation to the free movement of persons very little has been done to transpose and apply established EU law and practice. Despite progress in several areas, Bulgaria will still have to carry out major reforms in the area of legislation, policy and administration, if it is to conform to the European Union's rules in the medium term". It continues that "the Bulgarian Constitution puts all foreigners residing in Bulgaria and its own citizens on an equal footing, with the exception of a few specific areas for which Bulgarian nationality is required. Whilst equal treatment is guaranteed by the Constitution, in practice Bulgaria pursues a relatively restrictive immigration policy".[371] Overall, these considerations along with others have impeded the inclusion of Bulgaria in the first track of candidates for accession.

---

371 European Commission, Opinion on Bulgaria's application for membership, COM (97) 2008 final. Commission Report COM (98) 707 final.

The European Commission[372] considered that the *Czech Republic* has adopted important measures in relation to the free movement of persons but the new law on immigration and frontier controls has not been adopted. New legislation is needed to ensure, in particular, more effective surveillance of the frontiers and immigration movements. Member States, as discussed above, fear that an opening towards CEECs would lead to more pressure on their borders if these are not sufficiently controlled.

Estonia seems to meet the requirements imposed by EC law. "The European Commission considers that Estonia's legislation on freedom of movement of persons is fairly close to the rules in force in the European Union and should not present a major problem for accession to the EU in the medium term. In the case of the mutual recognition of professional qualifications, the preparation of legislative and implementing measures will have to be stepped up if they are to be ready to be applied in the medium term".[373] Such closeness of legislation has ensured to Estonia a place in the first group of states acceding to the EU. However, the Commission considers that "in view of the overall assessment which could be made of the current state and speed of progress in the various areas concerned, it is at the moment hard to imagine when Estonia would be in a position to adopt and implement all the instruments required to abolish checks at the internal borders and shift them to the external borders of the Union".

Hungary, in the Commission's opinion, needs to resolve important existing problems as regards the free movement of persons. "Under Hungarian law, access to employment for foreign nationals with relevant permits cannot be prohibited on grounds of nationality alone. In certain circumstances, however, preferential criteria for nationals may be imposed by statutory or collective instruments. Since the beginning of the 1990s, Hungarian legislation has imposed restrictions on the annual quota of immigration permits in order to boost employment of Hungarian nationals. Foreign nationals may only have access to employment if they have a work permit, which is subject to certain conditions. The current rules also require visas for the families of foreign workers. Provided migrant workers have a valid residence permit, they are eligible for social security. Members of the family of the foreign worker have access to education although, at least for higher education, the registration fees are higher for foreigners than for nationals. Members of a worker's family do not acquire a right to work". Finally "a substantial part of the acquis concerning the mutual recognition of diplomas and qualifications has already been taken on board and full approximation is expected of diplomas in

372 European Commission, Opinion on Czech Republic's application for membership, COM (97) 2009 final. Commission Report, COM (98) 708 final.

373 European Commission, Opinion on Estonia's application for membership, COM (97) 2006 final.

the medium term. Negotiations on the mutual recognition of diplomas are due to start soon, and, in particular, Hungary has expressed an interest in including in the discussion the medium level professional qualifications issued by vocational training centres".[374] Nonetheless, these concerns have not impeded Hungary from being successful in its application to be included in the first track for accession.

Latvia is required to make a number of changes to its legislation to comply with the Community acquis in relation to the free movement of persons. "Regarding mutual recognition of professional qualifications, sustained impetus and support will have to be given to the preparation of legislation and the relevant implementing measures if they are to be implemented in the medium term".[375] Latvia has only been included in the second track of candidates.

As regards *Lithuania*, notwithstanding the great progress made in the area related to the free movement of persons that has made it possible to adapt its regulations in the medium term Lithuania has been excluded from immediate accession.[376]

Poland is required to resolve outstanding issues regarding the free movement of persons in the medium term. "From an early stage of the reform process Poland has maintained a relatively open approach to the movement of persons into its territory, with visa requirements abolished for EU citizens. The right of residence is granted by the visa or a residence card equivalent to a resident permit. A residence permit is a precondition for a work permit. Work permits are granted depending on the local labour market conditions and further alignment will be required to improve access to employment for non-Polish nationals. Whilst nationality is not a sufficient reason to refuse work permits to EU citizens, the equal treatment of EU citizens will require further amendments to existing national legislation".[377] Poland is the biggest candidate and Poles represent the largest group that is trying to take advantage of the fall of the Iron Curtain to move in other Member States.

As far as *Romania* is concerned, the European Commission considers that unless major efforts are made to harmonise legislation and set up and strengthen implementing structures, it will be difficult for Romania to adopt EC/EU rules in

374 European Commission, Opinion on Hungary's application for membership, COM (97) 2001 final. Commission Report COM (98) 700 final.

375 European Commission, Opinion on Latvia's application for membership, COM (97) 2005 final.

376 European Commission, Opinion on Lithuania's application for membership, COM (97) 2007 final.

377 European Commission, Opinion on Poland's application for membership, COM (97) 2005 final. Commission Report COM (98) 701 final.

the area related to immigration.[378] Romania has been selected for the second round of accession.

As regards *Slovakia*, the European Commission considers that the necessary structures to facilitate the free movement of persons seem to be in place but it is not possible at this stage to assess their effectiveness fully. Legislation and the implementation/enforcement structures related to free movement of persons need to be adapted if Slovakia is too fully adopt the acquis in this area. Such adjustments are a feasible proposition in the medium term".[379]

Finally, "the European Commission considers that Slovenian policies on immigration and work permits are restrictive, but amendments to the law are being drafted. On mutual recognition of diplomas, some areas remain to be adjusted. *Slovenia* should adopt the necessary legislation in the medium term".[380] Slovenia has been included in the first track for accession to the Union.

Overall, even though all the candidates from Central and Eastern Europe could comply with the Community acquis concerning free movement of people it is very likely that a transitional period is established after the accession to delay the granting of EC free movement rights to the nationals of the new members.

This area is unlikely to produce many immigrants. The hordes of invaders from the ex-Communist countries, against the prediction made immediately after the fall of the Berlin wall, have not materialised. There has been an enormous increase in the amount of travelling taking place in the region but this has not taken the form of immigration and settlement.[381] However, what is feared is that these countries work as an open gate for migrants from further East towards the European Union. Great importance is, in fact, placed on the elaboration and enforcement of restrictive immigration rules to avoid that this happens.

378 European Commission, Opinion on Romania's application for membership, COM (97) 2003 final. Commission Report COM (98) 702 final.

379 European Commission, Opinion on Slovakia's application for membership, COM (97) 2004 final.

380 European Commission, Opinion on Slovenia's application for membership, COM (97) 2010 final. Commission Report COM (98) 709 final.

381 See on this point Stola D., The Social & Political Context of Migration between Central Europe and the European Union, in Guild E. (ed), *supra* note 115, 147-148.

VIII

ADMISSION FOR TCN'S FAMILY MEMBERS

VIII.1 FAMILY REUNION: THE INTERNATIONAL SETTING

The area related to family reunification is a particularly sensitive area in the already delicate field of immigration. Member States must combine the need to control migration flows into their territories and the commitment to guarantee the right to family life which is the source of the right to family reunion.

Since the oil crisis of 1973, Member States have individually adopted and enforced restrictive rules to reduce immigration, an attempt to regulate the flow of new entries, and in order to repatriate those already settled. Nevertheless the extra-Community population has not stopped growing. On the contrary, it is rising constantly. In this context the *family reunion* channel has become a crucial factor. After the 1973 crisis and the decision by the Member States to restrict new waves of TCN immigrants, TCNs legally settled in Western Europe have had to face the option of going back to their original countries, hit by general recession as well, taking advantage of the repatriation programme incentives and, generally, lose the possibility of returning, or the other option of having their families join them in the host state. Many chose the second option. Therefore, since the 1970s Member States have not only been unable to get rid of the foreign population already settled in their territory but they have also had to face the entry of more and more TCNs in their territory being virtually *powerless* to do anything about it.

Such "powerlessness" was caused partially by humanitarian concerns of not keeping families permanently separated but mainly by the need to respect international commitments. The right to family life which is the basis of the family reunion principle is in fact recognised and protected in many international agreements and declarations. As Guild recalls:[382]

> "The right to family life appears so consistently in human rights conventions as to qualify for consideration as norm of international law. Among the conventions inter alia protecting family life to which Member States are parties are found:
> The European Convention of Human Rights, Article 8, which requires states to respect the family and private life of all persons within their jurisdiction.
> The European Social Charter, Article 19(6), the obligation to facilitate the reunion of the family of a foreign worker defined as at least the spouse and dependent children under 21 years.
> The European Convention on the Legal Status of Migrant Workers, Article 12, requiring admission of spouses and unmarried minors, dependent children subject to available housing. Signatory states may introduce a waiting period but it may not exceed 12 months.
> ILO Convention 1443, Article 13 requiring states to facilitate reunification of families including spouses, dependent children and parents.
> Universal Declaration of Human Rights 12 and 16 enshrining the right protection of family life and to marry and found a family.
> International Covenant on Civil and Political Rights, Article 17 protecting the individual from interference with privacy or family.
> UN Convention on the Rights of the Child".

Among those instruments the most appropriate seems the European Convention of Human Rights (ECHR). First of all, because all the European countries are members and because it protects persons from states which are not member of the Council of Europe provided that the countries in which these persons reside have ratified the Convention, and secondly, because a system of judicial control and enforcement mechanisms are foreseen.[383]

A comprehensive analysis of the ECHR is outside the scope of the present research but a few remarks are nonetheless necessary. There is an express reference to this Convention in the TEU[384] and it seems that Member States in the elaboration and application of immigration rules are guided by the principles contained

382 Guild E., *The Developing Immigration and Asylum Policies of the European Union, Adopted Conventions, Resolutions, Recommendations, Decisions and Conclusions*, Kluwer Law International, 1996, 259-260.

383 Briefly, as regards the ECHR enforcement system, Article 25 allows for individual petitions and States which are analysed by the European Commission of Human Rights which tries to reach an agreement with the parties implied. In the case of failure the European Court of Human Rights, in Strasbourg, gives its judgment to which the parties are required to comply.

384 Old Articles F and K.2 TEU. The revised text only refers to the ECHR in Article 6 (ex Article F).

in the ECHR. Article 8(1) of the Convention states that "everyone has the right to respect for his private life and family life, his home and his correspondence". The formulation of Article 8(1) seems to confer an absolute right, but it must be interpreted with Article 8(2) which lists a great number of exceptions to the principle of family life. It is agreed that "there shall be no interference by a public authority with the exercise of this right except such as is in accordance with the law and is necessary in a democratic society in the interest of national security, public safety or the economic well-being of the country, for the prevention of disorder or crime, for the protection of health or morals, or for the protection of the rights and freedom of others". Moreover, in no case does the right to family life contained in Article 8 give a right to enter a country as it does not necessarily include the right to choose the geographical location of the family. And in fact, this right often encounters barriers when exercised. As Cholewinski observes:

> "Migrant workers, legally employed and lawfully resident in a country, other than their own, are often denied the right of reunion with their families in that country because such a right would conflict with the well-established principle of international law granting States control over the entry and exit of aliens".[385]

More importantly, the right to family life as enshrined in Article 8 has often been interpreted in a racist and sexist manner by the Member States. There is often a *racist* and *sexist* presumption that among TCNs communities wives must follow their husbands to the country in which they live. Unfortunately, such a vision was upheld by the Strasbourg Court. Accordingly TCN wives or brides have encountered great difficulties in being reunited with their husbands in Europe.[386] Women are discriminated against as it seems that they are not capable of having an independent role in the society. There is the presumption that they always have a subordinate role to their husbands.

Although, Member States often find legal loopholes to restrict the right of TCN migrants resident in their territory to be reunited with their families, the force of these international agreements and declarations must be not underestimated. In the last decade (1989/1999) Member States have put more and more emphasis, as seen in section I.6, on the respect and protection of human rights and funda-

385 Cholewinski R., "The Protection of the Right of Economic Migrants to Family Reunion in Europe", *International And Comparative Law Quarterly*, 1994, Vol. 43 569.

386 In the case of *Abdulaziz, Cabales, Balkandali v UK*, the Strasbourg Court held, although recognising sex discrimination in the UK immigration rules, that even in the case of a stateless person refusal by the immigration authorities to permit entry to the husband did not violate Article 8. European Court of Human Rights, 1985, Series A, No 94, 31.

mental freedoms in their external policy as well as their internal policy. There are therefore heavy pressures to honour such commitments.

VIII.2 EU REGULATION: AN EXCEPTIONS TO THE RESTRICTIVE ADMISSION PRINCIPLE?

For Member States, it has, therefore, become increasingly difficult to reconcile the desire to stop TCNs from coming into the EU and, at the same time, to respect the right of those settled to be reunited by their families. As far as the extra-Community population is concerned some remarks are necessary.

It should be noted that after years of family reunion immigration the features of the extra-Community population settled in the Member States has slowly changed, *from* a population dominated by young single men willing to carry out any type of work with very basic needs *to* a population increasingly made of families with different needs in terms of housing, school, health care, etc. Also the size of the foreign communities resident in the Member States has grown quickly both because of continued family reunion or family formation immigration and, generally, for the high fertility rate of certain ethnic groups compared to nationals. Moreover, family members, although the main reason for entry is to be reunited with the worker, eventually enter the labour market. Those who have lived the greater part of their lives in the host country and received their education there are not willing to do the dirty jobs as they have higher expectations.

All these considerations have raised serious concerns and have been largely used to motivate the closure of this channel as well. But apart from obvious economic worries justified by the late recession cycle, there are again racist factors which are shaping the desire to protect fortress Europe against "interminable" and "uncontrolled" flows of migrants. It is clear indeed, that the combined effect of a falling birth-rate of the European population and the high growth rate of the extra-Community population could eventually change the size and the ethnic composition of the European states as they are nowadays.

Presently, because of the *size* and especially for the *cultural distance* between some foreign communities and the national population, the "assimilation" of TCNs is becoming extremely difficult.

Assimilation policies, where assimilation concerns the adoption by the foreign population of the main values and culture of the host state, were partially successful in a few Member States, for instance in France. When the newcomers' cultures and traditions were not very dissimilar from those of the host country, their assimilation was easier and less traumatic, for instance Italians or Portuguese emigrating to France or Germany. The new migrants arrive from very distant countries, not only geographically but most importantly in terms of their culture, religion and traditions, therefore they find it very difficult to accept the new values.

Normally, therefore, TCN communities recreate their own "habitat" in the host country with their own customs and traditions which are occasionally parallel but often, opposite to those of the host country. This has provoked a widespread feeling at government level but also among EC citizens, that these communities have grown too large and are threatening the dominant culture. According to Eurobarometer, 40% of those interviewed considered that there were "too many" people from minority groups living in their country.[387] There is a European ethnocentric attitude which often alters the perception as regards the presence of foreigners in European countries. Only those Black TCNs, whether Asiatic, African, South American, as long as they are perceived as not belonging to the big European family and because of this, not assimilable, are deemed as undesirable and, therefore, are seen as a threat. As has been shown by Eurobarometer,[388] in 1997, 44.5% of those interviewed see TCNs as a cause of insecurity, and around 29% feel that minorities threaten their way of life. It should be noted that there has been a worsening of the situation as in 1993, only 22% of those interviewed among EU citizens felt embarrassed by people of a different nationality, race or religion.[389] Millions of TCNs are now firmly established within the Union. But instead of accepting some form of cultural pluralism, as an enriching factor, many Member States, in evaluating the impact of ethnic and cultural diversity of the new arrivals, have opted for stricter admission rules for family members. In the European Council, held in Brussels in June 1999, it was agreed that action must be taken in order to protect the family unit and prime importance was to be given to the integration of Long-term Residents in the sense of the respect of their cultural identity, but at the same time, it is stressed that "this needs to be matched by a readiness on the part of the third-country nationals to take an active part in their integration and to respect the fundamental values generally acknowledged by all Member States."[390] This is a positive sign that Member States are prepared to accept some form of cultural pluralism but Western values cannot be questioned.

Since the 1980s, Member States have also tried to adopt more restrictive regulations in this area. Notwithstanding the restrictive approach generally recorded in all Member States, rules and practice still differ widely. At European level, whether at intergovernmental level or EU level, efforts have been made to reach a certain

387 Eurobarometer Opinion Poll no 47, Luxembourg, 1997.
388 Ibidem.
389 Eurobarometer 1/1988 and 1/1992.
390 *Supra* note 312.

degree of harmonization, although at the lowest common denominator, and few steps have been taken which confirm the desire to reduce largely the pressure on this channel of immigration.

According to the draft Strategy Paper "the greatest challenge for Western Europe's migration policy in the next decade is the momentum of family reunification. On account of the policy on immigrant workers followed in the Member States over the past few decades, an exceptionally large group of single men have immigrated and who wish to reunite their families or start new ones. From a quantitative point of view, the demand for family reunification will certainly account for the major part of immigration pressure for a decade. A coordinated European procedure is advisable here. Family reunification will go ahead – as it should. The annual figures, conditions (waiting times, accommodation, income) and volume (nuclear family) must be determined on a uniform basis if irregularities and secondary migrations are to be avoided."[391]

Again, the draft strategy Paper clearly defines the "problem" and the "solution" where the solution is to avoid on a Union-wide basis new arrivals through this channel.

VIII.3 EU LEGAL BASIS FOR THE REGULATION OF FAMILY REUNION

This area of law is still governed largely by national rules and practices. However, since the late 1980s, Member States have agreed that this area also requires a minimum level of harmonization. Accordingly, in 1991, the Ministers responsible for Immigration reunited in London worked to adopt common guidelines to be included in a Resolution. This first attempt failed but eventually a Resolution on harmonization of family reunification[392] was adopted in 1993 at the Copenhagen meeting. This Resolution does not represent an EC instrument but it is the fruit of pure intergovernmental cooperation. Again, the decision to regulate a delicate area such as the one concerning family reunion whereby human rights are involved by a resolution and not by a more legal binding instrument, as for instance a convention, is further confirmation of the reluctance of the Member States to give up powers in the area of immigration. As Peers argues "the Resolution achieved no harmonisation whatsoever...there are no rules...there are options".[393]

391 See draft Strategy Paper, *supra* note 311.

392 Council document, Resolution on harmonization of family reunification, SN 2828. For the text see Bunyan T. (ed), *Key Texts on Justice and Home Affairs in the European Union*, Statewatch Publication, 1997, 98.

393 Peers S., *supra* note 28.

This area was later recognised as a matter of common interest in the Maastricht Treaty (Old Article K(1)(3)(b) TEU). Unfortunately, as is widely known, most matters concerning TCNs were included in the third Pillar outside EC competence. Family reunion issues have been shifted by the Amsterdam Treaty to the new Title IV EC. Article 63(3)(a) EC provides the legal basis for the adoption of measures relating to "conditions of entry and residence and standards on procedures for the issue by Member States of long-term visas and residence permits, including those for the purpose of *family reunion* (emphasis added)". However, the revised Article 63(3) EC (ex Article 73 k(3) EC) establishes an exception to the five year period within which, under Title IV EC (ex Title IIIa EC), the Council shall adopt new measures. In this area there is no agreed deadline. The absence of an agreed deadline deprives Article 63(3)(a) of any force to act and reduces it to no more than a political commitment. This exception is of great significance as the area related to family reunion is extremely important for the integration of TCNs settled in the Union. An active policy that ensures the settlement of the TCN's family is a clear sign of the desire to improve the integration of TCNs in the Union. The introduction of that exception in this sensitive area, likewise in other immigration areas moved from the third Pillar to the Community Pillar, is proof that there is a hidden objective of the new policy which is in antithesis with the one proclaimed. Member States still refuse to give up powers in this area and they have made sure that the new-born Community competence is limited. There are nonetheless positive signs in the Action Plan of the Council and the Commission on how best to implement the provisions of the Treaty of Amsterdam in the area of freedom, security and justice which established that measures implementing Article 63(3) (a) EC should be taken within five year.[394]

The communitarisation of the family reunion issues, it is hoped, will bring more order in this area, which is presently very chaotic. Apart from the 1993 Resolution, this area is regulated in other documents. First of all, as seen in section IV.4.3, the entry and stay of TCN family members of an EC citizen who exercise the right of free movement are governed by Regulation 1612/68/EEC. As regards TCN family members of a TCN legally resident within the territory of the EU, the Self-employed Resolution (*supra* section VI.6.2) expressly refers to the 1993 Resolution,[395] while the Workers Resolution (*supra* section VI.6.1) and the

394 *Supra* note 84.

395 The Self-employed Resolution states that "the spouse and unmarried children under the maximum age, varying between 16 and 18 years depending on the Member State concerned, of a self-employed person will in principle be admitted to join that person, subject to the conditions set out in the Resolution concerning family reunification adopted by the Ministers responsible for immigration questions of the European Union on 1 June 1993".

Students' Resolution (*supra* section VI.6.3) accord discretionary powers to the Member States that are free to grant the right to the TCNs resident in their territory according to their national law.[396]

Furthermore, the international agreements signed by the Community often confer rights to individuals. The most important is the EEA agreement which accords EEA nationals the same rights as those conferred to EC citizens. The recent agreement signed with Switzerland also confers the Swiss migrants' family members the same rights and protection afforded to EC citizens under Regulation 1612/68/EEC.

None of the other agreements signed by the Community confer the right of entry to family members. Decision 1/80 in the context of the EEC/Turkish Agreement contains a few provisions referred to the Turkish worker's family members. It does not confer any right of entry to them but after they have been admitted according to national rules, they are accorded limited rights. In particular, they are protected against expulsion and they have the right to work, if certain conditions are met (*supra* section VI.2.4).

Nowadays, the situation is confusing and chaotic. A first step to regulate the area more coherently has been taken by the Commission in the Convention on admission rules for TCNs which often resumes the provisions already adopted.

VIII.4 Regulation under the Immigration Convention

The proposal defines better the position of TCN worker's family members with the advantage of regulating their status in a single document. Also the Convention, proposed under the EU cloak, of which the provisions now fall under the Amsterdam Treaty, is to take the form of an EC directive and it will legally bind Member States.

The *personal scope* of the Convention is very broad but some categories are excluded, in particular, EC citizens' family members and those covered by specific agreements. TCN workers' and students' family members are now included.

The Convention does not contain an original regulation altogether, it indeed resumes, partially modified, provisions adopted previously under the 1993 Resolution.

396 The Workers' Resolution states that "Member States reserve the right to allow in accordance to their national law, the spouse and dependent children to accompany persons admitted in accordance with this resolution". The Students' Resolution states that "national provisions will apply as regards the possible admission of family members and the taking-up of employment or study by the spouse".

However, the personal scope, as seen above, is wider and more precise. It applies to all TCNs "provided that they have been legally resident in a Member State for at least one year and have the right of residence in that Member State for at least one year from the date they submit the application" (Article 23), while the 1993 Resolution excluded students and TCNs present in a Member State on a short-term basis.[397]

Protection is accorded to the TCN's spouse and children. In accordance with the Resolution, the Convention covers the spouse provided that the marriage is compatible with the fundamental principles of the law in the Member States. Expected progress in the area of the recognition of unmarried partners and same sex partners has not been made, which is also in line with EC legislation in this field (*supra* section IV.4.3).

As far as *children* are concerned, the Convention applies to all the couple's children whether natural or adopted. In this last case some precautions are taken to ensure that the departure of the child does not create legal problems. It was then decided that if the adoption decision was not taken by the authorities of the Member State concerned, it must be recognised by the competent authority there. Again, to guarantee legal certainty, in the case of children where only one of the spouses is the natural parent, they are covered by the Convention when the natural parent whether s/he is the resident or his/her spouse has the sole parental authority and s/he has been given custody of them and is responsible for them in practice. Children must be unmarried and they must have not reached the age of legal consent in the Member State concerned.

As regards the 1993 Resolution, more attention is given to the various forms a marriage can take, in particular, to a polygamous marriage. It must be assumed that in part not to create disruptive effects in the host society and as a way of controlling the entry of too many family members, it was agreed that the Member States reserve the right to refuse admission to a wife and her children for the purpose of family reunification if the marriage is polygamous, and either the children of another wife or another wife are resident in the territory of a Member State.

In must be noticed that while the relevance of the family reunification principle was recognised, a restrictive approach in the harmonisation was chosen by the Union.

397 The Resolution does not cover TCNs present in the territory of a Member State on a short-term basis (for example, students and persons admitted for employment for a fixed term). It only covers those TCNs lawfully resident within the territory of a Member State on a basis which affords them an expectation of permanent or long-term residence. It follows that the question of what constitutes an expectation of permanent or long-term residence is for determination by reference to national laws and policies.

The Resolution introduces a restrictive regime as regards the admission of family members in many aspects. Such an attempt is made more evident in comparison with the Community rules that regulate family members' admission within the Union.[398] The evident aim of the Resolution is to limit the pressure on this channel.

Very timid progress has been made in the Convention as regards other family members of the resident worker as it was decided that "Member States shall give favourable consideration to family reunion involving dependent relatives in the ascending line as well as other dependent relatives in the descending line" (Article 24). The Resolution limits Member States' discretionary powers as Member States may reserve the possibility of permitting the entry and stay of family members for compelling reasons which justify the presence of the person concerned. From a legal standpoint nothing has changed as Member States are still free to decide. They obviously have a wider room for manoeuvre than under EC rules where they shall admit, at least in principle, all relatives as long as they are dependent or living under the same roof in the country from where the migrant comes. But the approach under Regulation 1612/68/EEC is more positive as regards other relatives.

This new provision would have a great impact on certain ethnic groups. The tendency to maintain close links among relatives and to create big family units, more and more unusual in Western countries, is still very common in many developing countries. A generous policy as regards the entry of all family members has as a side effect the creation of several sub cultural worlds in the host society. This scenario is already visible in the main Western European cities where along with the dominant culture, other minority cultures such as Chinese, Maghrebies and Indians exist. The possibility of recreating by means of family links foreign customs and traditions within the territory of the host State is a serious threat to the programmes of integration, on the one hand, and programmes of repatriation, on the other hand, carried on in several Member States. It is very likely that Member States will use this power in a very discretionary way in order to discourage the entry of certain migrants.

Other barriers to entry of family members are surely those which oblige TCNs to furnish proof that they have suitable accommodation and adequate means to support their family when reunited (Article 26). Such requirements are absent under Regulation 1612/68/EEC. Although, Article 10 of Regulation 1612/68/EEC refers to the obligation on the worker to provide accommodation for the family it is, at the same time, prescribed that such accommodation should be considered in

398 See for a comparison of the Resolution as regards EC rules respect family reunion, Guild E., *supra* note 379, 261-272.

the light of the situation of national workers where the migrant is employed without discrimination. These guarantees are not present in the Convention.

Although the Convention presented by the Commission, which in general has a more liberal approach when dealing with TCNs, reflects the siege mentality present in all Member States about TCNs who, facing the impossibility of legal entry under EU strict rules, try to misuse any immigration channel, if available. It was agreed therefore that in the case of fraud of forgery used to elude admission controls, Member States shall refuse to admit a spouse or a child for the purpose of family reunion or withdraw their residence permit if they have been already admitted. If it is found that the *sole* purpose of the marriage or of the adoption was to enable the person concerned to be admitted into the Union, Member States may decide to refuse his/her admission or withdraw his/her residence permit if s/he is already within the Member State's boundaries. The wording of the Resolution was stricter as it was enough for Member States to refuse admission to family members that the marriage or the adoption were arranged solely or *principally* (emphasis added) to enter the Union. This offensive principle already present in some Member States[399] can seriously interfere with the formation of family life particularly among some ethnic groups.[400]

VIII.5 Arranged marriages in the Union

This is a very sensitive field as the European culture can clash with other cultures. It should also be noted that, nowadays, the family reunion channel has mainly taken the form of family formation immigration. There is a great distinction between family reunion and family formation. In the first case migrants residing in the receiving country reunite with their existing family (spouse, children or other relatives) while in the second there is a new marriage between a migrant (or migrant's child) living in the country of settlement, with a partner in the country of origin, leading to migration of the latter to the country of settlement of the former. Family reunification in the stricter sense of the term, including only TCNs already part of the family of the TCN worker before s/he arrived in Europe, started in the 1970s and it is almost finished. Presently, family formation immigration is the most important channel. In this context, the custom of arranged mar-

399 The primary purpose rule was in force in the UK where it was finally abolished in 1997.

400 For an comprehensive study of this principle in the UK context where this principle was very well developed, see Sachdeva S., *The Primary Purpose Rule in British Immigration Law*, Trentham Books, 1993.

riages, almost unknown in modern Western countries, has become of crucial importance. Such practice, in many developing countries, especially Moslem countries, is the most common way a marriage takes place. In the case of arranged marriages it is very difficult to evaluate whether they were contracted only for the purpose of circumventing admission rules and to gain entry into the Union. On this delicate issue the Council adopted a Resolution on measures to be adopted on the combating of marriages of convenience.[401] It was then agreed that when a marriage has not been arranged according to different customary culture but "with the sole aim of circumventing the rules on entry and residence of third-country nationals and obtaining for the third-country national a residence permit or authority to reside in a Member State", the residence permit or authorisation shall, as a general rule, be withdrawn, revoked and not renewed. It seems that in the final version of the Resolution, human rights concerns have been taken more seriously than in the previous drafts. First of all, the mention contained in the Preamble, completely absent in previous drafts (July 1997)[402] that the objective of the Resolution is not to introduce systematic checks on all marriages with TCNs but, on the contrary, checks are to be carried out where there are well-founded suspicions. This can be seen as a brake upon constant controls.

But more importantly, the Resolution states that the TCN concerned shall have an opportunity to contest or to have a review of, as provided for by national law, either before the court or before a competent administrative authority, any decision to refuse, withdraw, revoke or not renew a residence permit or authority to reside. Again, strong criticism must be made as regards the choice to regulate such an area by means of a Resolution which does not ensure a common interpretation and does not foresee a system of judicial supervision. Member States maintain great powers in this area to interpret these provisions in a discriminatory manner.

VIII.6 The Immigration Convention's new approach

In elaborating the proposal the Commission took into account the very restrictive trend also in this area, as was reflected in the 1993 Resolution on admission for TCN's family members. However, three modifications of the Convention seem very important. The proposal has eliminated the obligation for family members to live with the resident TCN which combined with the possibility of working after only six months after entry can greatly improve the situation of family members, in particular of migrant women. As noted in other sections of the research,

401 OJ 1997 C 382/1.

402 Council document, 9392/97.

spouses' rights are mainly women's rights. Many women arrived in the Union to be reunited with their husbands and they found themselves in a situation of both psychological and economic dependence on their partners. The possibility of working after six months anywhere in the host country without the obligation to live physically with the husbands would give them greater freedom and would represents an important step towards the integration of female migrants in the host society as individuals and not as appendages of the foreign worker.

However, the wording of the Article should have been more clear as it does not unfortunately impose a *maximum period* to give the right to work but only the minimum, i.e. six months.

Furthermore, the right to work and, therefore, to be economically independent combined with the possibility of living separated from their husbands may reduce the increasing number of cases of domestic violence against women. Again, domestic violence mainly affects women, who, in a position of general dependence on their husbands, are likely to endure very stressful situations.

The Convention goes even further as it envisages the possibility for family members to be accorded an independent status. Spouses, in particular, when separated, divorced or widowed do not face the immediate threat of deportation. Article 29 states that "where persons admitted for the purposes of family reunion are widowed, divorced or legally separated, lose their parents through death or reach the age of consent, they may submit an application for residence authorisation in another capacity. This application shall be examined in the Member State to which they have been admitted". As the Article has been worded it does not obviously represent an obligation on Member States to grant such permission. More importantly, the factors which the Member State concerned must take into account to grant such an independent status are not listed. However, it is to be hoped that cases of domestic violence especially in the light of the pressures by NGOs and, also, by some of the EU institutions will be considered as a determining factor by the competent authorities in the examination prior to the decision to grant such a status.

It should be remembered that unfortunately domestic violence is a widespread violation of women's rights and is not confined to specific groups but concerns all women, regardless of the status or class of the aggressor and the victim. Notwithstanding this, foreign spouses seem to be more vulnerable to suffer continued violence.

First of all, many female migrants, in particular from Moslem countries, often come from a very sexist culture which strongly influences them not to rebel against a violent husband. They also suffer strong psychological pressures as separated or divorced women are isolated in many migrant communities.

They must integrate in the host societies which are themselves to a certain extent *sexist* and also *racist*. Important steps have been taken to reach race and gender equality in Europe. The general non-discrimination provision introduced by the Amsterdam Treaty is the latest example of the efforts made at European level to protect the most vulnerable categories exposed to discrimination. However, EC provisions are generally worded so as to protect against discrimination in the *public sphere*.[403] Moreover, even when female migrants enter the labour market, EC law is not, in practice, able to offer the adequate protection and the fight against sex discrimination is a battle far from being achieved. Female migrants suffer continuous discrimination as is demonstrated by the fact that although highly-skilled and qualified they are employed in the lowest job categories engaged mostly in domestic and service work. *There*, they often experience violence in the form of rape, physical abuse and sexual harassment because of their gender and race by their employers. Separated or divorced spouses must face this double discrimination when integrating in the host society without the support of the group to which they belong.

But, the determining factor that makes a foreign spouse endure a situation of domestic violence seems to be the threat of deportation. Many have strongly criticised[404] the power that under these circumstances is given to husbands that to a certain extent have the control over their wives' fate. This critical situation has not been seriously taken into account by the Community legislators. Also, the ECJ, which is generally very liberal in the interpretation of EC rules, has refused to give an extensive interpretation of Decision 1/80 in the context of the EEC/Turkey Agreement when dealing with a case of domestic violence in the recent *Kadiman* case.[405]

The Commission's proposal, although expected to be more liberal and concerned with human rights, despite a few exceptions, has kept the very restrictive approach of the Member States in the immigration area. The very restrictive rules adopted have not been more *generous* in an area which affects fundamental rights as this one does. The several areas left unclear could interpreted more strictly by national authorities. Overall, as often is shown in the analysis of the immigration rules, the new rules *not only* do not protect the categories concerned against race and gender discrimination at European level but could worsen their situation.

---

403 For further comment Moebius I. & Szyszczak E., *supra* note 69.

404 See European Commission, Report of High Level Panel, *supra* note 185.

405 Case of *Kadiman, supra* note 304.

PART 4

THE REPRESSIVE SIDE OF IMMIGRATION POLICY: CONTROL AND EXPULSION MEASURES

IX

POLICING AND CONTROL MEASURES

IX.1 GENERAL REMARKS

The measures adopted so far to integrate resident TCNs and those regulating the entry of would-be migrants have been analysed. But it seems that the privileged area of cooperation among the Member States in the field of immigration is that concerning controls and forced repatriation of TCNs found to be unlawfully present in the territory of the European Union. Such cooperation includes both preventive and repressive measures.

This is an area where Member States have shown a very restrictive and repressive approach towards TCNs. Since the 1970s, the struggle to control the flows has resulted in increasing restrictive measures but it has only been in the last decade that a system of control has been developed at EU level. It is noteworthy that the entire system to gain control over migratory flows in Western Europe is based on the assumption that a very restrictive admission policy aimed at limiting new entries is the *prerequisite* to a successful and peaceful integration of those already settled within its boundaries. Also, according to the draft Austrian Strategy Paper the incessant influx of illegal migrants and the effect of migration crises on demographic policies have been major contributing factors to the absence of any prospect, even now, of uniform EU-wide rights of legal immigrants. Since these are the premises, a lot of energy obviously has been dedicated to adopting and improving control measures.

Such an approach has been criticised, in particular, as regards the Strategy Paper as "it is depressing to see the use of an unknown and unquantifiable concept "illegal immigrants" as a justification for failure to promote integration policies for the Community's long resident third country nationals."[406]

406 ILPA, *supra* note 328.

Also, the stepping up of controls is the direct consequence of the desire to create a frontier-free EU zone, which, it is claimed, requires a set of compensatory measures.

The restrictive system so created or under elaboration, can only efficiently work if those, *few*, who are legally admitted, and those who are lawfully present in the Union are protected *while*, on the contrary, those who held an illegal position as regards the right of entry, stay or work, are excluded and expelled. "The objective is to realise the area of freedom...fully taking into account the principles of the respect of human rights...to this end, increased efficiency in the security of the external borders and in combating illegal immigration will be required".[407]

It seems that the creation of an area of freedom naturally requires a severe parallel control system which often leads to the forced return of TCNs to their countries of origin.

But in the efforts to ensure the efficacy of such system of controls, these measures do not take into due account the human rights dimension of the problems related to illegal immigration. The tougher and stricter rules have in fact often made it impossible for migrants and asylum seekers to reach the European Union and for those already within its boundaries to legalise their position, when irregular.

IX.2 Migratory flows: Are the pull and push factors over?

The main problem when dealing with migration and, in particular, with illegal immigration is determined by the fact that, although caused by economic and social factors, it is generally addressed politically. As Collinson points out "illegal immigration probably fits the traditional models more easily than any other kind of international migration".[408] But as seen above, migratory flows respond to push and pull factors. Both factors are extremely important. Even in the eventuality that pull factors in Europe are over, the fact that the situation in the sending-migrants countries has not changed in that direction, means that migration pressures to Europe will continue at least in the short term.

However, the situation is far more complicated. As regards the *pull factors* in the Member States Van Amersfoort observes:

407 Council document, Draft Action Plan on establishing an Area of Freedom, Security and Justice, *supra* note 4.

408 Collinson S., *Europe and International Migration*, Pinter Publishers, 1993, 14.

"The State is not a homogenous entity: there are different interests in the society at large and even within the State bureaucracy itself. The multitude of parties prevents the formulation of a long-term regulation policy and interferes with the effective implementation of measures adopted".[409]

Often, Member States' governments and people in Europe feel that "the boat is full" and no more migrants can be admitted into the EU. Accordingly, those with an illegal status must be repatriated to their countries of origin but many sectors in the economy actually benefit from the presence of irregular workers. In many areas, "some employers find illegal immigrants an adaptable, hard working and uncomplaining workforce which is flexible, insecure and easily dispensable. Therefore, from these employers' point of view, illegal migrant workers are the ideally exploitable source of labour: low paid, unorganised and uncomplaining".[410] Agricultural economies with strong informal sectors, especially those in Southern Europe, seem to benefit the most from such presence and therefore make the demand for migrants, who when illegal are even more welcomed as they are deprived of any rights.

Governments, therefore, on the one hand, have adopted strong measures to stabilise the migratory flows of foreign labour or reduce them to a minimum but, on the other, since the irregular migrants are often a benefit for the rapid growth and competition of the domestic market, those measures have not been rigidly enforced. In particular, Southern European members, that only recently have become immigration countries, seem to allow the exploitation of the migration population to boost the economy and narrow the economic gap with the other Member States.

However, the official position at EU level, as seen above, is that none of the Member State is pursuing an active immigration policy. Officially, governments in the European Union have adopted very restrictive measures as regards admission. Southern countries as well have recently adopted immigration provisions to deal with their new status of immigration countries in line with the EU's official position. But migrants denied legal entry or the right to stay and work in the host country are likely to resort to illegal means to reach these objectives.

---

409 Van Amersfoort H., "Migration: The Limits of Governmental Control", *New Community*, 1996, 22(2), 250-251.

410 Wihtol de Wenden C., "The Absence of Rights: the Position of Illegal immigrants", in Layton-Henry Z. (eds), *The Political Rights of Migrant Workers in Western Europe*, Sage Publications, 1990, 27.

As a matter of fact, although very difficult to evaluate, the number of TCNs in an illegal position whether with respect to their entry, stay or work status, is generally increasing in the Union.

Obviously, no precise data on irregular migrants are available but their number is estimated to be around two million. Most irregular migrants seem to be concentrated in Southern European countries like Spain, Italy and Greece, due to these countries' geographical position and to their short experience as immigration-countries. Combating illegal immigration has become a major challenge in Member States' domestic and security policies.

Member States started co-operating in the 1970s, aware that given the international dimension of the problem a common answer was needed.

Furthermore, the abolition of the internal frontiers due to the completion of the Internal Market has required a common approach to all matters related to movements of people within and from outside the European Union. Once the objective of the Internal Market is achieved, immigration loses its national dimension and immediately becomes a common matter. Policies adopted by one member do indeed directly affect the rest of the Union's members.

The fear that more liberal policies could lead to a greater flow of migrants towards one state instead of another has led all Members to gradually adopt more and more restrictive measures. At European level, since such co-operation has began (1970s) the approach has been increasingly restrictive. Such an approach has been maintained although major changes were produced firstly by means of the Maastricht Treaty (1992) and recently through the Amsterdam Treaty (1997). The communitarisation of the area related to immigration envisaged in the Amsterdam Treaty does not imply a change in dealing with these subjects but a further confirmation. The creation of an area of freedom, security and justice needs more controls and policing.

The controls are carried out externally at the External Border but also inside Member States' territories. Indeed, checks at the former internal frontiers are forbidden but internal controls are still allowed.

According to the Strategy Paper "a model of concentric circles of migration policy could replace that of "fortress Europe." For obvious reasons, the Schengen States currently lay down the most intensive control measures. Their neighbours (essentially the associated States and perhaps also the Mediterranean area) should gradually be linked into a similar system which should be brought increasingly to line with the first circle's standards, particularly with regard to visas, border controls and readmission policies. A third circle of States (CIS area, Turkey and North Africa) will then concentrate primarily on transit checks and combating facilitator networks, and a fourth circle (Middle East, China, black Africa) on eliminating push factors."[411] The Paper continues "In the system as a whole, meeting the obligations arising in each respective role should have positive consequences for the country concerned: for example, the second circle must meet Schengen standards as a precondition for EU membership; for the third circle, intensified economic cooperation is linked to the fulfilment of their obligations; and the fourth circle, the extent of development aid granted can be assessed on that basis".[412]

The partial failure of control programmes so far has required a system of "concentric circles": the shift from the concept of fortress Europe to a system of fortifications whereby every non EU-country has a role to play. Their efforts will be rewarded in different forms from accession to the European Union to accession to international development programmes. In practice, Member States have already set up such a system of fortifications.

Once again, whether directly or indirectly, the new measures are likely to have a stronger impact on certain migrants, in particular those belonging to racial and ethnic minority groups, categorisable as Blacks, and especially female migrants. The discretionary powers, as seen so far, of the Member States to privilege some migrants and discourage others, have been shown to have very negative consequences on these categories of migrants. This latter group of migrants or would-be migrants is also the target of the provisions analysed in this last part of the research.

IX.3 CONTROLS ON ENTRIES

The controls carried out at the borders or in the countries of origin of the flows represent a desperate attempt to stop migrants from illegally entering the Union. But it is worth noting that, although the number of clandestine migrants is rising, the great majority of illegal migrants within the Union enter legally and then overstay or work without permission. By the stepping up of controls at the borders, Member States aim at limiting the illegal entry of clandestine migrants, on the one hand, and try to reduce the number of potential illegal TCNs, on the other.

Member States are presently caught in a very difficult position. As argued above, the majority of TCNs in an illegal position enter the Union through a tourist or a short stay visa, when inside they overstay and illegally start a new life in the host country. Once they are settled the procedure to expel them is difficult, expensive and unpopular. Examples of mobilisation of the public opinion in the

411 Draft Strategy Paper *supra* note 311.
412 Draft Strategy Paper *supra* note 311.

Member States against plans of forced repatriation of TCNs are frequent. For instance, in the summer 1996, in France, governmental efforts to deport hundreds of undocumented Africans migrants, "sans papiers", became a national crisis when some of these migrants occupied a Parisien church. Other examples are daily news all around Europe. However, "public and publicised opinion...oscillates between the desire for humanitarian solutions in individual cases and the call for more rigidity towards potential migrants in general."[413]

In general, therefore, even if declared illegal, TCNs have a few chances of not being expelled for humanitarian reasons. In particular, asylum seekers who do not qualify as refugees according to the Geneva Convention are often granted leave to stay.

This situation explains *why* major efforts are made to create an unreachable fortress Europe. These measures are elaborated in order to prevent entry or sometimes to discourage some specific migrants from even approaching Europe. "An effective entry control concept cannot be based simply on controls at the border but must cover every step taken by a third country national from the time he begins his journey to the time he reaches his destination".[414] This restrictive policy is often discriminatory and based on prejudice against TCNs belonging to racial and ethnic minority groups and it disregards the most basic human rights concern, namely that protection must be guaranteed to TCNs seeking asylum.

As regards the controls, Member States have elaborated a very intensive system of successive barriers, "concentric circle theory", in order to prevent entry. For many TCNs who happen to belong to a racial and ethnic minority group deemed as undesirable, reaching Europe has become an impossible task.

In general Blacks from Africa and South-East Asia are the most unwanted.

Many controls are carried out *in* the departure countries *before* the arrival of the TCN at the Union's external frontiers,. The first important filter is represented by the requirement of a visa to enter the Union for nationals of certain third countries. The analysis of the EU visa policy has already been the object of discussion in section VII.5. Member States have commonly agreed by Regulation 574/99 to introduce an integrated partial system related to visas. Notwithstanding the existence of different instruments, the often strict requirements to obtain a visa to travel to Europe can work as a first filter and a barrier. In fact, the majority of immigrant-sending countries are included on the visa list (see annex II). Again, it should be remembered that the greatest number of countries included in the

413 Münz R., "A Continent of Migration: European Mass Migration in the Twentieth Century", *New Community*, 1996, 22(2), 201-226.

414 Draft Strategy Paper *supra* note 311.

visa list are Black countries. Besides economic considerations, i.e. Black countries are generally a big reserve of emigrants, there is a high degree of white ethnocentrism in the decision to require a visa for the nationals of these countries. The fear of being swamped by immigrants who threaten the dominant culture is very strong. The assumption is that in order to maintain the right equilibrium between EC nationals and the extra-Community population inside the Union and, at the same time, to prevent racism and xenophobia, measures must be elaborated to keep the number of Black foreigners very low in the host countries. Few say it loudly but many are convinced of it. Visa requirements are the first barrier TCNs, mostly Blacks, encounter in the long way to Western Europe. As often in this area, cooperation among Member States has constantly improved to combat unauthorised immigration. On April 1999, the Council adopted a Recommendation for the detection of false or falsified documents in the visa departments of representations abroad and in the offices of domestic authorities dealing with the issue or extension of visas[415] where the Member States agree on improving the conditions for issuing visas, in particular, by ensuring that staff are increasingly better trained to detect false or falsified documents in order to prevent document abuse when third country nationals enter and stay in the territory of the Member States.

Furthermore, as far as visas are concerned, in 1996, the Council adopted a Recommendation relating to local consular cooperation regarding visas.[416] Waiting for an integrated visa policy to be adopted at EU level, it is for individual Member States to issue visas to TCNs. By means of this Recommendation, it is clear, Member States try to control and prevent clandestine immigration. This Recommendation has been analysed in section VII.5.6, but here it should be noted that it contained clear indications of the effort to control and prevent clandestine migration. For this goal "consular services should exchange information to help determine the good faith of visa applicants and reputation". It appears that an examination of the real intentions has become necessary given the number of those TCNs that enter the Union by legal means thanks to a transit or short stay visa but with secondary aims, with the intention, on the contrary, to immigrate into the Union. But this is a very interesting provision as it could introduce a highly subjective discriminatory criteria when issuing visas which can be used by officials to discriminate certain TCNs on the basis of their physical appearance. At this stage, a TCN suffering discrimination is judicially unprotected. Furthermore, measures to control migratory flows by stepping up the checks carried out in the departure countries were agreed in the Council in the Joint Position on pre frontier assistance

415 OJ 1999 C 140/1.

416 Council Recommendation relating to local cooperation regarding visas, *supra* note 356.

and training assignments.[417] There are examples of travellers with valid visas who have been denied passage without any plausible reason. It was decided that taking into account that checks carried out at embarkation on flights to Member States would be a useful contribution to the aim of combating unauthorised immigration by TCNs, specialist officers could, in agreement with the competent authorities of the third country concerned, assist the officers who carry out the controls. Such assistance assignments may be of varying duration. For this purpose, a list of airports at which joint assignments are to be carried out on a temporary or permanent basis is to be drawn up.

Since the main objective is the fight against illegal immigration, these specialist officers are likely to be placed in those third countries that are the main reserve of potential illegal migrants. There will therefore be a great concentration in developing countries. It is hard to imagine this sort of cooperation in departure countries such as Canada, Australia or the United States. A Black TCN travelling to Europe after obtaining a visa which implies that the good faith and reputation tests have been satisfied, must pass the checks of both nationals and EU officers. Again, it is very likely that more severe controls will be based of the physical appearance of the traveller with great discrimination of Black TCNs.

At least, it is to be hoped that the severity of these controls will lessen the pressure on carriers.

IX.3.1 Carriers' liability

In the desire to control the flows, Member States are shifting immigration controls from the public to the private sector. Measures which envisage fining carriers for failure to carry out proper controls on foreigners were foreseen in the External Border Convention and in the Schengen Agreements. The proposed External Borders Convention would have imposed penalties for carriers transporting foreigners without the requisite documentation (Article 14) and it would have obliged the carrier to return a person to the State from which the clandestine migrant was transported if admission were refused.[418] These provisions have been commonly criticised. First of all, they are against the Chicago Convention on International Civil Aviation which foresees that its members shall not fine operators in the event that passengers are found inadmissible, unless there is evidence to suggest that the carrier was negligent in taking precautions to the end

417 OJ 1996 L 281/1.

418 Similar provisions are foreseen by the Schengen Agreement (1990), Article 26.

that the passengers complied with the documentary requirement for entry into the receiving State.[419]

Besides, only the competent authorities should be in the position to decide who may exercise the right of free movement and, most importantly, to apply for asylum.[420] By transferring the burden of the control and of the return to the country of departure, in the case of lack of admission, the end result could be the rise of arbitrary refusals to embark TCNs who for subjective reasons appear not to satisfy the entry requirements. Fears that airlines' decisions are arbitrary and influenced by elements like the appearance of the passenger have shown to be correct.

In his study, Cruz observes that in the carrying out of the controls certain parameters do stand out:

> "The passenger concerned is hardly ever 'white'; frequently, airline staff do not appear to be sufficiently familiar with relevant laws and rules; staff are in a position of authority, so they can assert their stance, however untenable, over the customer, sometimes even if they know they are wrong; calling a superior may trigger off some response in magnified form, also because the tendency to protect one's own kind becomes a factor; this means that pseudo-ethnic bonding of airline staff vs. customer actually reinforces ethnic prejudices."[421]

This discretionary power conferred upon airline staff is less acceptable as supervision of the decisions is not foreseen and consequently TCNs are left judicially unprotected in the case of refusal of embarkment as they cannot take any action against the carrier. Effort are presently being made to harmonise Member States' laws on carriers' liability.

The proposed External Borders Convention and the Schengen Agreements envisaged the harmonisation of these measures and some Member States have implemented these measures into their national law.

Instead of abolishing the responsibility for carriers, the way undertaken in the Union is that of training airline staff as "improving the checks carried out on embarkation by airline staff is a useful instrument in combating unauthorised migration by TCNs".[422] Accordingly, airline staff should be trained in the prin-

---

419 See O' Keeffe D., "Reflection on a European Immigration Policy", in Korella G.D. & Twomey P.M. (eds), *supra* note 168, 22.

420 See EP, Resolution on the incompatibility of passport checks carried out by certain airlines with Article 7a of the EC Treaty, OJ 1994 C 91/316.

421 Cruz A., *Shifting Responsibility: Carriers' Liability in the Member States of the European Union and North America*, Trentham Books Limited, 1995.

422 Council document, Draft Council Act adopting a Joint Action on the training of airline staff, 4617/95.

ciples and the rules of entry as well as methods of checking the validity of the documents required to enterthe Union in a sort of duplication of the immigration authorities. The Action Plan adopted by the Council and the Commission,[423] lists among the priorities to implement the Amsterdam Treaty "further harmonising Member States' laws on carriers' liability" showing that there has not been a change in the area.

IX.3.2 Controls at the external borders

As far as the controls at the external borders are concerned, "the wall has come down, but only a few still dream of a Europe without borders. Much larger is the number of those advocate for more technical border equipment and armed border troops".[424] The proposed External Borders Convention established that "all persons crossing the external frontiers shall do so at authorised crossing points permanently controlled by the Member States".[425] The Schengen Agreement (1990) in Articles 6 to 8 also refers to severe checks at the borders: "Cross-border movement at external borders shall be subject to checks by the competent authorities...checks on persons shall include not only the verification of travel documents and of the other conditions governing entry, residence, work and exit but also checks to detect and prevent threats to the national security and public policy of the Contracting Parties".

The External Border Convention would have imposed penalties for crossing at any point other than those authorised.[426]

Member States agreed to keep the external borders under effective and constant surveillance by mobile units or other appropriate means.[427] Again, the Schengen Agreements also had similar provisions "the competent authorities shall use mobile units to exercise surveillance on external borders between crossing points; the same shall apply to border crossing points outside normal opening hours. This surveillance shall be carried out in such a way as not to encourage people to circumvent the checks at crossing points".[428] Although the External Border Convention was never signed and the Schengen Agreements were in force only in some Member States, all members have slowly moved towards reinforcing the

423 Council document, *supra* note 84.

424 Mynz R., "Where did they all come from? Typology and Geography of European Mass Migration in the Twentieth Century", *European Population Conference*, Milano 4-8-Settembre 1995.

425 Article 2 of the External Border Convention.

426 Article 2 of the External Border Convention.

427 Article 3 of the External Border Convention.

428 Article 6 of the Schengen Agreement (1990).

surveillance of their borders so as to reduce the entry of clandestine migrants into their territory to a minimum level.

> "In fact a series of Western countries have deployed armed forces along the borders formerly protected by the Iron Curtain. Where this fortification once shielded the West from Eastern immigrants, and Western public opinion was indignant at shooting at would-be migrants and the antipersonnel mines in the border areas, there are now Finnish border patrols, the Swedish coast guard, and Germany's special border police."[429]

Vast amounts of time and money have been dedicated to improving the technology of control at the borders.[430]

Besides this system of successive barriers, which, at least, complicate reaching Europe's external borders for many foreigners, other controls are envisaged at the external frontiers.

Member States have been elaborating the standardisation of documents with validity throughout Europe to ease border officials' work, such as a uniform format of visas, uniform formats for residence permit and others.

Moreover, programmes to improve the preparation of officials have been approved at EU level. Among those, the *Sherlock* programme[431] which was aimed at establishing a framework for training, information, study and exchange to improve officials' familiarity with the techniques applied in the production and checking of identity documents in other Member States. It was absorbed by the *Odysseus* programme[432] which has the more general aim of cooperation in the field of immigrants crossing external borders. Also the *Stop* programme more concerned with the fight against trafficking in human beings,[433] offers a framework for co-operation among officials against illegal entries. Nonetheless, many countries, especially Southern members, are struggling against a "continuous tide" of new illegal arrivals.

---

429 Mynz R., *supra* note 421.

430 For more information see Webber F., *Crimes of Arrival: Immigrants and Asylum-seekers in the New Europe*, Statewatch Publications, 1995.

431 Joint Action introducing a programme of training, exchange and cooperation in the field of identity documents OJ 1996 L 287/7.

432 Proposal for a Council Decision on a Joint Action adopted by the Council introducing a programme of training, exchanges and cooperation in the field of asylum, immigration and crossing of external borders OJ 1997 C 267/74.

433 Joint Action adopted by the Council establishing an incentive and exchange programmeme for persons responsible for combating trade in human beings and the sexual exploitation of children OJ 1996 L 322/7.

IX.4 SUCCESS OF CONTROLS? THE RISE OF ILLEGAL IMMIGRATION

Control policies have become a high priority in the field of immigration. Although important annual resources are designated to development aid towards third countries, major efforts, in terms of money and persons involved, are dedicated to enforce such legislation.

> "In order to ensure an orderly immigration system within the European Union, all possibilities for circumventing the immigration rules must be excluded or provisions must be made for appropriate penalties".[434]

In this respect, the draft Strategy Paper reconfirms this tendency and states "the measures taken should range from applying a penal and police policy of zero tolerance towards those who facilitate illegal immigration, to effectively confiscating any proceeds, seizing all assets used in facilitating and preventing anyone from enjoying the rewards of such activities".

Despite the increasing and toughening of the controls carried out by Member States both in the countries of departure and at Member States' borders, illegal immigration into Western Europe continues. It seems that immigrants denied legal means of entry do not hesitate in resorting to illegality in order to enter into the Union.

As noted above, only a minority actually enters the European Union illegally, but the number is growing.

The wide range of controls aimed at stopping illegal entries into the EU are too often ineffective thus increasing Member States frustration as they face a real impossibility of halting migratory flows into the EU. Considering that the vast majority of this illegal migrant population is made up of "visible" nationals of developing countries with a different ethnicity (not for instance by poor US citizens), the failure to regulate the flows has seriously increased national xenophobic attitudes.

As discussed above, controls to *save* the Fortress Europe from migratory flows in reality only make reaching Europe more difficult and dangerous. Clandestine immigrants, indeed, resort to illegal and very hazardous forms of travel.

It should be noted that apart from very few cases where TCNs organise their illegal entry into the Union individually, the vast majority of clandestine migrants

434 Council document, Supplementing the Convention on rules for the admission of third-country nationals to the Member States of the European Union, 9584/98.

relies upon international networks. They normally buy a complete "package" in the country of departure which normally includes travel, accommodation and work in the country of destination.

Smuggling people has become a very important business. Criminal organisations take advantage of the economic hardship of emigrants, who are prepared to pay huge amounts of money to escape desperate situations and be smuggled in. It is evident that the tougher the controls, the higher the price.

This situation has already caused a large number of deaths. Many migrants have already died or have been seriously injured as a result of being transported to Europe in dangerous and inhuman conditions by unscrupulous persons for profit.[435] Daily news report about migrants who are promised entry and who are then left near the border coasts of the Union where many, generally the most vulnerable such as women and children, meet their death. Networks that organise the illegal entry for immigrants are concerned with making money and not with the safety of the system of transportation.[436] These networks, because this trade is highly profitable, have become more and more powerful and are using more channels and devices to smuggle in migrants. The fight against illegal immigration represents a top priority. In Tampere, the European Council stressed "the need for more efficient management flows at all their stages.' In particular, it called "for the development, in close cooperation with countries of origin and transit, of information campaigns on the actual possibilities for legal immigration, and for the prevention of all forms of trafficking in human beings." Finally, it was agreed "to tackle at its source illegal immigration; especially by combating those who engage in trafficking in human beings and economic exploitation of migrants."

IX.5 Trafficking in human beings: a growing form of illegal immigration

Trafficking in human beings is neither a new phenomenon in Europe nor world wide. Since the beginning of this century measures have been taken at international level to combat this odious trade.[437] However, only in the nineties, has this trade attracted the attention it deserves at EU institutional level. The Parliament, the Commission and Council have approached this area from different angles of

435 EP, Resolution on illegal migrants, OJ 1997 C 115/173.

436 Statewatch, *supra* note 318.

437 See on this point International Movement against all Forms of Discrimination and Racism (IMADRIS), *Strengthening the International Regime against the Traffic in Women,* A Working Paper presented to the Working Group on Contemporary Slavery, May 1998.

analysis. Although outside the coverage of the present research, trade in persons is becoming a major concern for specialists in the immigration field not only because trafficking in human beings is closely linked to clandestine immigration but also due to the concerns that this trade represents a fundamental breach of human rights.

The Council has approached the area from the angle of illegal immigration and has adopted a rigid stance against it since the networks that organise the trafficking are becoming more and more powerful and dangerous – the profits are often reinvested in other criminal activities – and the number of clandestine migrants has risen. The European Commission and, in particular, the EP have been concerned with the effects on the victims of the trade, which both institutions regard as a serious breach of fundamental human rights.

In this area, special attention must be given to the delicate position of women. *Women* seem to be the most affected by this trade.

As discussed in other parts of this research, female migrants must face the double discrimination due to their gender and their belonging to an ethnic minority group. They are, when admitted, limited in the types of work they can perform: normally low-paid, low-skilled and low-status jobs. Immigration policies elaborated in Western Europe encourage, in practice, white highly skilled migrants. Women who face the impossibility of immigrating *legally* into the European Union, often, do not hesitate to find illegal means to elude the stricter controls. This explains why many women are caught in trade networks. In particular, because while many occupations are closed off in Europe for female migrants, others, such as domestic labour, entertainment and the sex industry, are wide open.[438]

Trade in human beings, particularly women, has become a common practice outside the regular international labour migration channels and it has grown since the fall of the Berlin wall. According to the International Organisation for Immigration (IOM) "the trafficking of women from East to West is increasing rapidly. This form of exploitation and abuse of human rights is no longer confined to women from developing countries...trafficking in women from East to West is increasing because it is easier and cheaper for traffickers to bring women from Central and Eastern Europe to Western Europe than to recruit women from developing countries. Women do not have to travel so far and legal entry as a tourist is easy, as visa restrictions no longer apply to many (although not all) citizens from Central and Eastern Europe".[439]

---

438 Ibidem.

439 IOM, *Trafficking and Prostitution: the Growing Exploitation of Migrant Women from Central and Eastern Europe*, 1995. Several IOM studies examine the growing problem of trafficking in women to Western Europe. Among those IOM, *Trafficking in Women from the Dominican Republic for*

TCNs, especially women, are therefore recruited to work in the European Union from elsewhere in the world and find themselves subject to abuse and slavery and, are often, forced to work in brothels. Criminal networks, whether with deceit or not, bring women into the Union and, given their illegal position, have complete control over them. The victims of this ignominious trade, afraid of and often blackmailed by traffickers, menaced with expulsion and threatened to be humiliated in front of their families, rarely escape and denounce their situation to the police.[440]

In the past, attention was focused on the fight against clandestine migrants and that has made this trafficking so lucrative: "...the risks for the traffickers are not great. Sentences against traffickers are light, and there are few successful convictions. This is partly because many countries deport victims immediately, thereby losing valuable witnesses".[441] In fact, trafficked migrants, when caught by the police were often automatically expelled from the territory of the European Union to their country of origin.

Nowadays, Member States are aware that the only effective way to combat illegal immigration is by directing their actions against the organisers of the illegal trade and not against its victims. Immediate deportation of trafficked migrants will not prevent future trafficking, it will only make illegal migrants more dependent on traffickers.[442]

Member States have also recognised the importance of cooperation in this area because "trafficking often involves persons of several nationalities working in different European countries who can shift their activities from one country to the next at short notice."[443] National measures to tackle this problem are insufficient and, therefore, greater international co-operation is required. Accordingly, cooperation among national competent officials has been set up or improved.

The commitment to fight trafficking in human beings is now contained in many important documents adopted in the area of immigration.

Sexual Exploitation, 1996; IOM, *Trafficking in Women to Italy for Sexual Exploitation*, 1996; IOM, *Trafficking in Women to Belgium for Sexual Exploitation*, 1996; IOM, *Trafficking in Women to the Netherlands for Sexual Exploitation*, 1996; IOM, *Trafficking in Women to Switzerland for Sexual Exploitation*, 1996; IOM, *Trafficking in Women to Austria for Sexual Exploitation*, 1996.

440 IOM (1995) ibidem.

441 Ibidem.

442 Ibidem.

443 Ibidem.

IX.5.1 Regulation prior to Maastricht

Until recently, there was no specific legal basis, under either the EC Treaty or the EU Treaty, to fight trafficking in human beings, but since the trade in persons, although with specific features, is to be considered closely linked to illegal immigration, this area was incidentally covered.

Measures were first taken in 1992 by the Ministers responsible for Immigration through the Recommendation regarding Practices followed by Member States on expulsion (London, 30 November-1 December 1992)[444] in order to enable legal procedures against people who deliberately facilitate, or try to facilitate the entry or passage, who deliberately offer accommodation to illegal foreigners, especially, those who perform such acts for payment or as an organisation. The approach of the Member States was clear: a very strict and severe position against the traffickers had to stop the trade itself.

However, under the provisions of the 1992 Recommendation, it seems that Member States went too far as it must be assumed that people who also act on *humanitarian grounds*, and are not part of any criminal organisation, are reserved the same treatment as those people who are involved in illegal immigration rackets. Only those who smuggle people into the European Union for their benefit and part of criminal networks should be the target of these measures.

Otherwise, once again TCNs pay the price for this policy. In Germany, for instance, there is a criminalisation of taxi-drivers who carry undocumented immigrants as passengers. This obliges taxi-drivers to turn into unwilling immigration control agents. Many taxi drivers are indeed likely to refuse to pick up foreign-looking passengers to avoid incurring in fines or worse imprisonment. Lacking any immigration control expertise, they will make their decision on the sole appearance of the passenger, affecting mainly TCNs.[445]

TCNs are also more likely to suffer from the provisions contained in the 1992 Recommendation because it was agreed "considerations should also given to the question whether it would be appropriate to have the power to expel people subject to immigration/alien provisions who have been involved in the facilitation, harbouring or employment of illegal immigrants." This means that TCNs, even when they are not part of a criminal network if caught facilitating, harbouring or employing clandestine migrants are expelled, if so it is agreed, while nationals would not be subject to such a punishment.

---

444 For the text see Bunyan T., *Key Texts on Justice and Home Affairs in the European Union*, *supra* note 389, 77.

445 See on this point Campaign Against Racism and Fascism, 1999, No 48, 5.

Special attention was paid to the problem related to illegal immigration into the Member States, outside the Community framework, under the Schengen Agreements. Therefore, the transportation of illegal aliens to the Schengen territory for the pursuit of gain was to be made a statutory offence in each of the countries concerned. Article 27 (1) stated "the Contracting Parties undertake to impose appropriate penalties on any person who, for purpose of gain assists or tries to assist an alien to enter or reside within the territory of one of the Contracting Parties contrary to the laws of that Contracting Party on the entry and residence of aliens". Here, the reference made to "purpose of gain" better defined the meaning of traffickers and it reduced the number of those to be prosecuted. However, it would have been advisable to indicate exactly how by the expression "purpose of gain" sould be interpreted. Again, it is difficult to draw a clear dividing line.

> "There is no straight divide between humanitarian and commercial trafficking – for example, two German priests who were recently imprisoned in Germany for escorting a Kurdish refugee into Denmark charged nothing. However, an Iranian shepherd, Turkish fisherman or Polish taxi driver might charge a fare across a border: the question is whether they should therefore be classed as international criminals".[446]

However, in the elaboration of common rule in the area of immigration, Member States, whether under EC/EU law or under intergovernmental cooperation, have been more concerned with measures directed at controlling and stopping migratory movements towards the Union than the impact of such measures on TCNs.

IX.5.2 Maastricht and post-Maastricht regulation

The Maastricht Treaty, which brought the most relevant aspects of immigration under EC/EU competence, did not include a specific reference to the fight against trafficking in human beings. This did not hamper the discussion of these themes at EU level and the elaboration and adoption of specific measures. Targeted measures were envisaged in the Recommendation on trade in human beings for the purpose of prostitution, adopted in 1993. The Council, in this Recommendation, stressed the importance of cooperation among competent national authorities to fight the trade in human beings for prostitution but it was also decided that the "work carried out in this area must be extended and intensified in the area of

---

446 Morrison J., *The Cost of Survival. The Trafficking of Refugees to the UK*, The Refugee Council, July 1998, 1.

administrative and police cooperation, law enforcement, immigration and entry into national territories". Importance was also given to the collection and distribution of information in this field in the Union and abroad from the countries from which the victims of prostitution networks come. The 1993 Recommendation focused on the prevention, control and fight against trafficking in persons mainly for the purpose of prostitution but it neglected to consider the victim's side. As noted above, traffickers bring aliens to the Union by deceit or by using the force to exploit them in the black economy. Trafficked aliens are the victims and they should be treated as such. However, the 1993 Recommendation did not provide any assistance or rehabilitation for these victims.

On the contrary, the EP and the Commission have paid attention to the victims when addressing this problem. As far as the EP is concerned, it adopted a Resolution on trafficking in human beings,[447] in February 1996, wherein it stressed the importance of fighting against such a trade as this has become a preferred area of activity for international crime. It affirmed the importance to grant protection to the illegal migrants, the very victims of this trade and, at the same time, it called on the Member States in order to include the explicit penalisation of this crime in their respective penal codes. A few months later the European Commission presented a Communication to the Council and the EP on trafficking in women for the purpose of sexual exploitation.[448] As stated by the same Commission the purpose of this Communication was to stimulate a broad policy debate, and to promote a coherent European approach on these issues. The Commission is more focused than the EP in the Communication and it considers only women and it also limits its analysis to trafficked women for the purpose of exploitation but it shares as the EP the same humanitarian concerns: "Any initiative to combat this from of international organised crime must devote central attention to the devastating effect it has on the victims...The Communication will thus be limited to the particularly serious abuse of human right which is involved in trafficking for sexual purposes". The European Commission also analysed the problem related to the trade in persons in the Communication incorporating equal opportunities for women and men into all Community policies and activities.[449] In this last Communication, the Commission stressed the importance of the prevention of the trafficking of women in prostitution networks, as well as on the adoption of appropriate measures in order to develop programmes aimed at reintegrating the victims into society.

---

447 EP, Resolution on trafficking in human beings, *supra* note 367.

448 COM (96) 0567 final.

449 *Supra* note 85.

Both the EP and the Commission concentrate more on the violence suffered by women and, in general, by the victims of the trade.

But apart from considerations that action must be taken in order to stop a trade which often implies sexual abuse, there is a growing concern, at EU level, that trafficked aliens are an increasing part of the illegal migrant population in Europe.

From this perspective, the JHA Council adopted a Joint Action concerning action to combat trafficking in human beings and sexual exploitation of children,[450] in February 1997. This Joint Action is a further step towards regulating this area and limiting the illegal entry of trafficked human beings.

The Joint Action has a broader personal scope which covers all trafficked persons, regardless of their sex or the reasons they have been trafficked. It does not make any distinction between trafficked persons and, therefore, it does not include only women. But unlike the EP Resolution it stresses the sexual objective of the trade, excluding others that are just as important. It is indeed confined to trafficking only for the purpose of sexual exploitation.[451] It is worth noting that defining the term "traffic in women" is a difficult task. According to IOM "there seems to be a great deal of confusion about what precisely is meant by the term...the lack of clarity in use of terminology is partly because trafficking covers a wide variety of situations, not all of which involve illegal migration or exploitation...confusion over the use of the term "trafficking" is exacerbated by the fact that it does not necessarily refer to a situation in which the person trafficked has been exploited or can be described as a victim... "trafficking in women" however is usually used to describe extreme cases wherein fundamental human rights and freedoms are violated".[452]

According to a note from the EUROPOL Working Group to the K4 Committee "traffic in human beings means subjection of a person to the real and illegal sway of other persons by using violence or by abuse of authority or intrigue."[453]

While taking into account the great number of situations that could be covered by the term "trafficking in women", so that a restriction of the scope of the Joint Action was necessary, such a strict limitation, absent in the EP Resolution, must nevertheless be criticised because although trafficking mainly involves TCNs, largely women, for the purpose of prostitution, pornography or sex tourism, it

---

450 OJ 1997 L 63/2.

451 According to EP "trafficking in human beings should be defined as any act or any activity aimed at drawing a person into prostitution, pornography or a degrading job or at keeping them in those situation, possibly by taking them away from their homes either within or outside the country, sometimes with their consent or by means of deceit, threats, coercion or other methods EP, Report on trafficking in human beings, A4-0326/95.

452 IOM (1995) *supra* note 436.

453 Council document, Trafficking in human beings, 8663/2/97.

is also directed at recruiting immigrants to work in degrading conditions in factories, farms, the hotel trade, restaurants and even in households.

The Joint Action argues that trafficking in human beings for the purpose of sexual exploitation by using coercion, deceit or by abuse of authority or other pressure must be made a criminal offence punishable by effective, proportionate and dissuasive criminal penalties. Although it would have been advisable to include more specific provisions of what had to be considered as a criminal offence, at least, by considering trafficking as a crime many Member States have been forced to modify their national legislation in order to recognise traffickers as criminals and prosecute them.

According to the Commission,[454] all Member States have presently criminalized trafficking in women.

Finally, a clear distinction is made between the victims and the criminals. The most significant element is the right to a provisional residence status to be granted, although only in *appropriate* cases, to the victims of this trade in order to enable them to protect their rights. No mention is made of the possibility envisaged in the EP Resolution to the right for trafficked migrants to remain in the territory of the Member State concerned for humanitarian reasons where repatriation could seriously endanger their lives. This is a particularly sensitive area due to the many interest involved. From the *human rights perspective*, the protection of the victims would require a permit to stay in the host country as after years of sexual slavery returning to the country of origin could be the source of more traumas and problems for the victims. Many TCNs, especially trafficked women, often come from poor and traditional societies that taking into account their past experiences may exclude and marginalise them. But, nowadays, Member States are struggling to reduce, not to say stop, immigration, so granting a residence right to the victims of this intolerable trade is against their actual immigration policies especially because this right could easily be misused by immigrants and become another channel to elude stricter immigration rules. Member States have demonstrated great concern in respect of this traffic but only in the perspective of stopping a new channel of illegal immigration. From the analysis of the provisions contained in the Council Joint Action, in particular compared to the proposed Resolution of the EP, it is evident that the measures which adopted are meant to be an instrument to tackle such a new channel while the EP proposed measures stressed the importance of readjustment and rehabilitation of the victims.

The fight against trafficking in human beings is considered, at present, a primary goal of the co-operation under Title VI. JHA Ministers have in several

---

454 Council Press Release, 8654 (Press 168).

occasions, affirmed their commitment to maximising co-operation in the fight against trade in human beings[455] and to take all necessary measures to protect those most vulnerable in the society. More importantly, since the trade in persons has been recognised as a problem with distinctive features in the wider area of illegal immigration, the TEU, as revised by the Amsterdam Treaty, expressly includes among its objectives the achievement an area of freedom, security and justice, the fight against trafficking in human beings (Article 29 TEU) and it provides a legal basis for action under the EU framework.

Whether from the angle of the violence suffered by the victims or only to tackle illegal immigration in this new form, Member States at EU level, are investing great efforts to combat such a trade.

IX.5.3 Development of cooperation among national officials

Member States still consider trafficking in human beings as a problem which requires repressive and tougher measures, more control and cooperation. Since 1994, Member States have agreed, in order to improve international cooperation, to include the fight against the trade in persons in the Convention establishing EUROPOL. Only on 1 July 1999, did EUROPOL become fully operational, but before that date competence was accorded to EUROPOL Drug Unit (EDU).

Efforts have also been made to improve cooperation among officials to combat this trade. A specific programme *Stop*[456] (Sexual Trafficking in Persons) has been created to ensure a framework of cooperation among officials to work in the exchange of information and training. The *Daphne* programme set up by the Commission and designed to finance measures relating to violence against women, young persons and children, can also be used as a tool to help the victims of the trade in persons. Within a more general programme of cooperation among officials in the area of immigration "*Odysseus*" – which aims at establishing the training, exchanges and cooperation in the field of asylum, immigration and crossing of external borders – it was agreed in the 1999 programme that measures had to be taken to prevent trafficking in human beings.

455 See Agence Europe No 6821, 28.9.96, No 6862, 28.11.96 and No 6865, 2/3.12.96.
456 *Supra* note 318.

IX.6 THE EXTERNAL RESPONSE TO ILLEGAL IMMIGRATION: THE READMISSION AGREEMENTS

In the nineties, migration issues became an integral element of the external policy of the Member States. The concept of an "integrated approach" is elaborated to respond to migration pressures: "a wide variety of foreign, external economic, development, social and home affairs policy measures need to be combined for this purpose."[457] According to the "concentric circle" approach suggested in the draft Strategy Paper, Member States, whether individually or within the EU framework, must reach agreement with the other "circle" countries.

Member States have elaborated and signed agreements with third countries which, at least in principle, are sending-emigrant or transit states, concerning the readmission of irregular migrants as well as other matters. The main element of these agreements is that through them Member States have found a way to externalise the controls on migratory movements. Many Members States have, therefore, initiated negotiations with third countries in order to control, prevent and stop the migratory flows.

There is general consent among the Member States on the necessity to include specific clauses in the text of new mixed agreements to prevent and control migratory flows.[458] Member States have signed important multilateral and bilateral agreements with third countries that oblige these countries to take back those foreigners who have no right to stay in Member States' territory, regardless of their nationality, whether they are nationals of the country concerned or not.

The Agreement on the readmission of illegal immigrants and illegal residents signed in 1991 between Poland and the Schengen States is one of the most important. But other bilateral conventions between Member States and third countries have been signed or are under discussion.[459]

The majority of these agreements have been signed by the Member States and not by the European Community, as such, but the Council nonetheless set out the principles to be used by the Member States as a basis for negotiations

---

457 *Supra* note 312.

458 See Council document, Conclusions on clauses to be inserted in future mixed agreements, 4272/96.

459 In December 1996 Spain concluded an agreement with Morocco to co-operate in the fight against illegal immigration, EL Pais, 22.3.97. In February 1997 Belgium signed a Treaty with Poland to prevent Poland acting as an entry gate into the Union, see Statewatch, 1997, Vol. 7 No 1. Italy signed a readmission agreement with Switzerland in September 1998, Migration News Sheet, October 1998. Italy has also been trying to negotiate an agreement with Albania in order to stop the massive migratory flows of the last few years, La Repubblica 18.3.98.

with third countries on the conclusion of readmission agreements.[460] The Treaty of Amsterdam unequivocally confers competence to the Community to conclude readmission agreements in Article 63 (3) EC, which includes among other objectives of a common immigration policy the *repatriation* of persons residing unlawfully in a Member State. The debate as to whether such competence was exclusive or wether it could be shared with the Member States has been clarified by the Presidency of the Union which declared that the Community's responsibility with regard to the conclusion of readmission agreements with third states is not exclusive. This declaration is important only from a political standpoint as the Presidency, it is known, does not have any competence to define EC's external powers. A Member State can continue to conclude readmission agreements with third states provided that the Community has not concluded with the third state concerned or has not concluded a mandate for negotiating such an agreement. In individual cases, Member States may also conclude bilateral agreements after the conclusion of a Community agreement or after the opening of the negotiations, for instance, where the Community agreement or the negotiating mandate contains only general statements on readmission but one or more Member States require more detailed arrangements on the matter. The Member States may no longer conclude agreements if these are detrimental to existing Community agreements."[461] Such readmission agreements are increasingly seen as a significant contribution to combating illegal immigration, especially, in cases where the lack of an agreement with a third country can hinder the quick and effective return of illegal migrants.

The long-term aim is the creation of a more secure fortress Europe by creating a buffer zone and a system of fortifications at its borders to prevent non-EU countries becoming an open gate to Western Europe. In fact, although each Contracting Party agrees to readmit at the request of another party and without any formality persons who do not, or who no longer, fulfil the conditions in force for entry or residence in its territory, the counterflow will be only one way. It is hard to imagine many European citizens illegally entering or residing in EU's neighbouring countries such as Poland or Morocco.

Readmission clauses are therefore often incorporated in general association and cooperation agreements signed between the Community and third countries.

460 Council Recommendation of 30 November 1994 concerning specimen bilateral readmission agreement between a Member State and a third country, OJ 1996 C 274/20 and Council Recommendation of 24 July 1995 on the guiding principles to be followed in drawing up protocols on the implementation of readmission agreements, OJ 1996 C 274/25.

461 Council Press Release, *supra* note 450.

IX.6.1 Mediterranean countries

As regards the Mediterranean countries the process started back in the 1980s.[462] Some Southern European countries have since then signed formal or informal agreements with their neighbours which envisage the obligation for the Parties to take back illegal migrants. These agreements are of great importance as immigrants from the Maghreb and more generally Northern Africa are a source of anxiety and hostility in Europe for their presumed cultural distance compared to Europeans. Moreover these countries often serve as a gateway for immigration from more distant southern African countries.

IX.6.2 Central and Eastern European Countries

Several Central and Eastern European countries have signed important readmission agreements with the Member States and the Community. However, the approach followed by the Member States towards these states has been more open. Economic reasons seem to justify the different treatment: these countries have managed to adapt to the Western model in only a few years. They have been very receptive to Western European influence and, in less than a decade, have made gigantic steps to becoming market economy democracies so that the migratory flows expected from this part of Europe have not take place. As some authors have highlighted even when movements take place in the European Eastern border "they can be conceived more in terms of mobility than migration[463]". Member States are only partially concerned and threatened by Central and Eastern European countries' nationals moving to the European Union, who they consider as belonging to the European family, but they fear movement from further East from the ex-Soviet republics and Asia. In many CEECs immigration rules still accord a favourable treatment to countries once belonging to the Soviet bloc, much more generous than the one in force between Community members towards those same countries. This is why Member States are pushing CEECs to adopt stricter rules on admission and tougher controls in order to avoid these countries from becoming another "open gate" to the Union. CEECs are required to accept the Community acquis before accession entirely as well as the area related to JHA cooperation. This insistence for the adoption of the EU acquis could create complications, not

---

462 For more information on the evolution of this process, see Collinson S., *Shore to Shore, The Politics of Migration in Euro-Magreb Relations,* Royal Institute International Affairs, 1996.

463 See Wallace C. & Chmouliar O. & Sidorenko E., "Mobility in the Buffer Zone", *New Community,* 1996, 22(2), 258-286. See also Stola D., "The Social and Political context of Migrations between Central Europe and the EU", in Guild E. (ed), *supra* note 115, 139-140.

only because of the enormous costs for these countries in order to seal off their frontiers, but, in particular, because of the resistance of some candidates to adopt EC/EU immigration rules and jeopardise their good relations with the ex-Soviet republics.

In the perspective of the enlargement with Central and Eastern European countries, Member States have signed important accords with the new candidates, which commit these countries to improving their systems of border controls in order to resist to migratory pressures at their borders as well as readmission agreements, taking into account that the Eastern external frontier of the European Union after the accession is to be moved further East.[464]

The result has been the toughening of the controls on migrants by Europe's counterparts: these States want to avoid the burden of accepting illegal migrants or residents back. In particular, Central and Eastern European countries have been seriously toughening, with some exceptions, their immigration policies and adjusting them to the Western European model in order to gain access to the Union.

Other non-EU countries have accepted to adopt much stricter controls at their borders in exchange for development aid and financial support.

IX.7 INTERNAL CONTROLS

As argued at the beginning of this last part of the research, Member States are attempting to create a system where there is no longer a place for illegal migrants.

This explains the gigantic efforts made to adopt measures to control the migrant population as well as to enforce such measures. By means of this policy, whether through *preventive* or *repressive* measures, Member States try to ensure a high level of security in a freer Europe. People must feel free and safe. According to the Draft Action Plan on establishing an area of freedom, security and justice "the Treaty of Amsterdam also opens way to giving "freedom" a meaning beyond free movement of people across the internal borders. It is also freedom to live in a law-abiding environment in the knowledge that public authorities are using everything in their individual and collective power...to combat individuals and contain those who seek to deny or abuse that freedom. Freedom must also be complemented by the full range of fundamental rights, including protection from any form of discrimination..."[465] It seems that in order to reach freedom

464 For more information on this point, see Statewatch, Vol. 7, No 3, 1997.

465 Council document, Draft Action Plan on Establishing an Area of Freedom, Security and Justice, *supra* note 4.

and security, several and continuous controls must be carried out. As regards this process in Europe, Foucher points out:

> "On the one hand, frontier functions are disintegrating in a spatial sense. On the other hand, in certain respects, the entire national territory is now being treated as an expanded frontier zone."[466]

Simultaneously, there has been a *criminalisation* of TCNs whether legal or illegal migrants. Illegal presence in Europe is now a crime in many States it is considered to be a threat to the stability and security of Western European democracies. But this is not always the case. Only a small percentage of the clandestine migrants are involved in criminal activities such as terrorism, drug trafficking and others, which can obviously threaten the well established public order or security or also health of the host country. More often they are the first victims of their illegal status as they are exploited by landlords, employers or criminal networks. But as Foblets recalls:

> "Third country nationals, asylum seekers, drug dealers, criminals and potential terrorists are handled more or less in the same terms".[467]

Therefore as Huysman argues, recently migration and asylum are dominantly governed by a *security logic*: illegal migrants are increasingly seen as a threat to the internal security rather than to the economies of the host States.[468]

The crusade against illegal immigration, which is becoming a serious burden on Member States' finances, has often disregarded the fact that the majority of illegal aliens are "harmless".

It should be noted, however, that this process of criminalisation of the migrant population has been combined by a parallel *racialisation* process. As a matter of fact, it is not the entire migrant population that is suffering for such a stigmatisation. Rather, mainly Black migrants are the target of these security concerns in the Member States. They are therefore most likely to be affected by these policies. Firstly, they make up the vast majority (around 70%) of the whole extra-Community population. Secondly, as seen above, due to the new restrictive rules, many have lost their legal status in the states of residence. Taking into account the fact that the natural consequence of such controls on the irregular

466 Foucher M., The Geopolitics of European Frontiers, in Anderson M. & Bort E., *supra* note 23.

467 Foblets M.C., "Europe and its Aliens after Maastricht. The Painful Move to Substantive Harmonization of Member States' Policies Towards Third-country Nationals", *American Journal of Comparative Law,* 1994, Vol. 42, No 4, 783-805.

468 See Huysman J., *supra* note 109.

position of migrants is expulsion, these new rules could maintain the control on a growing Black community within EU boundaries. It seems a very drastic solution to tackle the problem of assimilation and integration of TCNs inside the Union and a disguised attempt to protect the cultural identity of the host societies threatened by an increasing number of migrants belonging to minority ethnic groups, which are "difficult" to assimilate.

The security argument has been *instrumentalised* so to fight the presence of certain migrants. In particular, concerns have been directed against those considered to be undesirable, because they are non Europeans, in order to keep the homogeneity of Western Europe from changing into a multi-cultural and multi-ethnic society.

Such attempts to regulate immigration risk to fail due to the impossibility of concretely carrying out controls of TCNs.

As regards illegal entrants, individually and under the EU umbrella, Member States have dedicated major energies to stop or, at least, reduce migratory flows towards the Union. But as noted above, many TCNs enter regularly and only afterwards does their presence become unlawful in respect of their right to stay or work.

Indeed, the largest portion of the TCNs illegally present within the Union enter its territory legally with a transit or short-stay visa, often as tourists or students, and then overstay or work without the necessary permission. Many of them are family members, asylum seekers or just economic migrants that resort to illegality in order to escape the restricted immigration regime, slowly introduced from the late eighties. Furthermore, as the EP observes, the same immigration rules enforced in Western Europe have caused the illegality of many migrants as "developments in the immigration laws of certain European Union's Member States have led to a considerable deterioration in the situation of certain immigrants ... and a large number have lost their right of residence and therefore become illegal".[469] In fact, Member States decide the dividing line between a legal and illegal migrant. The adoption of stricter rules has meant that many TCNs who held a legal status or who were able to gain legal status in the host State have suddenly become illegal and lost the possibility to regularise their position.

It is worth noting that, notwithstanding the fact that numbers on the exact presence of the illegal TCN population can only be approximate, there is an over-representation of women and young people among the illegal population. According to Wihtol de Wenden:

---

469 EP, Resolution on expulsion of illegal immigrants, OJ 1996 C 320/198.

> "This suggests that many legally recruited foreign migrants often have difficulty obtaining permission for their wives and children but send for them nevertheless".[470]

Member States have therefore put great emphasis, also, on the fight against illegal migrants within their boundaries. Such a fight is based on the stepping up of internal controls and on expulsion measures. Removal of internal border controls, notably envisaged in the Single European Act, has finally been reached under the Amsterdam Treaty, which has created an area of freedom, security and justice. The Amsterdam Treaty has finally overcome the opposition of the UK[471] to any project that envisaged the elimination on internal barriers and thirteen Member States have finally been able to carry out that project under EC competence. The UK's opting out solution has been regulated by a Protocol annexed to the TEU.

EC citizens, as well as TCNs, are allowed to move freely within the Union. As made clear by the new Title IV, three factors must work simultaneously, namely freedom, security and justice. Freedom must therefore be combined with the other two elements, in particular security requirements. And security reasons seem to justify the stepping up of internal controls.

Member States, therefore, convinced that the suppression of the internal controls could favour the illegal presence of TCNs, have decided that controls at the borders must be abolished *but* national authorities are still empowered to carry out internal checks in order to verify the legal position of TCNs. The elimination of the internal borders and of the formalities to which persons at the crossing points were obliged does not exclude the possibility of carrying out internal controls by the police on foreigners according to national law. It should be underlined that these controls should take the form of spot checks and they may not be carried out in a systematic, arbitrary or unnecessarily restrictive manner.[472] Through these checks national police forced must avoid the spread of crime across Member States but, at the same time, they must control illegal migrants. Controls verify the legal position of aliens in respect of residence and work permits in the state concerned. According to Zolberg:

> "Internal controls are mainly of two kinds: policing the physical presence of foreigners and the more complex undertaking of policing their activities. Among liberal democracies, the first of these entails a very cumbersome process, hemmed in by legal and political constraints, whose overall costs probably outweigh whatever returns are

470 Wihtol de Wenden C., *supra* note 407, 31.

471 The UK and Ireland have been given an opt out solution regulated in two different Protocols.

472 The ECJ restricted the possibility to carry out controls only in a sporadic and unsystematic way. Case 321/87 *Commission v Belgium* [1989] ECR 997.

> achieved. In most instances, the police cannot check individuals except for cause; moreover, since the carrying out checks is very costly, policing must be carried out in an economical manner. Systematic sweeps are therefore ruled out, except in very special circumstances ... A shortcut is available where the 'suspect' group is somatically distinct as, for example, Africans and Asians in a 'white' country ...".[473]

There are deep concerns that the shortcut is taken so that racial and ethnic minority groups will often be harassed with controls *just* because of their foreign appearance, that now becomes as a presumption of illegality. This *evolution* is particularly regrettable as it regards not only national police forces but also other authorities concerned with the controls of the legal status of the TCN worker or resident.

IX.8 Controls on legal workers or residents

As far as internal controls are concerned, Member States have adopted a few recommendations against illegal immigration, In particular, in 1993, the Recommendation concerning checks on and expulsion of third country-nationals residing and working without authorisation[474] and, in 1995, the Recommendation harmonising means of combating illegal immigration and illegal employment and improving the relevant means of control.[475] Both Recommendations are directed at further harmonising the means for checking on foreign nationals to verify their legal position as regards their right to entry, to stay and work in the Union. Among the declared aims is the fight against illegal immigration. Through these controls national authorities must ensure that the position of the migrant concerned is in order.

As well as the external border checks, internal controls have been highly improved. There must be more cooperation and exchange of information among national police forces. For this aim EUROPOL was foreseen by the Maastricht Treaty (Article K.1.9). EUROPOL, it should be noted, is not a European Police force by analogy with the American FBI but a "Union-wide system for exchanging information".[476]

---

473 Zolberg A.R., "Are the Industrialised Countries under Siege", in Luciani G. (ed), *Migration Policies in Europe and the US, supra* note 278, 71.

474 Council document, SN 3017/93. For the text see Bunyan T. (ed), *supra* note 389, 81.

475 OJ 1996 C 5/1.

476 Den Boer M., "Moving between Bogus and Bona Fide: the Policing of Inclusion and Exclusion in Europe" in Miles R. & Tränhardt D., *supra* note 93, 92-111. Also of the same author "Police Cooperation in the TEU: Tiger in a Trojan Horse? *Common Market Law Review*, 32, 1995, 555-578.

The 1993 Recommendation foresees that "measures should be taken with a view to ensuring that third-country nationals do not remain beyond the period for which they have been admitted or given permission to remain and that they do not work without authority to do so". Similar provisions are contained in the 1995 Recommendation.

Any person, now, can be asked to identify himself which implies the obligation to show identity documents.

More dangerously for the privacy of individuals is the fact that the number of computerised data systems to control undesirable TCNs have increased in the last years. Among those, special mention must be made to the Schengen Information System (SIS), which for lack of accord among the Member States has been allocated under the third Pillar of the Union, the European Information System (EIS) drafted on the basis of the SIS, although never agreed, and EUROPOL.

Also Eurodac, a planned EU-wide computerised system can be listed in this section. It was originally created for storing and accessing fingerprints of asylum seekers but it has been extended to include irregular migrants. Article 8 of the proposed Eurodac Convention[477] creates an obligation for each Member State to take the fingerprints of any third country national or stateless person aged fourteen years or over who is caught in connection with an irregular crossing of the border of that Member State with a third country. Article 11 of the Eurodac Convention creates a facility for Member States to use Eurodac if they wish to do so to check whether a person found illegally present within its territory has previously claimed asylum in another Member States. However, Article 11, contrary to Article 8, *does not* create an "obligation or a power in Community legislation for a Member State to fingerprint persons found illegally present within its territory. The Member State in question can only take the fingerprints of the person in question if it is permitted to do so under national law."[478]

Furthermore, controls must be carried out not only by national police forces but also by the migrants' employers or public service providers. By means of the 1995 Recommendation public services, when providing benefits, in particular, in the area of health, retirement, family or work, are required to *verify* the residence and employment status of the TCNs concerned. As seen in other section, there is a deep concern about *misuse* and *abuse* of the Member States' welfare system by poor TCNs. It has already been said that although TCNs normally have a very low economic status, the percentages of those who actually benefit from welfare

477 European Commission, Proposal for a Council Regulation concerning the establishment of "Eurodac" for the comparison of the fingerprints of applicants for asylum and certain other aliens, COM (99) 260 final.

478 European Commission, Eurodac Regulation, Explanatory Memorandum, ibidem.

provisions are a small number. Besides as Moore and Wallace argue, in the British context:

> "Allegations of supplementary benefit abuse, and illegal immigration itself, are marginal features of the social scene but they command disproportionately great attention and an actual maldistribution of administrative efforts and other public resources".[479]

Such considerations can be extended to other European States.

Along with the controls carried out by the police and public services also employers wishing to recruit foreign nationals should be encouraged to verify that their residence or employment situations are in order by requiring them to present the document(s) by virtue of which they are authorised to reside and work in the Member State concerned. Penalties are foreseen for those employers who hire unauthorised TCNs. This suggests that Member States should introduce measures against those employers who hired illegal TCN workers. The labour market plays a crucial role because so long as TCNs are able to find a job whether legal or illegal they will arrive. For every TCN in an illegal position in the labour market there is also an illegal employer.

These rules are directed at ensuring the establishment of an area of security so that EC citizens are both free and safe. But the connection of crime with illegal migrants and with Blacks, as seen above, is likely to create a policing system against the Black community within Western Europe whether migrants or EC citizens. The same wording of the Recommendations offers a basis for checks based on prejudice and racist justifications.

The 1993 Recommendation states that "checks should be in particular, be carried out in respect of persons who are known or *suspected* (emphasis added) of staying or working without authority....Member States shall examine the types of checks which would be the most appropriate to introduce with a view to detecting TCNs who are residing or working illegally". Also the 1995 Recommendation foresees that where an identity check is carried out on a TCN "at least where a person appears to be residing in the country unlawfully, his residence situation should be verified". These provisions deserve severe criticism because they link the check on TCNs to their *appearance* of illegality (although in a number of specified situations). This second factor is a completely subjective element which can lead to arbitrary controls by national polices forces on TCNs belonging to black or ethnic groups. They are, in fact, more physically recognisable compared

479 Moore and Wallace quoted in Den Boer M., "Moving between Bona fide and Bogus", *supra* note 473.

to other foreigners. Examples of discriminatory controls carried out by the police are frequent: after the Metro bombing in Paris an estimated one million north Africans have had their legal status checked by the French police.[480]

Moreover, these provisions give an implicit power to carry out frequent checks among TCN communities. As Guild observes:

> "There is no limitation on the frequency with which checks may be undertaken. Third country nationals are entitled to dignity and respect just as nationals of the Member States. The increasing differentiation of treatment of third country nationals lawfully residing on the territory by way of reporting requirements and checks which seems to be foreseen...is unlikely, in the longer term, to be conducive to good community relations. Depending on the frequency and circumstances, such checks may even constitute degrading treatment prohibited by Article 3 ECHR".[481]

The EP suggested better training of police officers so that they have a better knowledge of the immigrant population in order to prevent any blunders or irregularities, particularly during identity checks.[482]

However, as discussed above, employers and public service providers also have the responsibility for such controls. In particular, *private employers* must check that the situation of the TCN they wish to hire is in order. Once again, Member States agreed to shift the control from the public sector to the private sphere. Like for the fining of air carriers for bringing TCNs without the necessary documents into the Union, the penalties imposed upon companies found to be employing unauthorised workers may result in arbitrary and racist-motivated refusals by employers to hire TCNs. Employers when in doubt may decide to refuse to hire a TCN to avoid risks and incurring in the fine.

Also, *public service providers* may refuse assistance or offer it with delays to TCNs belonging to ethnic minority groups or even EC citizens on the basis of their "suspicious look".

Measures are also foreseen against those who benefit from the presence of illegal TCN residents. The 1993 Recommendation foresees that Member States may expel those people who are subject to immigration/aliens provisions who have been involved in the facilitation, harbouring or employment of illegal migrants.

While measures against traffickers, landlords, employers and whoever else takes advantage of the particularly vulnerable position of TCNs illegally present

480 For further examples see Webber F., *supra* note 427.

481 Guild E., *supra* note 379.

482 EP, Resolution on the Status of non-member countries in the EU, A3-0332/93.

in the EU, must be adopted, these measures seem inappropriate. First of all, they are disproportionate, as the punishment for breaking the rules is expulsion, which is an extreme measure, especially because the persons involved may have acted in good faith. But, the inappropriateness is particularly due to the fact that this provision is likely to discriminate against the TCN population compared to nationals as the sanction of expulsion, established by the Recommendation is applicable only "to those people who are subject to immigration/aliens provisions" while no similar sanctions are foreseen for nationals.

Finally, the illegality in the situation of migrants can be referred to their right to work. In fact a TCN could have the right to reside in the host country, as for instance a migrants' family member, but not to work. A TCN legally employed under a restrictive agreement who is employed in a manner not authorised by the agreement, is also to be considered an illegal migrant, for instance under the EEC-Turkey Agreement a Turkish worker who works for different employers before the expiration of one year.

Taking into account that the irregular position of TCN workers can distort the correct functioning of the Internal Market, and affect the social integration of those TCNs lawfully working in the Union, Member States have decided to allow internal checks to verify the residence but also the employment situation of apparently unlawful TCNs. By means of these checks Member States also attempt to stop the illegal presence of foreigners within the Union. But, fears of being hired or when in employment of being fired make many TCNs hostages of unscrupulous employers who force their foreign employees to accept "unacceptable" conditions such a mixture of low pay, long hours and no holidays and sick pay. In the past, being an illegal worker was considered a criminal offence in many Member States while no sanctions for employers who hire illegal workers were established. Nowadays, most Member States have adopted legislation in this area. It should be remembered that according to the 1993 Recommendation, the sanction for a TCN employing illegal workers is expulsion. Such a provision gives a very wide discretionary power to Member States because, as has been discussed above, even in the case of good faith of the TCN employer, a national authority can opt for immediate expulsion.

Measures against the exploitation of illegal workers by unscrupulous employers must be welcomed, even though in the case of TCN employers involved such measures seem, again, to be disproportionate. Furthermore, these measures are likely to cause great side effects that could affect minorities strongly. In such an atmosphere of control and policing an increasing number of employers may simply refuse to contract TCNs on the basis of their appearance.

X

EXPULSION MEASURES

The crusade against illegal immigration in the European Union has influenced measures relating to expulsion of TCNs illegally present in its territory. Over the last few years, the Council has adopted several measures that ensure that the expulsion of illegal TCNs is carried out *effectively* and *speedily*. "The criteria of speed, efficiency and economy should be taken into account at all times when carrying out expulsion measures."[483] This is, indeed, an area where Member States have been particularly active as "it needs constant close cooperation by all Member States".[484]

X.1 LEGAL BASIS

The toughening of expulsion measures appears *necessary* because the whole restrictive regime adopted in the immigration field by the Member States would be meaningless if those who do not have the right to enter, stay or work within the EU breach the rules and notwithstanding that they are able to stay. The increase in the number of persons unlawfully present within the Union is the constant nightmare for EU governments.

The presence of millions of illegal TCNs – data are all but exact – would therefore require massive deportation from Europe to third countries. Forced deportation has taken place, in particular, in southern Europe, against the tide of illegal immigrants that these countries face. However, massive deportation, a distinctive feature of totalitarian regimes, has not taken place and is not foreseen in the near future. This drastic solution to the immigration problem seems to be used more as a threat than as a concrete measure, although some authors point out that "the spirit of deportation is very much at the heart of Community immigra-

483 Council document, Assistance in cases of transit for the purpose of expulsion by air, 14348/98.
484 Ibidem.

tion ideology".[485] It should be noted that collective expulsion of aliens is forbidden under Protocol No 4 Article 4 ECHR but apart from that clause "the express provisions of the Convention provide little comfort to an alien who faces deportation, especially if that individual is in a State which has not ratified the relevant additional protocols."[486]

The lack of competence of Community law has not impeded, Member States cooperating since the eighties to discuss, elaborate and adopt measures on expulsion of several categories of illegal TCNs, such as clandestine entrants, illegal residents or workers, along with few other specific categories.

The legal basis for expulsion can be found in several instruments outside the EC framework. The proposed External Border Convention stated that "a person who illegally crosses an external frontier without a residence permit or who does not fulfil, or no longer fulfils, the conditions of residence in a Member State shall normally be required to leave the territory of the Member State without delay, unless his stay is regularised".[487] It followed that where such a person had not left voluntarily, he must be expelled, according to the legislation of the Member State concerned, *to* his country of origin.

The Schengen Agreement (1990) contained similar provisions and its Article 23 stated "an alien who does not fulfil or no longer fulfils the short visit conditions applicable within the territory of a Contracting Party must in principle leave the territories of the Contracting Parties without delay...where such an alien has not left voluntarily or where it may be assumed that he will not so leave or if his immediate departure is required for reasons of national security or public policy, he must be expelled from the territory of the Contracting Party within which he has been arrested".

The Recommendation regarding practices followed by Member States on expulsion adopted in 1992 (London 30 November – 1 December 1992)[488] stated that "people found to have entered or remained unlawfully in Member States (where their stay has not been regularised)...should be expelled, unless there are compelling reasons, normally of a humanitarian nature, for allowing them to remain. In addition, consideration should be given to the question whether, in appropriate circumstances, a person who has been working in breach of immigration/alien or related provisions should be expelled". The Recommendation concerning checks on and expulsion of third-country nationals residing and working

485 Ward I., *supra* note 109, 112.

486 Sherlock A., "Deportation of Aliens and Article 8 ECHR", *European Law Review,* 1998, 23, 9.

487 Article 15.1 and 2 on illegal crossing of an external frontier.

488 Council document, SN 4678/92 see for the text Bunyan T (ed)., *supra* note 389.

without authorisation, adopted in 1993,[489] stated that "measures should be taken with a view to ensuring that third-country nationals do not remain beyond the period for which they have been admitted or given permission to remain and that they do not work without authority to do so". Moreover, the 1993 Recommendation includes, as seen above, the possibility to expel "those people who are subject to immigration/alien provisions who have been involved in the facilitation, harbouring or employment of illegal immigrants".

All these measures have no legal binding effects in the Union because some were included in the External Border Convention, which was never signed, others were part of the Schengen acquis, only applicable to some Member States, and the rest of the measures were adopted by means of recommendations and resolutions, notably without any legally binding effect. But the guidelines included in those instruments have been by and large included in Member States' national legislation.

X.2 The impact on TCNs of repatriation measures

The new trend is very much likely to affect ethnic minorities and women.

Blacks due to their number and the toughening of immigration rules are more likely to be in an illegal situation and, consequently, they are more concerned by these measures.

A strong presence in the illegal population in Europe is made up of women. Many of them are family members of TCN migrants settled in the Community that due to the stricter rules on family reunification, have been denied legal means of entry, stay or work, resort to illegality to join and live with their husbands. It is widely known that, notwithstanding the fact that the right to family life is recognised Union-wide, national legislation generally requires long periods for migrants to be joined by his/her family members and longer periods are required to be granted permission to enter the national labour market. The logic of deportation is likely to overshadow all considerations of respect for family reunion rights, as was made evident in the *Demirel* case.[490]

But what is worth noting most is the fact that in reality race and wealth factors play an important role in Member States' policies. "Although there are related provisions for the expedited return of unskilled migrants to Poland, there do not seem to be any comparable measures for the expedited or "stimulated" return of

489 Council document, SN 3017/93 see for the text Bunyan T. (ed), *supra* note 389.
490 *Demirel supra* note 66.

skilled or wealthy immigrants with white skin".[491] This seems to suggest that the targeted group is made up of poor immigrants belonging to minority groups more than combating the presence of illegal migrants within the EU.

X.3 Practical arrangements for expulsion

Member States have agreed that expulsion measures must be brought in without delay. The 1992 Recommendation stated that "expulsion should take place as soon as possible after the decision to expel has been taken". It is important to note that factors like speed, economy and efficiency overcome concerns such as the respect of human rights and fundamental freedoms.

But time is necessary in order to prepare the "departure" of the illegal migrants. Member States may decide to detain them until expulsion.[492] Unfortunately, no maximum period is prescribed but "any restriction on liberty should be limited to the period necessary to effect expulsion, including identification, the making of any necessary arrangements and the provision of tickets, travel documents and escorts". This provision alone justifies a long detention period.

Considering that an illegal migrant who violates immigration rules cannot however be treated as a criminal "appropriate places of custody should be available, where possible providing accommodation separate from those used by prisoners". But normally Member States have no adequate structures to "welcome" illegal migrants until their departure and, on the contrary, the structure at their disposal are more like detention camps with severe police controls, barbed wire, etc. According to the plan set out by the Schengen members, adopted in December 1997, "such holding centres should prevent illegal immigrants disappearing until their identity has been established or until the implementation of necessary police measures...[and allow for] immediate repatriation/readmission of illegal immigrants if they have not been granted temporary leave [to remain]".[493]

In order to avoid delays, TCNs who have deliberately brought about their illegal position, particularly by refusing to supply travel documents, should be subject to penalties. Frequently, TCNs deliberately destroy their personal documents in order to make checks on their illegal position more difficult and to hamper the control procedure by immigration authorities in the hope of receiving legal status

491 O' Keeffe D., cited in Ward I., *supra* note 105, 112.

492 The detention procedure of illegal migrants is a very common practice in the Member States. See on this point Webber F., *supra* note 427.

493 Schengen Plan, December 1997, see for a comment Statewatch, 1998, Vol.8, No 1.

in the meantime. In the past, indeed, Member States have occasionally granted legal residence status to illegal migrants either individually or by means of amnesties.

Also, without proper documentation the national authorities cannot deport the illegal migrant concerned to any State but they can just issue an order to leave the country, unless as seen above the person concerned represents a serious threat to public policy or public security. Many clandestine migrants, therefore, just wait to be given such an order to leave and then disappear and work on the black economy in that country or just leave that country for a neighbouring Member State. This practice is still in force in Italy: when clandestine migrants are caught by the police, the impossibility to ascertain their identity is solved by an order to leave the country in 15 days, but they are not detained.

Proposals are under discussion to extend the fingerprinting to all illegal migrants whose identity cannot be established by the EU's Eurodac computerised fingerprint database in order to avoid these *strategic disappearances.*

Guarantees against expulsion measures are foreseen. The 1992 Recommendation provided that "people being expelled should be notified in an appropriate manner of the reasons for the decision unless the interests of national security make such notification undesirable". It followed that "whenever there is any doubt about a person's ability to understand the language in which an interview is being conducted, consideration should be given to the provision of an interpreter". Finally "there should be a right to be represented and appropriate means to challenge expulsion decisions". Unfortunately, Member States too often execute their expulsion orders neglecting such guarantees and deportations are brought about in a completely extra-judicial context.[494]

X.4 Cooperation in carrying out forced repatriations

As the measures adopted by a Member State can seriously affect the others, the Council adopted a Recommendation on concerted action and co-operation in carrying out expulsion measures.[495] The main purpose of the Recommendation is to achieve the effective carrying out of expulsion measures without delays. The greatest difficulties in bringing about expulsion measures are encountered by Member States because of the lack of travel or identity documents of the TCNs obliged to leave. It has therefore been decided to co-operate in order to make the

494 Ward, I., *supra* note 105, 112.

495 Council Recommendation on concerted action and cooperation in carrying out expulsion measures, OJ 1996 C 5/3.

acquisition of the necessary documentation easier and quicker. Several measures are foreseen in order to obtain such documentation, such as the consultation of the consular authorities of the third state to which the TCN is to be expelled. As a last resort, Member States facing the impossibility of carrying out the expulsion through these means, can issue a standard travel document valid for a single journey to a third state outside the Union.[496]

The issuing of such a document is based on too many suppositions. As Guild observes:

> "The Agreement of such a standard document is necessarily based on a number of suppositions:
> That the identity of a third country national with no travel document can be determined to a reasonable degree of certainty;
> That the third country national subject to expulsion order possesses a nationality and that nationality can be determined with a reasonable degree of certainty;
> That the State to which the third country national is being expelled accepts the two preceding determinations by the Member State;
> That the State to which the person is to be expelled accepts the validity of the standard travel document."[497]

By these Recommendations Member States want to close off the loophole for undocumented migrants: once the expulsion order has been made the lack of identity or travel documents does not hamper the effective carrying out of such measures. But this effective theoretical structure may, for practical reasons, prove inadequate for such aims. Moreover, it is feared that efficacy requirements are carried out at the expense of those subject to the order of expulsion.

Another element that produced costs and delays in bringing about the forced departure of illegal TCNs was the lack of agreement on transit measures. It is generally agreed that expulsion from a Member State must be not to another Member State but to the country of origin or to any other country to which the individual may be admitted: where a person is being expelled on public policy or national security grounds this should not be to another Member State unless the individual has a right of residence there.[498]

---

496 Council Recommendation concerning the adoption of a standard travel document for the expulsion of TCN to improve the efficiency with which the measures of expulsion are executed. OJ 1996 C 274/18.

497 See Guild E., *supra* note 379.

498 Recommendation regarding practices followed by Member States on expulsion, SN 4678/92, see for text Bunyan T. (ed), *supra* note 389, 77.

However, the expulsion of a TCNs to a third state often implies transit through another Member State. Member States, therefore, agreed to co-operate in this area and adopted the Recommendation concerning transit for the purpose of expulsion,[499] which includes a series of measures directed at increasing the speed, efficiency and economy of the entire operation of expulsion.

Measures are under discussion within the Council in order to ensure more co-operation by all Member States concerned with expulsion, in particular transit countries. It is noted that "experience has shown that failure could have been avoided in many cases had the accompanying officials been given adequate support at the transit airport by the local security forces. The accompanying officials do not themselves have any authority to use direct methods of restraint on an aircraft in order to prevent any resistance but must obey the orders of the flight captain who has absolute authority on board the aircraft...If necessary, the accompanying officials have a right to self defence. The fact that accompanying officials depend wholly on the active support of those with local jurisdiction is an incentive to the person being expelled to take advantage of the situation and use violence to break free."[500]

The wording of this passage is outrageous as it completely neglects any humanitarian considerations. Many TCNs who are asked to leave are asylum seekers who have been refused entry because of the strictly interpreted rules of the Geneva Convention or "economic migrants" who have left their countries to escape hardship but they are not criminals. The majority of those ordered to leave the territory of the Union have not committed any criminal offence except for the fact they are there illegally.

Finally, deportation measures are made easier by the signature by the Member States of several agreements with third countries (*supra* section IX 6). These Agreements oblige the Contracting Parties to readmit irregular migrants on their territory, this is to say migrants who have entered or overstayed in another member's territory. The obligation includes not only nationals of the Contracting Parties, but also non-nationals as long as the illegal migrant has entered a signatory member from another member. The 1992 Recommendation expressly referred to these agreements and it states that "insofar as re-admission agreements do not already exist, consideration should be given to establishing them with appropriate States. Where possible, such agreements should be multilateral, but where is not possible bilateral agreements should be considered".

---

499 OJ 1996 C 5/5.
500 Ibidem.

It appears that all these measures have solved the problem of forced deportation. In fact, many formal and practical matters have been addressed and solved but many still require a solution. Although many migrants have very few possibilities of escaping these new rules when caught in an illegal position or when their asylum request is rejected, they will try to do everything in their power to stay. But once the European machine is turned on, it is very difficult to stop it. Only on a few occasions has the mobilisation of the public opinion for specific cases stopped it but sometimes only when it was too late.
According to the Campaign Against Racism & Fascism only in 1998:

> "Out of the total of 45 deaths, 29 were of asylum seekers or undocumented workers whose deaths, we believe, arose a direct consequence of immigration and asylum policies which deny individual human rights. Institutionalised racism played a part in many of the remaining sixteen cases documented".[501]

X.5 THE WAY FORWARD: FORCED DEPORTATION?

This is a very sensitive area, because, as discussed above, the whole restrictive structure would fall down if measures to expel those who do not have a right to stay were not severely enforced and illegal migrants were nevertheless allowed to remain.

The tension is therefore very high as, on the one hand, it is commonly agreed that illegal migrants should be sent away, especially because they are used as scapegoats for the illness of societies, but all the same deportation encounters great difficulties as it is contrary to the democratic values of Western societies. As Wihtol de Wenden remarks:

> "There is a contradiction in democratic societies which claim to uphold civil liberties and humanitarian values to hunt down and deport people who have worked, brought up their families, been law-abiding and maintained themselves independently of the state, in some case for many years".[502]

Public opinion while generally adverse to the presence of illegal migrants has nevertheless been mobilised to face concrete deportations. Therefore, while forced deportation is considered necessary and it is often carried out in relation to ir-

---

501 Campaign Against Racism & Fascism, Institutionalised racism and human rights abuses. A special investigation into 45 deaths in Europe in 1998, http://www.carf.demon.co.uk/deaths98/.

502 Wihtol de Wenden, *supra* note 407, 45.

regular migrants who refuse to leave the Union, great efforts are made in order to encourage their voluntarily departure. According to the Commission "expulsion whilst it may be judged to be a necessary component of immigration control, may be regarded as an instrument of last resort in relation to persons in an irregular situation who are not prepared to depart voluntarily".[503]

Member States have individually elaborated programmes to repatriate both illegal and legal TCNs. Within the Council, Member States also agreed on the exchange of information concerning assistance for the voluntary repatriation of TCNs.

In a recent proposal in the area of asylum[504] the Commission points out that smuggled people often claim asylum in order to remain in the territory of the Member States, although they do not satisfy the strict requirements to be recognised as refugees. When they cannot classify as asylum seekers they are automatically seen, with few exceptions, as economic migrants. In this case they are less protected against expulsion. But the Commission in its proposal recognises that "such people would be given the opportunity to participate in projects which could lead them voluntarily to withdrawing their asylum applications and returning permanently to their countries of origin".[505]

This way is the one that has been privileged lately as it is the least traumatic for all involved. Member States are dedicating important resources in the form of covering transport costs associated with repatriation of the irregular migrants or those who wish to return, measures to support the reintegration in their country of origin and also post repatriation monitoring. The flood of refugees caused by the Kosovo war has brought the attention in more general terms to the problem of voluntarily repatriation of refugees, displaced persons and asylum seekers from the Member States to their countries of origin and their reintegration there. The Council adopted a Joint Action on April 1999[506] which envisages measures to assist the voluntary repatriation of the above mentioned categories. These measures cover important areas such as the collection and dissemination on all information relevant to the return, training and education providing the TCN is willing to return the skills to reintegrate in the country of origin and counselling to those TCNs who are evaluating the possibility of returning as well as those who have already decided to do so.

503 European Commission, Proposal for a Council Decision on a Joint Action establishing measures to provide practical support in relation to the reception and voluntary repatriation of refugees, displaced persons and asylum applicants, COM (98) 733 final.

504 Ibidem.

505 Ibidem.

506 OJ 1999 L 114/2.

CONCLUSIONS

The analysis has covered fifty years of Community immigration history. In this period migratory movements and their regulation have both changed. However, until the late eighties, TCN's presence within the Community and migratory pressures at Member States' frontiers were largely neglected at EC/EU level and their regulation was mainly left to national legislation. Over the last decade (1989-1999) immigration matters have jumped to the top of EC/EU political agenda and they have become a major political issue for the European Union. Accordingly, there has been frenetic activity and many measures have been adopted concerning the most important aspects in this field.

The research has shown that the evolution towards a common European immigration policy has followed often difficult and uncoherent paths. The reason is to be found mainly in the multitude of political actors, the EC institutions and the Member States, called upon to draw up such a policy, that very often do not share the same positions on which direction to follow in this area.

Also, the existence of conflicting interests in this field as well as the labyrinth of regulations in force to which the Member States and the Community are bound, have impeded a completely new start and approach.

Although the analysis carried out in the research has shown the complexity of this area, with few exceptions, the trend recorded is to create a Fortress Europe, a *White* Fortress. The approach in the discussion, elaboration and adoption of new measures is by and large very restrictive. The emerging European immigration policy is therefore a serious challenge for Western Europe's declared values of democracy and respect of human rights and fundamental freedoms. In particular, the research has demonstrated that the new measures have racial and gender implications that undermine the liberal and non- discriminatory commitments of the Member States and of the European Union itself.

The reform brought about by the Treaty of Amsterdam is largely further confirmation of this trend. Nonetheless a few concessions have been made, which can produce unexpected and probably unwanted effects in the future. The shift of the most relevant aspects related to immigration from the third Pillar to the Community Pillar, with a consequent increasing involvement of the European Parliament and the Commission, may impose a more liberal perspective.

The analysis of the *immigrant policies and rules* has clearly shown the evolution that has taken place in the Community in this area. As regards the EC rules, old measures only incidentally covered TCNs, which was an area considered of national competence.

The economic approach was evident and TCN workers were seen as just *labour* and not people. This is confirmed by the several agreements signed in the past by the Community with third countries, which never included provisions dealing with social and cultural implications of the presence of foreign labour. Economic concerns are still present but it has been demonstrated that *these* have been accompanied by security and, most recently, racial factors. Few measures have been adopted therefore for the integration of the extra-Community population settled within the European Union.

There is a willingness to close Western Europe off against what is perceived as being *foreign contamination.* But Europe is already a multi-cultural and multiracial society and it will be probably more and more so in the future. To stand up against such a natural evolution of the European society and to adopt a policy of self-confinement is an anti-historical position. But, with the exception of a few gaps, mainly due to the pressure coming from the European Parliament and the Commission, the measures are restrictive and repressive.

The most recent agreements signed with third countries by the Community, especially with Central and Eastern European countries, mirror these concerns. The vast majority of the accords recently concluded were not formulated to have any direct effect nor to include provisions concerning labour. The few concessions accorded under the Europe Agreements, EEA agreement and, finally, the Agreement with Switzerland, have been possible thanks to the *closeness* of these countries with the Member States.

In the area of *immigration policies and rules,* the restrictive approach has been demonstrated with more clarity. The majority of the measures analysed have been adopted over the last decade and the strategy is more coherent. None of the Member States has a positive and open policy towards new immigration movements. Consequently, admission policies are directed at sealing off the borders with strict requirements for all categories of TCNs, including migrant workers, asylum seekers and family members seeking entry into the European Union. The Treaty of Amsterdam has shifted these matters from the third Pillar to the first Pillar but by and large they have escaped Community methods. The Action Plan on how best to implement the provisions of the Amsterdam Treaty contains the commitments of the Commission and the Council, analysed in detail, to take action within five years from the date of the coming into force of the Treaty however this is no more than a political declaration. Presently, therefore, this area is largely regulated by means of Regulations and Recommendations with no legally binding effect, which are often highly incompatible with fundamental human rights, in particular, they do not comply with EC/EU commitments against race and sex discrimination. The measures adopted often have a disproportionate impact on TCNs from Black countries.

In the last part of the research concerning *control and expulsion measures*, very few concessions have been made on humanitarian grounds. In general, the rules adopted were restrictive and repressive. The Treaty of Amsterdam confirms this approach: by the creation of an area of freedom, security and justice, Member States have stressed the importance of the security factor. This implies the stepping up of controls and the very strict enforcement of current legislation. Again, the impact of the new restrictive measures is greater upon TCNs from Black countries as well as TCN female migrants .

This research represents a contribution in the ongoing debate on how to build a common immigration policy. It is the first attempt to analyse in a single work all the measures related to TCNs, adopted under EC/EU law in a systematic way. The legal analysis is accompanied by a socio-political approach, which is essential to evaluate the real effect of the emerging immigration rules on racial and ethnic minority groups and women. Through the study of the various documents, the research demonstrates that, although some gaps in the labyrinth of European regulation remain, the main trend, imposed principally by the Member States, is towards the creation of a Fortress Europe.

BIBLIOGRAPHY

ACKERS L., "Women, Citizenship and European Community Law: The Gender Implications of the Free Movement Provisions", *Journal of Social Welfare of Family Law*, 1994, 391-406.

ALEXANDER W., "Free Movement of Non-EC Nationals. A Review of the Case-Law of the Court of Justice", *European Journal of International Law*, 1992/3, 53-64.

ANDERSON M. & DEN BOER M (eds)., *Policing Across National Boundaries*, Pinter, 1994.

ANDERSON M. & BORT E. (eds), *The Frontiers of Europe,* Pinter, 1998.

BALDWIN-EDWARDS M., "Recent Changes in European Immigration Policies", *Journal of European Social Policy*, 1992, 2(1), 53-71.

BALDWIN-EDWARDS M. & SCHAIN M. A., "Special Issue in the Politics of Immigration in Western Europe", *West European Politics*, 1994, Vol. 17, No 2, 127-196.

BALDWIN-EDWARDS M., "The Emerging European Immigration Regime: Some Reflections on Implications for Southern Europe", *Journal of Common Market Studies*, 1997, Vol. 35, No 4, 497-519.

BALLARD R., *Desh Pardesh, The South Asian Presence in Britain*, C. Hurst & Co Publishers, 1994.

BARRY B. & GOODIN R. E. (eds), *Free Movement: Ethical Issues in the Transnational Migration of People and of Money*, Harvester Wheatsheaf, 1992.

BEGHÈ LORETI L., *Rifugiati e Richiedenti Asilo nell'Area della Comunità Europea*, CEDAM, 1990.

BEYANI C., *Human Rights Standards and Freedom of Movement of Peoples Within States*, Oxford, Clarendon Press, forthcoming.

BHABHA J. & SHUTTER S., *Women' Movement: Women under Immigration, Nationality and Refugee Law*, Trentham Books, 1994.

BIEBER R. & MONAR J. (eds), *Justice and Home Affairs in the European Union, The Developing of the Third Pillar*, European Interuniversity Press, The Bruges Conference 1995.

BÖHNING W.R., "Integration and Immigration Pressures in Western Europe", *International Labour Review*, 1991, Vol. 4, 445-458.

BROWN T.A., *Migration and Politics*, The University of North Carolina Press, 1988.
BUECHLER H. C. & BUECHLER J.M., *Migrants in Europe. The Role of Family, Labor, and Politics*, Greenwood Press, 1987.
BULMER M. & REES A.M., *Citizenship Today*, UCL Press, 1996.
BUNYAN T., "Towards an Authoritarian European State", *Race and Class*, 1991, 32(3), 19-27.
BUNYAN T. (ed), *Statewatching the New Europe: a Handbook on the European State*, Statewatch Publication, 1993.
BUNYAN T. (ed), *Key Texts on Justice and Home Affairs in the European Union*, Statewatch Publication, 1997.

CARTER B., GREEN M. & HALPERN R., "Immigration Policy and the Racialization of Migrant Labour: the Construction of National Identities in the USA and Britain", *Ethnic and Racial Studies*, 1996, Vol. 19, 135-157.
CASTLE S. et al (eds), *Here for Good. Western Europe's New Ethnic Minorities*, Pluto Press, 1984.
CESARANI D. & FULBROOK M. (eds), *Citizenship, Nationality and Migration in Europe*, Routledge, 1996.
CHALMERS D. & SZYSZCZAK E., *European Union Law Two. Towards a European Polity?*, Ashgate, 1998.
CHOLEWINSKI R., "The Protection of the Right of Economic Migrants to Family Reunion in Europe", *International and Comparative Law Quarterly*, 1994, Vol. 43, 568-598.
CHURCHES COMMISSION FOR MIGRANTS IN EUROPE, *Immigrant Women and Integration:Towards Equal Opportunities*, CCME Briefing Paper, No 21, 1995.
CLOOS J. et al (eds), *Le Traité de Maastricht: Genèse, Analyse, Commentaires*, Bruylant, 1994.
CLOSA C., "The Concept of Citizenship in the Treaty on European Union", *Common Market Law Review*, 1992, Vol. 29, 1137-1169.
COLLINSON S., *Europe and International Migration*, Pinter Publishers, 1993.
COLLINSON S., *Beyond the Borders: West European Migration Policy Towards the 21st Century*, Royal Institute of International Affairs, 1995.
COLLINSON S., *Shore to Shore. The Politics of Migration in Euro-Maghreb Relations*, The Royal Institute of International Affairs. 1996.
CRAWLEY H., *Women as Asylum Seekers: A Legal Handbook*, ILPA, 1997.
CREMONA M., "Citizens of Third Countries: Movement and Employment of Migrant Workers Within the European Union", *Legal Issues of European Integration*, 1995/2, 87-113.
CROCKER D.A., "Insiders and Outsiders in International Development Ethics", *Ethics & International Affairs*, 1991, Vol. 5, 149-173.
CRUZ A., *Shifting Responsibility:Carriers' Liability in the Member States of the European Union and North America*, Trentham Books, 1995.
CULLEN D. & MONAR J. (eds), *Co-operation in Justice and Home Affairs. An Evaluation of Third Pillar in Practice*, College of Europe, Working Series, 1996, No 23.

CURTIN D. & MEIJERS H., "The Principle of Open Government in Schengen and the European Union, Democratic Retrogression?", *Common Market Law Review*, 1995, Vol. 32, 391-442.

CURTIN D. M., "La Coopération dans le Domaine de la Justice et des Affaires Intérieures au Sein de l'Union Européenne: Une Nostalgie d'Avant Maastricht?", *Revue de Marché Unique Européen*, 1995, No 3, 13-34.

CURTIN D., "The Constitutional Structure of the Union: A Europe of Bits and Pieces", *Common Market Law Review*, 1993, Vol. 30, 17-69.

DALLEN J.R., "An Overview of European Economic Protection of Human Rights with Some Special Reference to the UK", *Common Market Law Review*, 1990, Vol. 27, 761-790.

DE FILIPPO E. & PUGLIESE E., "Le Nuove Migrazioni Internazionali e i Modelli Migratori nei Paesi del Sud Europa", *Mediterraneo,* Luglio-Settembre, 1996, 49-71.

DEKNOP J. & RAES K., "Schengen, Mars 95: Ebauhe d'une Libre Circulation en Europe", *Revue de Marché Commun et de l' Union Européenne*, 1996, 282-286.

DE MARCHI B. & BOILEAU A.M. (eds), *Boundaries and Minorities in Western Europe,* Franco Angeli Editore, 1982.

DEN BOER M., "Police Co-operation in the TEU: Tiger in a Trojan Horse?", *Common Market Law Review*, 1995, Vol. 32, 555-578.

DUFF A., PINDER J. & PRICE R., *Maastricht and Beyond: Building the Union*, Routledge, 1994.

DUMMETT A., "Racial Equality and 1992", *Feminist Review*, 1991,Vol. 39, 85-90.

ESSED P., *Diversity. Gender, Color, and Culture*, Braun-Brumfield, 1996.

EVANS A., "Nationality Law and European Integration", *European Law Review*, 1991, Vol. 16, 190-215.

EVANS A., "Third Country Nationals and the Treaty on European Union", *European Journal of International Law*, 1994, Vol. 5, 199-219.

FEKETE L. & WEBBER F., *Inside Racist Europe*, Institute of Race Relations, Russell Press, 1994.

FENWICK H. & HERVEY T.K., "Sex Equality in the Single Market: New Directions for the European Court of Justice", *Common Market Law Review*, 1995, Vol. 32, 443-470.

FITZPATRICK P. (ed), *Nationalism, Racism and the Rule of Law*, Dartmouth Publication, 1995.

FRIDLIZIOUS S. & PETERSON A., *Stranger or Guest? Racism and Nationalism in Contemporary Europe*, Almqvist & Wiksell International, 1996.

FOBLETS M.C., "Europe and its Aliens After Maastricht. The Painful Move to Substantive Harmonization of Member States' Policies Towards Third-Country Nationals", *American Journal of Comparative Law*, 1994, Vol. 42, No 4, 783-805.

GARBAGNATI M. L., "Immigrazione, Diritto di Asilo e Libertà di Circolazione delle Persone nella Prospettiva dell'Unione Europea", *Diritto Comunitario e degli Scambi Internazionali*, 1995, Vol. 34, 7-45.

GEDDES P., "Immigrant and Ethnic Minorities and the EU's Democratic Deficit", *Journal of Common Market Studies*, 1995, Vol. 33, 197-203.

GREENWOOD C., "Nationality and the Limits of the Free Movement of Persons in Community Law", *Yearbook of European Law*, 1987, No 7, 185-210.

GROENENDIJK K., GUILD E. & DOGAN H., *Security of Residence of Long-Term Migrants. A Comparative Study of Law and Practice in European Countries,* Centre for Migration Law University of Nijmegen, Strasbourg, 1998.

GUILD E., "Towards an European Asylum Law. Developments in the EC Law", *Immigration & Nationality Law & Practice*, 1993, Vol. 7, No 3, 88-92.

GUILD E., "Protecting Migrants' Rights and Community Law: the Co-operation Agreements with Algeria, Morocco and Tunisia", *Immigration & Nationality Law & Practice*, 1993, Vol. 7, No 1, 15-18.

GUILD E. (ed), *The Developing Immigration and Asylum Policies of the European Union*, Kluwer Law International, 1996.

GUILD E., *A Guide to the Right of Establishment under the Europe Agreements*, Baileys Shaw & Gillet in association with the Immigration Law Practitioners' Association, 1996.

GUILD E. (ed), *The Legal Framework and Social Consequences of Free Movement of Persons in the European Union*, Kluwer Law International, 1999.

HAGENDOORN L., "Ethnic Categorisation and Outgroup Exclusion: Cultural Values and Social Stereotypes in the Construction of Ethnic Hierarchies", *Ethnic and Racial Studies*, 1993, Vol. 16, 26-51.

HAILBRONNER K., "Visa Regulation and Third-country Nationals in EC law", *Common Market Law Review*, 1994, Vol. 31, 969-995.

HAILBRONNER K., "European Immigration and Asylum Law Under the Amsterdam Treaty", *Common Market Law Review,* 1998, Vol. 35, 1047-1067.

HALL S., "The European Convention of Human Rights and Public Policy Exceptions to the Free Movement of Workers Under the EEC Treaty", *European Law Review*, 1991, Vol. 16, 466-488.

HALL S., *Nationality, Migration Rights and Citizenship of the Union*, Martinus Nijoff Publisher, 1995.

HALL S., "Loss of Citizenship in Breach of Fundamental Rights", *European Law Review*, 1996, Vol. 21, 129-143.

HAMILTON K.A. (ed), *Migration and the New Europe*, Centre for Strategies and International Studies, 1995.

HAMMAR T., *Democracy and the Nation State-Aliens, Denizens and Citizens in a World of International Migration*, Avebury, 1990.

HANDOLL J., *Free Movement of Persons in the EU*, John Wiley & Sons, 1995.

HEPPLE B.A. & SZYSZCZAK E. (eds), *Discrimination: The Limits of Law*, Mansell Publishing Limited, 1992.

HERVEY T. & O'KEEFFE D. (eds), *Sex Equality Law in the European Union*, John Wiley & Sons, 1996.
HERVEY T., *European Social Policy*, Longman, 1998.
HONDIUS F.W., "Legal Aspects of the Free Movements of Persons in Greater Europe", *Yearbook of European Law*, 1990, 291-307.
HOOGENBOOM T., "Symposium: The Status of Non-Community Nationals in Community Law", *European Journal of International Law*, 1992, No 3, 36-52. HREBLAY. V., *La Libre Circulation des Personnes, les Accords de Schengen*, Presse Universitaire de France, 1995.
HUYSMANS J., "Securitising Europe, Europeanising Security, the Construction of Migration in the EU", Paper presented at the Conference "Defining and Protecting Europe's Identity: Issues and Trade Offs", The Graduate Institute of International Studies, Geneva, 21-22 March 1996.

JOHNSON E. & O'KEEFFE D., "From Discrimination to Obstacles to Free Movement: Recent Developments Concerning the Free Movement of Workers 1989-1994", *Common Market Law Review*, 1994, Vol. 31, 1313-1346.
JOLY D. (ed), *Scapegoats and Social Actors. The Exclusion and Integration of Minorities in Western and Eastern Europe*, MacMillan Press LTD, 1998.
JOPPKE C. (ed), *Challenge to the Nation-State. Immigration in Western Europe and the United States*, Oxford University Press, 1998.

KING R. (ed), *The New Geography of European Migrations*, Belhaven Press, 1993.
KING T., "The European Community and Human Rights in Eastern Europe", *Legal Issues of European Integration*, 1996, Vol. 2, 93-125.
KNOCKE W., "Migrant and Ethnic Minority Women: The Effects of Gender-Neutral Legislation in the European Community", *Social Politics*, 1995, Vol. 3, 225-238.
KORELLA G.D. & TWOMEY P.M. (eds), *Towards a European Immigration Policy*, European Interuniversity Press, 1993.
KOSER K. & LUTZ H. (eds), *The New Migration in Europe, Social Constructions and Social Realities*, MacMillan Press LTD, 1998.
KRENZLER G.H., *The EU and Central-East Europe: the Implications of Enlargement in Stages*, The Robert Schumann Centre, Policy Paper 97/2, European University Institute, 1997.
KUBÁT D. (ed), *The Politics of Migration Policies: Settlement and Integration: the First World into the 1990s*, Centre for Migration Studies, 1993.

LABAYLE H., "La Coopèration Européenne en Matière de Justice et d'Affaires Intérieures et la Conference Intergouvernamentale", *Revue Trimestrelle de Droit Européen*, 1997, Vol. 1, 1-37.
LAYTON-HENRY Z. (ed), *The Political Rights of Migrant Workers in Western Europe*, Sage Publications, 1990.

LEHNING P. & WEALE A. (eds), *Citizenship, Democracy and Justice in the New Europe*, Routledge, 1997.

LENAERTS K., "Fundamental Rights to Be Included in a Community Catalogue", *European Law Review*, 1991, Vol. 16, 367-390.

LEPOIVRE M., "Le Domaine de la Justice et des Affaires Intérieures dans la Perspective de la Conference Intergouvernementale de 1996", *Cahier de Droit Européen*, 1995, Vol. 3, 323-343.

LIROLA DELGADO M. I., Libre Circulaciòn de Personas y Uniòn Europea, Editorial Civitas, 1994.

LUCIANI G. (ed), *Migration Policies in Europe and the United States*, Kluwer Academic Publishers, 1993.

LUDLOW P., "Beyond Agenda 2000, EU Enlargement Issue", *Centre for European Policy Studies Review*, 1997/98, No 5, 1-9.

MARIA E.A., *European Citizenship*, European Institute of Public Administration, 1994.

MARTIN D. & GUILD E., *Free Movement of Persons in the European Union*, Butterworths, 1996.

MEEHAN E., *Citizenship and the European Community*, Sage Publication, 1993.

MCLEAN S. & BURROWS N. (eds), *The Legal Relevance of Gender. Some Aspects of Sex-Based Discrimination*, MacMillan Press LTD, 1988.

MCMAHON R., "Maastricht's Third Pillar: Load Bearing or Purely Decorative?", *Legal Issue of European Integration*, 1995, Vol. 1, 51-64.

MEIJERS M. et al (eds), *A New Immigration Law for Europe? The 1992 London and 1993 Copenhagen Rules on Immigration*, Standing Committee of Experts in International Immigration, Refugee and Criminal Law, 1993.

MEISSNER D. M. et al (eds), *International Migration Challenges in a New Era: Policy Perspective and Priorities for Europe, Japan, North America and the International Community: A Report to the Trilateral Commission*, The Trilateral Commission, 1993.

MERON T. (ed), *Human Rights in International Law, Legal and Policy Issues*, Oxford Clarendon Press, 1989.

MILES R. & THRÄNHARDT D. (eds), *Europe, A New immigration Continent Policies and Politics in Comparative Perspective*, LIT 1992.

MILES R. & THRÄNHARDT D. (eds), *Migration and European Integration in Europe*, Pinter, 1995.

MOEBIUS I. & SZYSZCZAK E., "Of Raising Pigs and Children", *Yearbook Of European Law*, forthcoming.

MONAR J. & MORGAN R. (eds), *The Third Pillar of the European Union Co-operation in the Fields of Justice and Home Affairs*, European Interuniversity Press, 1994.

MONAR J., "Justice and Home Affairs in the Treaty of Amsterdam: Reform at the Price of Fragmentation", *European Law Review*, 1998, Vol. 23, 320-334.

MOROKVASIC M., "Fortress Europe and Migrant Women", *Feminist Review*, 1991, Vol. 39, 69-83.

MÜLLER-GRAFF P. C., "The Legal Basis of the Third Pillar and its Provision in the Framework of the Union Treaty", *Common Market Law Review*, 1994, Vol. 31, 493-497.
MÜNZ R., "A Continent of Migration: European Mass Migration in the Twentieth Century", *New Community*, 1996, 22(2), 201-226.

NASCIMBENE B., *Nationality Law in the European Union*, Giuffrè Editore, 1996.
NEUWAHL N.A. & ROSAS A. (eds), *The European Union and the Human Rights*, Martinus Nijoff Publishers, 1995.
NIESSEN J. & MOCHEL F., *Les Relations Extérieures de l'Union Européennes et les Migrations Internationales*, Migration Policy Group, 1999.

O'KEEFFE D., "Recasting the Third Pillar", *Common Market Law Review*, 1995, Vol. 32, 893-920.
O'KEEFFE D., "The Emergence of a European Immigration Policy", *European Law Review*, 1995, Vol. 20, 20-36.
O'KEEFFE D., "The Free Movement of Persons and the Single Market", *European Law Review*, 1992, Vol. 17, 3-19.
O'KEEFFE D. & TWOMEY P.M. (eds), *Legal Issues of the Maastricht Treaty*, Chancery Law Publishing, 1994.
O'LEARY S., "Nationality Law and Community Citizenship: A Tale of Two Uneasy Bedfellows", *Yearbook of European Law*, 1992, No 12, 353-384.
O'LEARY S., *European Union Citizenship. The Options for Reform*, Institute for Public Policy Research, 1996.
O'LEARY S., Employment and Residence for Turkish Workers and Their Families: Analogies with Case-Law of the Court of Justice on Article 48 EC, in Scritti in Onore di Giuseppe Federico Mancini, Vol.II, Diritto dell'Unione Europea, Giuffrè Editore, 1998.

PAPADEMETRIOU D.G., *Coming Together or Pulling Apart? The European Union's Struggle with Immigration and Asylum*, Carnegie Endowment for International Peace, 1996.
PEERS S., "The Common Market Harmonisation of Laws", *European Law Review*, 1996, Vol. 21, 150-155.
PEERS S., "Towards Equality: Actual and Potential Rights of Third-Country Nationals in the European Union", *Common Market Law Review*, 1996, Vol. 33, 7-50.
PEERS S., "Undercutting Integration: Developments in Union Policy on Third-Country Nationals", *European Law Review*, 1997, No 22, 76-84.
PEERS S., "Aliens, Workers or Humans? Judicial Activism and Turkish Nationals in the EU", Paper delivered at the Sociology of Law Symposium, Onti, Spain, September 1997.
PEERS S., "Building Fortress Europe: The Development of EU Migration Law", *Common Market Law Review,* 1998, Vol. 35, 1235-1272.
PEERS S., *EU Justice and Home Affairs Law*, Longman, forthcoming.
PIETERSE J.N., "Fictions of Europe", *Race and Class*, 1991, Vol. 32(3), 3-10.

PLENDER P., "Competence, European Community Law and Nationals of Non-Member States", *International and Comparative Law Quarterly*, 1990, 599-610.

RASMUSSEN H. K., *No Entry. Immigration Policy in Europe*, Copenhagen Business School Press, 1997.

RATTANSI A. & WESTWOOD S. (eds), *Racism, Modernity & Identity*, Polity Press, 1994.

RENAULT G., Schengen, un Modéle pour l'Europe Pénale?, *Les Dossiers du Journal des Tribunaux*, Maison Larcier s.a, No 6, 1996.

REX J. & DRURY B., *Ethnic Mobilisation in a Multi-Cultural Europe*, Avebury, 1994.

ROCHE M. & VAN BERKEL R. (eds), *European Citizenship and Social Exclusion*, Dames, 1997.

ROSSILLI M., "The European Community's Policy on the Equality of Women", *European Journal of Women's Studies*, 1997, Vol. 4, 63-82.

RUDOLF H. & MOROKVASIC M., *Bridging States and Markets. International Migration in the Early 1990s*, Sigma, 1993.

SACHDEVA S., *The Primary Purpose Rule in British Immigration Law*, Trentham Books, 1993.

SCHERMERS H.G. et al (eds), *Free Movement of Persons in Europe*, Martinus Nijhoff Publishers, 1995.

SCHNAPPER D., *L'Europe des Immigrés. Essai sur les Politiques d' Immigration*, Éditions François Bourin, 1992.

SHAH P., "Refugees and Safe Third Countries", *Immigration & Nationality Law & Practice*, 1995, Vol. 9, No 1, 3-13.

SHAW J. & MORE G., *New Legal Dynamics of European Union*, Clarendon Press, 1995.

SIMPSON G., "Asylum and Immigration in the European Union after the Treaty of Amsterdam", *European Public Law*, 1999, Vol. 5, 91-124.

SPENCER M., *State of Injustice: A Guide to Human Rights and Civil Liberties in the European Union*, Pluto Press, 1995.

THRÄNHARDT D., "European Migration from East to West: Present Patterns and Future Directions", *New Community*, 1996, Vol. 22(2), 227-242.

TORIELLO F., *La Condizione dello Straniero. Profili di Diritto Comparato e Comunario*, CEDAM, 1997.

UÇARER E.M., & PUCHALA D. J. (eds), *Immigration into Western Societies: Problems and Policies*, Pinter, 1997.

UGUR M., "Freedom of Movement vs. Exclusion: A Reinterpretation of the 'Insider'-'Outsider' Divide in the European Union", *International Migration Review*, 1995, No 29, 964-968.

VAN AMERSFOORT H., "Migration: The Limits of Governmental Control", *New Community*, 1996, Vol. 22(2), 243-257.

VERSCHUEREN H., "EC Social Security Coordination Excluding Third Country Nationals: Still in Line With Fundamental Rights After the Gaygusuz Judgement?", *Common Market Law Review*, 1997, Vol. 34, 991-1017.

VIGNES, "Plaidoyer pour le IIIème Pilier", *Revue du Marché Commun et de l' Union Européenne*, 1996, 272-281.

VINCENZI C., "European Citizenship and Free Movement Rights in the United Kingdom", *Public Law Review*, 1995, 259-275.

WALLACE C., CHMOULIAR O. & SIDORENKO E., "The Eastern Frontier of Western Europe: Mobility in the Buffer Zone", *New Community*, 1996, Vol. 22(2), 259-286.

WARD M.L., "Pre-Conditions in European Law", *Journal of Law and Society*, 1996, Vol. 23, No 2, 198-212.

WARD I., *The Margins of European Law*, MacMillan Press LTD, 1996.

WARD I., "Law and the Other Europeans", *Journal of Common Market Studies*, 1997, Vol. 35, 79-96.

WARD A. & GREGORY Y., *Women and Citizenship in Europe. Borders, Rights and Duties*, Trentham Books, 1992.

WEBBER F., "From Ethnocentrism to Euro-racism", *Race and Class*, 1991, Vol. 32(3), 11-17.

WEILER J.H.H., "Thou Shalt Not Oppress a Stranger: On the Judicial Protection of the Human Rights of Non-EC nationals- A Critique", *European Journal of International Law*, 1992, Vol. 2, 53-64.

WEILER J.H.H., "The European Union Belongs to its Citizens: Three Immodest Proposals", *European Law Review*, 1997, Vol. 22/2,150-156.

WEINER M., "Security Stability and International Migration", *International Security*, 1993, Vol. 17/3, 91-126.

WILLIAMS F., "Race/Ethnicity, Gender, and Class in Welfare States: A Framework for Comparative Analysis", *Social Politics*, 1995, 127-159.

WINN D.B., *Third Country Nationals in the European Union*, ILPA, 1995.

WRENCH J. & SOLOMOS J.(eds), *Racism and Migration in Western Europe*, Berg Publishers LDT, 1993.

ZOLBERG A.R., Keeping Them Out: Ethical Dilemmas of Immigration Policy, in Myers R.J. (ed), *International Ethics in the Nuclear Age*, Carnegie Council on Ethics and International Affairs, University Press of America Inc, 1987, 261-298.

ANNEXES

I

TABLE OF EQUIVALENCE BETWEEN THE PREVIOUS AND THE NEW NUMBERING OF THE TREATY OF AMSTERDAM[507]

TREATY ON EUROPEAN UNION

Previous numbering	New numbering
Title I	Title I
Common Provisions	*Common Provisions*
Article A	Article 1
Article B	Article 2
Article C	Article 3
Article D	Article 4
Article E	Article 5
Article F	Article 6
Article F.1[508]	Article 7
Title VI[509]	Title VI
Provisions on police and judicial cooperation in criminal matters	*Provisions on police and judicial cooperation in criminal matters*
Article K.1	Article 29

507 In accordance with Article 12 and the Annex to the Treaty of Amsterdam, the articles, titles and sections of the Treaty on European Union and of the Treaty establishing the European Community are renumbered. The new renumbering is effective since 1 May 1999, on which date the Treaty of Amsterdam has entered into force.

508 Article introduced by the Amsterdam Treaty.

509 Title reorganised by the Amsterdam Treaty.

Title VI bis[510]	Title VII
Provisions on closer cooperation	*Provisions on closer cooperation*
Article K.15	Article 43
Title VII	Title VIII
Final provisions	*Final provisions*
Article L	Article 46
Article M	Article 47
Article O	Article 49

TREATY ESTABLISHING THE EUROPEAN COMMUNITY

Previous numbering	New numbering
PART 1 *Principles*	PART 1 *Principles*
Article 2	Article 2
Article 3	Article 3
Article 3b	Article 5
Article 4	Article 7
Article 6	Article 12
Article 6a[511]	Article 13
Article 7a	Article 14
PART 2 *Citizenship of the Union*	PART 2 *Citizenship of the Union*
Article 8	Article 17
Article 8a	Article 18
Article 8b	Article 19
Article 8c	Article 20
Article 8d	Article 21

510 Title introduced by the Amsterdam Treaty.
511 Article introduced by the Amsterdam Treaty.

PART 3	PART 3
Community policies	*Community policies*
Title III	Title III
Free movement of persons, services and capital	*Free movement of persons, services and capital*
Chapter 1	Chapter 1
Workers	*Workers*
Article 48	Article 39
Article 49	Article 40
Article 50	Article 41
Article 51	Article 42
Chapter 2	Chapter 2
Right of establishment	*Right of establishment*
Article 52	Article 43
Article 53 (repealed)	-----------
Article 54	Article 44
Article 55	Article 45
Article 56	Article 46
Article 57	Article 47
Article 58	Article 48
Chapter 3	Chapter 3
Services	*Services*
Article 59	Article 49
Article 60	Article 50
Article 61	Article 51
Article 62 (repealed)	-----------
Article 63	Article 52
Article 64	Article 53
Article 65	Article 54
Article 66	Article 55

Title III bis[512]	Title IV
Visas, asylum, immigration and other policies related to the free movement of persons	*Visas, asylum, immigration and other policies related to free movement of persons*
Article 73i	Article 61
Article 73j	Article 62
Article 73k	Article 63
Article 73l	Article 64
Article 73 o	Article 67
Article 73p	Article 68
Article 73 q	Article 69
Title V	Title VI
Common rules on competition, taxation and approximation of laws	*Common rules on competition, taxation and approximation of laws*
Chapter 3 Approximation of laws	Chapter 3 Approximation of laws
Article 100c (repealed)	------------------
Title VII	Title IX
Common commercial policy	*Common commercial policy*
Article 113	Article 133
Title VIII[513]	Title XI
Social policy, education, vocational training and youth	*Social policy, education, vocational training and youth*
Chapter 1 Social provisions	Chapter 1 Social provisions
Article 117	Article 136
Article 118	Article 137

512 Title introduced by the Amsterdam Treaty.
513 Title reorganised by the Amsterdam Treaty.

Article 118a	Article 138
Article 118b	Article 139
Article 119	Article 141
Title IX	Title XII
Culture	*Culture*
Article 128	Article 151
PART 5	PART 5
Institutions of the Community	*Institutions of the Community*
Title I	Title I
Provisions governing the institutions	*Provisions governing the institutions*
Chapter 1	Chapter 1
Institutions	Institutions
Section 4	Section 4
The Court of Justice	*The Court of Justice*
Article 169	Article 226
Article 173	Article 230
Article 175	Article 232
Article 177	Article 234
PART VI	PART VI
General and final provisions	*General and final provisions*
Article 228	Article 300
Article 235	Article 308
Article 238	Article 310

II

LIST OF THIRD COUNTRIES WHOSE NATIONALS ARE REQUIRED A VISA WHEN CROSSING MEMBER STATES' EXTERNAL BORDERS[514]

I. STATES

Afghanistan
Albania
Algeria
Angola
Armenia
Azerbaijan
Bahrain
Bangladesh
Belarus
Benin
Bhutan
Bulgaria
Burkina Faso
Burma/Myanmar
Burundi
Cambodia
Cameroon
Cape Verde
Central African Rep.
Chad
China
Comoros
Congo
Côte D'Ivoire
Cuba
Democratic Republic of the Congo
Dijbouti
Dominican Republic
Egypt
Equatorial Guinea
Eritrea
Ethiopia
Federal Republic of Yugoslavia
Fiji
Former Yugoslav Rep. of Macedonia
Gabon
The Gambia
Georgia
Ghana
Guinea
Guinea-Bissau
Guyana
Haiti
India
Indonesia
Iran
Irak
Jordan
Kazakhstan
Kyrgystan
Kuwait
Laos
Lebanon
Liberia
Libya
Madagascar
Maldives
Mali
Mauritania
Mauritius
Moldavia
Mongolia
Morocco
Mozambique
Nepal
Niger
Nigeria
North Korea
Oman

514 Source Council Regulation 574/99 OJ 1999 L 72/2.

Pakistan
Papua New Guinea
Peru
Philippines
Qatar
Romania
Russia
Rwanda
Sao Tomé and Principe
Saudi Arabia
Senegal
Sierra Leone
Somalia
Sri Lanka
Sudan
Suriname
Syria
Tajikistan
Tanzania
Thailand
Togo
Tunisia
Turkey
Turkmenistan
Uganda
Ukraine
United Arab Emirates
Uzbekistan
Vietnam
Yemen
Zambia

II TERRITORIAL ENTITIES AND AUTHORITIES NOT RECOGNISED AS STATES BY ALL THE MEMBER STATES

Taiwan

III

LIST OF THIRD COUNTRIES WHOSE NATIONALS ARE NOT REQUIRED A VISA WHEN CROSSING MEMBER STATES' EXTERNAL BORDERS.[515]

Andorra
Argentina
Canada
Chile
Czech Republic
Cyprus
Hungary
Iceland
Japan
Liechtenstein
Malta
Mexico
Monaco
New Zealand
Norway
San Marino
Singapore
Slovenia
South Korea
Switzerland
Uruguay

515 European Commission, Commission Communication in pursuance of Council Regulation 574/1999 determining the third countries whose nationals must be in possession of visas when crossing the external borders of the Member States, OJ 1999 C 133/19.

IV

LIST OF THIRD COUNTRIES WHOSE NATIONALS ARE REQUIRED A VISA IN ONE OR MORE MEMBER STATES WHEN CROSSING ITS EXTERNAL BORDERS

Antigua and Barbuda
Australia
Bahamas
Barbados
Belize
Bolivia
Bosnia-Herzegovina
Botswana
Brazil
Brunei
Colombia
Costa Rica
Croatia
Dominica
Ecuador
El Salvador
Estonia
Grenada
Guatemala
Honduras
Israel
Jamaica
Kenya
Kiribati
Latvia
Lesotho
Lithuania
Malawi
Malaysia
Marshall Islands
Micronesia
Namibia
Nauru
Nicaragua
Northern Marianas
Panama
Paraguay
Poland
Seychelles
Slovak Republic
Solomon Islands
South Africa
St Kitts and Nevis
St Lucia
St Vincent and Grenadines
Swaziland
Tonga
Trinidad and Tobago
Trust Territory of the Pacific Islands (Palau)
Tuvalu
United States of America
Vanatu
Vatican State
Venezuela
Western Samoa
Zimbabwe

List of dependant territories of the Member States whose nationals are subject to the visa requirement by one or more Member States.

Territories under UK administration

Bermuda
Montserrat
St Helena

Territories under Portuguese administration

Macao

V

LIST OF THIRD COUNTRIES WHOSE NATIONALS ARE REQUIRED A TRANSIT VISA[516]

Afghanistan
Ethiopia
Eritrea
Ghana
Irak
Iran
Nigeria
Somalia
Sri Lanka
Democratic Republic of Congo (ex-Zaïre)

516 Source Joint Action 96/197/JAI OJ 1996 L 63/

TABLE OF TREATIES AND LEGISLATION

Treaty on European Union

EC Treaty

TREATY ON EUROPEAN UNION
(AFTER THE ENTRY INTO FORCE OF THE AMSTERDAM TREATY)

EC TREATY
(AFTER THE ENTRY INTO FORCE OF THE AMSTERDAM TREATY)

TABLE OF EC LEGISLATION

Regulations

INDEX

INDEX

Immigration and Asylum Law and Policy in Europe

1. E. Guild and P. Minderhoud (eds.): *Security of Residence and Expulsion*. 2000 ISBN 90-411-1458-0
2. E. Guild: *Immigration Law in the European Community*. 2001 ISBN 90-411-1593-5
3. B. Melis: *Negotiating Europe's Immigration Frontiers*. 2001 ISBN 90-411-1614-1

Kluwer Law International – The Hague / London / Boston